Decisive writing

Decisive writing
AN IMPROVEMENT PROGRAM

L. P. DRISKILL
Rice University

MARGARET SIMPSON
San Jacinto College

New York
OXFORD UNIVERSITY PRESS
1978

Library of Congress Cataloging in Publication Data

Driskill, Linda, 1940-
Decisive writing.
1. English language—Rhetoric.
I. Simpson, Margaret, 1935- joint author. II. Title.
PE1408.D73 808'.042 77-21588
ISBN 0-19-502121-5

Printed in the United States of America

We would like to thank the following persons and firms for allowing us to use material from their writings and publications.

Julina Bach Literary Agency, Inc.: from "The Best-Traveled Man on Earth" by Jan Morris (*Horizon*, Summer 1975). Copyright © 1975 by Jan Morris.

Paul Boesch: from his *The Womanly Art of Self Defense.*

Thomas Y. Crowell Company, Inc.: from *A History of Greece* by Cyril E. Robinson.

Doubleday & Company, Inc.: "Memorial Day" from *Poems, Essays and Letters* by Joyce Kilmer. Copyright 1914 by George H. Doran.

Forbes Magazine: from "Wheat: Will the Rains Come? Or The Russians?" by Stanley W. Angrist (*Forbes Magazine*, April 1, 1976). Reprinted by permission of the publisher and Stanley W. Angrist.

Dr. Alice Ginott: from *Between Parent and Teenager* by Dr. Haim G. Ginott.

Grove Press, Inc.: from *Games People Play* by Eric Berne. Copyright © by Eric Berne.

Harcourt Brace Jovanovich, Inc.: from *Character and Conflict* by Alvin B. Kernan.

Harper & Row, Publishers, Inc.: from *Here Is New York* by E. B. White (1949); from *Why We Can't Wait* by Martin Luther King, Jr.

Harper's Magazine: material adapted from "The Advertising Game" by John Fischer (*Harper's Magazine*, October 1973).

Holt, Rinehart and Winston, Publishers: "Design" from *The Poetry of Robert Frost*, edited by Edward Connery Lathem. Copyright 1936 by Robert Frost, copyright © 1964 by Lesly Frost Ballantine, copyright © 1969 by Holt, Rinehart and Winston.

Houston Chronicle and Monroe K. Spears: excerpt from Monroe K. Spears' review of Robert Lowell's *Selected Poems* (*Houston Chronicle*).

Ludlow Music, Inc.: "A Home on the Range," collected, adapted and arranged by John A. Lomax and Alan Lomax TRO, copyright © 1938 and renewed 1966 by Ludlow Music, Inc.: "Starving to Death on a Government Claim," collected, adapted and arranged by John A. Lomax and Alan Lomax TRO, copyright © 1947 and renewed 1975 by Ludlow Music, Inc., New York, N.Y.

Macmillan Publishing Co., Inc.: from "Sex and Secularization" in *The Secular City* by Harvey Cox, Revised Edition. Copyright © 1965, 1966 by Harvey Cox.

William Morrow & Co., Inc.: from *Zen and the Art of Motorcycle Maintenance* by Robert Pirsig. Copyright © 1974 by Robert Pirsig.

The Nature Conservancy: from a Nature Conservancy brochure written by Steve Enke.

Oxford University Press, Inc. and Richard Emil Braun: from *Antigone* by Sophocles, translated by Richard Emil Braun (The Greek Tragedy in New Translations Series). Copyright © 1973 by Richard Emil Braun.

Psychology Today: from "The Styles of Loving" by John Alan Lee (*Psychology Today*, October 1974). Copyright © 1974 by the Ziff-Davis Publishing Company.

Random House, Inc.: "The Shield of Achilles" by W. H. Auden from *Collected Shorter Poems 1927–1957*, copyright 1952 by W. H. Auden; from *The Environmental Handbook*, edited by Garrett De Bell, copyright © 1970 by Garrett De Bell; from *The Holiday Guide to West Germany* by the Editors of *Holiday*, copyright © 1976 by The Curtis Publishing Co.

Charles Scribner's Sons: from "Cervantes" by George Santayana in *Essays in Literary Criticism of George Santayana*, edited by Irving Singer; "My Old Man" by Ernest Hemingway from *In Our Time*, copyright 1925 by Charles Scribner's Sons.

Sierra Club: letter from the Sierra Club Southern Plains Regional Conservation Committee.

Simon & Schuster, Inc.: from *Our Bodies, Our Selves* by The Boston Women's Health Book Collective, copyright © 1971, 1973, 1976 by the Boston Women's Health Book Collective, Inc.; from *The Pleasures of Philosophy* by Will Durant.

Texas Monthly: from "Bringing Up Lyndon" (*Texas Monthly*, January 1976) and "The Only Game in Town" (*Texas Monthly*, March 1975) by Larry King. Copyright respectively 1976 and 1975 by Mediatex Communications Corporation, P. O. Box 1569, Austin, Texas 78767.

Vital Speeches: from "But Then Came Man" by Stewart L. Udall (*Vital Speeches of the Day*, Vol. 33, July 1967).

To those I love

L.P.D.

For those who have something to say
and
For Miss Dorothy Rushing, who taught me how to teach

M.S.

Preface

Most good writing results from a set of decisions made by the writer about his subject, his audience, his intentions, and his various writing options. A good writer's decisions are guided by the questions he has learned to ask. Too often students hope to improve without understanding that they must take a critical stance toward their own writing if they are to succeed. As numerous studies have shown, intensity and frequency of evaluation by the teacher have little impact on the student's progress. So long as the student confines himself to the center of the page and the teacher writes in the margin, the writing in the center of the page remains the same week after week.

The crucial problem in writing improvement is how to help the student master the decision-making process of writing, a task that traditional texts have not made easy. A famous semanticist once remarked that the trouble with writing examples in traditional texts is that the examples are already written; learning from them to improve one's writing is like "learning to bake a cake by eating one." The aim of this book is to make the writer aware of the nature of decisions made in writing and to help him or her develop a set of criteria with which to judge the effectiveness of such decisions. Once the writer has learned to take the critical view from the margin he can begin to make more appropriate and more personally expressive writing decisions. The language in the center of the page will become more vivid, precise, and purposeful. The more effective his judgments, the more likely his writing is to be strong and decisive. This book is about decisions and its aim is to create decisive writers.

This book employs an innovative writing improvement procedure. The chapters define the important decisions governing writing, illustrate the results of both poor and effective decisions in the writing of others, and then lead the writer through his own decisions into improved writing. Each chapter introduces the student to the questions he must consider before he can write effectively. After the questions are applied to evaluate samples of student and professional writing, the questions are reviewed and the student is asked to use them in making decisions about his own writing. Through this process, the writer internalizes the standards of good writing often left to a text, a teacher, or an editor. He becomes both creator and critic of his own writing.

The structure of this book follows the writer's necessary growth in decision making. Chapters One through Four identify the preliminary decisions concerning purpose, content, tone, and order. Chapters Five through Eight explain how to choose the organization and argumentation necessary to implement these preliminary decisions. Chapters Nine and Ten concern the decisions involved in the presentation of the whole essay. Finally, Chapters Eleven through Thirteen explain those modifications of the basic decisions demanded by special writing situations.

In whatever learning situation, the student who follows this program of writing improvement will develop a sense of confidence, a degree of competence, and a set of criteria for evaluating his own writing and that of others. We cannot transform people by decree. It is not enough to say "Be expressive; write what you mean." Each person must learn to define what he wishes to create and to control the process that can fulfill that desire. This book offers a new procedure for writers who want to be free, expressive, and effective, an improvement program for becoming a more decisive writer.

Acknowledgments

At every stage of its development, the writing project at Rice University has benefited from the support of many friends—good scholars and writers who believed that decisive, interesting writing is the core of a university education and the mark of a mature person. The members of the English Department supplied frequent encouragement and assistance. Chairman Joseph Ward and Chairman Walter Isle took care of the many administrative arrangements so essential for a successful experimental program. The Committee on Undergraduate Teaching provided funds to develop and test materials. The Dean of Humanities, Dr. Virgil K. Topazio, the Provost of the University, Dr. Frank Vandiver, and the President, Dr. Norman Hackerman, gave us leadership and support. Ideas and programs can only flourish in an environment that encourages well-planned innovation, and we are grateful to have had such an opportunity.

We owe debts to friends everywhere, among faculty members who sent clippings of both irksome and enlightening examples, cheerful cartoons, and student papers for review. Lynn and Martin Bloom loaned private drafts and materials and led us to a consideration of student decision-making in writing. Kay Smith at the University of Massachusetts at Amherst generously read early versions of these materials and suggested improvements, as did Dr. Robert Entzminger. Long discussions with Dr. Stewart Baker helped to clarify goals and approaches in the early stages of the project.

Our student assistants in the writing laboratories made many contributions to the quality of the instructions for exercises by reporting where students asked for additional explanation and which examples were most effective. The proctors to whom we owe a special thanks include Janice Hartrick, Brenda Kocian, Alan Van Fleet, Daryl Drickman, Ed Stone, Berne Kluber, Nita Vandiver, Charles Zelnick, Paul Shinkawa, Jeanne Ann Whittington, Dodie Wilson, Betsy Bergtholdt, Gary Thompson, Carolyn Dahl, Andrew Kappel, and Diana Weihs. Audrey Handley's excellent graphic sense and typing skills put the materials in good order for their early classroom use and her hospitality and willingness to type far into the night helped us meet the deadlines for various revisions.

During the book-making process we relied heavily on the keen judgment and experience of our editor, Ellie Fuchs. The best reward of the publication experience has been the friendship, sustaining wit, and rigorous intellect of John Wright, College English Editor, of Oxford University Press.

Throughout the long process of writing and revising the materials for the Rice writing program, which eventually became the chapters of *Decisive Writing*, my husband Frank Driskill and my daughter Lorinda have tolerantly adjusted their schedules and plans to accommodate the project and have been liberal with love and encouragement, as have my brother, Bob Phillips, and my mother, Lorane Phillips. At the beginning of a new undertaking it is easy to feel alone, but at the end one finds that the journey has been made in the generous and gracious company of friends.

To the instructor

Texts are written, or they ought to be, to serve the needs of those who teach as well as those who learn. We have tried to make *Decisive Writing* serve the needs of teachers partly for selfish reasons, because we wanted the book to work well in our own classes. As we used these materials in different classroom situations and writing laboratories, we changed the text to achieve more fully a set of objectives that we hope other instructors will also value:

1. *To make the chapters suitable for a variety of learning formats.* Because students learn to improve their writing under various of learning conditions, we have prepared this book so that it can be used alone in a traditional presentation-and-discussion classroom situation, in writing workshops and writing laboratories, in conjunction with essay anthologies, and in other formats. The materials have been used in various settings and modified to meet a variety of demands.

2. *To make the instructions adequate for students working independently or with miniumum guidance.* When instructions are sketchy and must be interpreted or supplemented by comments to several individual students, precious time is lost. The instructions in this text are detailed and complete.

3. *To teach logically and understandably the way to structure arguments and papers.* Too often writing texts simplify the

organization of essays to "writing three paragraphs in support of the thesis, building up to the most important reason." In *Decisive Writing* we have linked organizational patterns to thesis sentence structure and have shown students how to combine these patterns effectively.

4. *To help students recognize the importance of the audience in academic as well as professional writing, so that composition will not be a vain exercise in "writing for no one."* We have explained the difference between the audiences for academic and professional writing, emphasizing the requirements that the academic audience places on the writer.

5. *To help students see the relevance of composition to other studies and situations by using examples that deal with the subjects and issues of other academic disciplines.* It is scarcely surprising that students and teachers suspect a course has limited value when the text recommends a thesis sentence answering a question no academic discipline would ever ask about a topic. When a textbook author suggests such thesis sentences as "Cats are really man's best friend," "A broccoli patch is a lesson in economics," or "Nominalism is not as inscrutable as one would suppose," the student knows immediately that no professor would ever pose the questions these sentences imply. Students cannot respect the skills we teach unless we respect these abilities also and show their value beyond the doors of our own classrooms. Although we have sought variety in our topics and examples, we have insisted upon intellectual validity and appropriateness.

6. *To reconcile those who have for some years argued over whether writing is a process or a product.* To us, the division between the "product" and the "process" champions has seemed unfortunate and unproductive. We have tried to make it easier for the teacher to show how decision making is related to the quality of the product or essay so that the student will produce the kind of essay he wanted. Making the right decisions early in the writing process assures the quality of the written product.

Contents

Preliminary decisions

1. *Writer, subject, and audience,* 1

Writers, subjects, and audiences, 1
The reason for writing, 1 Preliminary decisions about the audience, 2 Preliminary decisions about the writer's role, 7

Asking questions and making decisions, 12

2. *Complete expression,* 16

Inclusive and particular terms, 16
Degrees of inclusiveness, 17 Inclusive-particular patterns, 19

Complete expression and audience needs, 22

Asking questions and making decisions, 28

3. *The thesis sentence,* 34

The thesis and the topic sentence, 34
Limiting a topic, 35 Choosing a controlling idea, 36

Evaluating thesis sentences, 38
Viability, 38 Clarity, 40 Accuracy, 44

Asking questions and making decisions, 45

4. *Coherence,* 47

Coherence, 47
Coherence through space order and time order, 48 Coherence through logical order, 50 Coherence through repetition, 51 Coherence through transition, 53

Asking questions and making decisions, 56

Implementing decisions

5. *Comparison*, 60

Using comparison, 61
Choosing bases of comparison, 61   Organizing comparisons, 64
Using sentence structure in comparison, 69   Combining dominant
and subordinate comparisons, 71

Asking questions and making decisions, 76

6. *Causes and consequences*, 80

Cause-and-effect reasoning, 81
Inductive reasoning, 81   Forming a hypothesis, 84   Testing the
hypothesis, 88

Asking questions and making decisions, 95
Organizing cause-and-effect writing, 98

7. *Analysis and definition*, 105

The writer's perspective, 105
Using models, 108   Internal and external models, 109   Choosing
appropriate models, 113   Using analysis and definition, 115

Asking questions and making decisions, 116

8. *Organizing the essay*, 126

The thesis sentence as guide to organization, 127
1. Definition pattern, 127   2. Analysis pattern, 128   3. Time or
space pattern, 129   4. Comparison pattern, 129   5. Cause and/or
effect pattern, 129   6. Interpretive generalization pattern, 130
7. Recommendation pattern, 131

Choosing a dominant pattern of organization, 132
Using an outline, 136
Asking questions and making decisions, 141

9. *Introductions and conclusions*, 144

Evaluating introductions, 145
Evaluating conclusions, 151
Asking questions and making decisions, 155

10. *The whole essay: decisions from start to finish*, 163

Preliminary decision-making, 163
Audience awareness, 164   Choosing a topic, 172   Making decisions about the thesis, 173

Implementing your decisions, 175
Organizing the essay, 175   Planning the introduction and conclusion, 178   Drafting the essay, 179   Revising the essay, 179

Special situations

11. *Research*, 182

Step 1: Limiting a topic, 183
Step 2: Finding possible sources of information, 184
Step 3: Collecting information, 187
Step 4: Organizing the final paper, 188
Step 5: Writing and documenting the paper, 190
A research paper: The Individual's Right to Die, 194

12. *Critical essays*, 203

Critical intentions, 203
Interpretive essays, 205   Judgmental essays, 208   Correlational essays, 210   Supporting critical arguments, 213

Asking questions and making decisions, 221

13. *Technical writing*, 247

Reader-oriented technical writing, 247
Techniques for reader-oriented writing, 248   Technical writing style, 248   Visual emphasis through listing, 249

Technical correspondence, 253
Process descriptions, 255
Technical reports, 256
Physical research report, 257   Laboratory report, 260   Progress report, 264   Feasibility report, 264

Decisive writing

1 *Writer, subject, and audience*

Objectives

Decisive writing, the goal of this writing improvement program, invites a reader to share the information and ideas of a writer who knows his purpose, subject, and relationship to the reader. Decisive writing transports energy from one mind to another, preserving in the exchange the excitement of discovery and the vigor of conviction. Decisive writing pleases the reader and fulfills the writer because it shows keen appreciation of the reader's needs and achieves the writer's purpose.

To begin improving your writing, you must learn to ask the questions that guide a writer's preliminary decisions. These questions concern the reason for writing, the choice of a subject, the identification of an audience, and the choice of a role appropriate to the particular writing situation.

Writers, subjects, and audiences

The reason for writing

Every writer has a reason for picking up his pen. He may respond to the needs of a particular audience, or to the demands of a situation, or to his own personal need for self-expression. Consider what would happen after an auto accident. The insurance company and the police would require a written report from the driver detailing the conditions and events leading up to the accident. The investigating officer at the scene would also hand in a written report to the state highway department. A newspaper reporter covering the accident would file a story to satisfy the larger audience, the public, and a smaller audience—the city editor, who could fire him for bad reporting. Later, for personal reasons, the driver might write a letter to a friend about the accident. The letter would differ from the formal reports and the newspaper story in tone, style, and perhaps content. In each of these examples—report, news story, and letter—the specific reason for writing would lead to a series of preliminary decisions affecting the tone, style, and content of the written product. Students who write on demand—for class assignments—also need a clear sense of their purpose, the writing situation, and their instructor's expectations.

Each writer's reason for writing prompts him to tell something specific about the topic. An essay about the supersonic Concorde passenger jet would include different information as written for an aeronautical engineering course, an ecology course, or a course in English composition. For the aeronautics assignment the writer might describe how the Concorde works, how its design and operation differ from those of earlier, smaller, slower planes. For the course in ecology the same writer would treat the subject differently: he might examine how the Concorde affects the ozone layer of the atmosphere, or how it contributes to noise pollution. For the composition course the writer would tackle the subject in still another way, describing how it feels to cross the Atlantic in three hours, or comparing a Concorde crossing with Charles Lindbergh's original flight to Paris. The implicit demands of each particular writing situation help the writer decide on the selection of evidence, the most useful order, and essential argumentative points.

Preliminary decisions about the audience

Before he writes, the writer must make some preliminary decisions about his audience. First he must identify his prospective readers. Some audiences are clearly defined, with well-known characteristics. The writer may be preparing a proposal to the local city council or sending a letter to a close friend. In these cases he knows his audience as individuals, and he can tailor his message to fit their particular backgrounds and points of view. A writer preparing an article for the Sierra Club newsletter cannot identify his audience as individuals, but he can expect them to share certain values and interests: a strong commitment to the preservation of wilderness areas and wildlife, familiarity with proposed legislation affecting the environment, and an understanding of pollution problems. Similarly, a student might know (or want to know) a great deal about the professor for whom he is writing—the professor's area of specialization, the approaches and methodologies he likes best, and so forth. Sometimes, however, a writer's knowledge of his audience is limited. The author of a Red Cross lifesaving manual expects his readers to want clear and exact instructions for rescue work, but he knows nothing else about them.

The more a writer knows about his audience, the more certain he can be of accomplishing his writing goals. Therefore, the decisive writer will discover as many relevant facts about his audience as he can. Different audiences make different demands on a writer. Before he begins his actual writing, he must consider the audience's knowledge of the subject, their experiences and attitudes, and their probable response to his message. A person trying to convince fourth graders of the value of recycling might compose the following paragraph:

Litterbugs cause problems for all of us. Litterbugs throw cans and bottles any place they feel like. When they do, the mess isn't pretty to look at. Broken glass and rusting cans can be dangerous, and every time people throw away a can made of aluminum, there is less aluminum for people to use in the future.

The same writer would present his case very differently to environmental engineering students:

Thinking of wastes as raw materials can solve the long-term problems of resource demand and solid-waste disposal. Each ton of paper, aluminum, or iron reclaimed from waste takes the place of a ton that would have to be taken from our mines and forests. Furthermore, society and industry can benefit greatly. The ton of recycled material can cost less than the ton from the earth. In the case of aluminum, for example, much of the original cost derives from the immense amount of electrical energy needed to refine the ore. The cost of preparing a ton from aluminum items collected for recycling is much lower, making recycling economically feasible. Reynolds Aluminum Corporation's new plants . . .

Addressing the paragraph meant for the college students to the fourth graders would be a bad mistake. The words would be too difficult and the information would be useless. The difference in cost of newly refined and recycled aluminum would have little to do with their sphere of action, which is helping in trash pick-up drives and recycling projects. This example may seem extreme, but any writer who assumes his audience knows more than they do will fail to supply necessary explanations. A writer who says too much, repeating what his audience already knows, will bore them—they won't bother to finish what he has written.

Different audiences also approach what they read with different attitudes, different standards for satisfaction, and different ways of responding to what they have read. Schoolchildren like to live in clean, pleasant surroundings; they don't want to get hurt, and they want to have cans full of soda available whenever they are thirsty: so it is possible to convince them to participate in trash pick-up drives and recycling projects. The engineering students, on the other hand, are motivated more by their desire to be good engineers. They want to feel pride in knowing that the recycling systems they will design for their employers are economically feasible and environmentally sound.

The first decisions a writer makes depend on the assumptions made about the audience:

1. Who are the audience?
2. What are their assumptions about the subject?
3. How much do they know about the subject?
4. How do they feel about the subject?
5. Do their language skills enable them to understand the material?
6. How do they feel about the writer?

These questions cannot always be answered accurately or in detail, but the writer should always keep them in mind, because the more he knows about the audience, the more fully he can satisfy them.

Exercise: Analyzing the audience

In this exercise you will analyze what the writers decided about their audiences *before* they began writing. Preliminary decisions about the audience shape the writing itself. In every passage there will be clues to what the writer thought about his audience. How did the authors of the following passages answer the six questions listed above? The first passage serves as an example. Follow the same procedures for the other passages.

Example

I tell you frankly that if you are attacked by a man your chances of survival without injury are not good. Therefore I repeat: do not expect miracles of physical strength to well up within you when you need them. Concentrate on staying out of trouble and places where trouble breeds.

Make no mistake about it, whether you call the art wrestling, judo, karate, dirty fighting, or self-defense, it takes long hard hours of practice to develop an effective technique. Few men have the time to devote to it unless they are dedicated amateurs or professionals. Fewer women have either the time or the physical and mental equipment necessary to become "experts" in self-defense. There is no easy solution; no "instant expert" method. The things you are about to be told to do may shock you. But, how often have you been shocked when you read what happened to a woman who was unable to defend herself? (Paul Boesch, *The Womanly Art of Self Defense*)

Sample questions and answers

1. *Who are the audience?* The audience addressed here is composed of women—specifically, women with no previous experience in combat who want to learn how to defend themselves. The writer uses the second person pronoun "you" for people who will receive instruction in self defense, so the readers must be learners.

2. *What are their assumptions about the subject?* The writer thinks these women may assume they would suddenly experience great strength to fight off attackers. He has also decided that they think there is a quick and easy way to learn self defense.

3. *How much do they know about the subject?* The writer seems to have decided the audience knows very little about the topic. He says they may be shocked by what he tells them, implying that this information will be entirely new to them.

4. *How do they feel about the subject?* The writer expects the women to be fearful but willing to learn.

5. *Do their language skills enable them to understand the material?* At first the audience might not know the technical vocabulary of self defense. The author has been careful not to use any unusual terms.

6. *How do they feel about the writer?* The writer's tone of authority indicates that he thinks the audience is looking for an expert. He has cast himself in this role, and he expects the audience to accept his authority.

Now analyze these passages for preliminary decisions about the audience:

a. Before buying a canoe, you should become familiar with the range of sizes and designs on the market. Certain design features that offer advantages in one situation become disadvantages in another. Understanding the consequences of design features can help you buy a canoe that will suit your needs best. In general, a good canoe has a long hull or body—because the greater the ratio of length to width, the easier the canoe will be to paddle. The long hull is more stable, draws less water, and has a greater capacity. A hull with sharp entry lines splits the water more efficiently than a blunter, rounder design. The low, sharp bow at the front also offers less wind resistance, an advantage on windy days. But in white water or in going over drop-offs this lower, sharper bow will "nose under," slicing into the waves and taking on water; whereas the higher bow will ride above the spray, and be less likely to swamp. A keel, a flat center strip running the length of the canoe, will allow the canoeist to maintain a straight course on a lake in spite of wind; but in white water the keel will drag on rocks and inhibit quick maneuvering. With the proposed type of canoeing in mind, you can assess the various designs to your advantage.

b. To cope with our own anger, we need to admit openly, and accept graciously, that anger is here to stay. Fifty million American parents cannot be wrong—they all get angry at their children. Our anger has a purpose: it shows our concern. Failure to get angry at certain moments indicates indifference, not love. Those who love cannot avoid anger. This does not mean that our teenagers can withstand torrents of rage and floods of violence. It does mean that they can benefit from anger which says: "Enough is enough. There are limits to my tolerance."
   . . .

There are certain concrete ways to deal with our anger. The first step in any annoying situation is to describe clearly how it affects us, adding nothing else. When Gary, age fifteen, started clinking his fork on a plate, his mother said, "The noise makes me very uncomfortable." Gary gave several more clinks and stopped. This method was effective because mother did not tell her son what to do. She described her discomfort and took it for granted that he would respond. Compare this approach to a more prevalent one. "What's the matter with you? Don't you have anything better to do? Can't you sit still? Do you have to give me a headache? Stop it this minute, P-L-E-A-S-E!" (Dr. Haim G. Ginott, *Between Parent and Teenager*)

Preliminary decisions about the writer's role

Having evaluated the audience and the demands of the writing situation, the writer must decide what effect he wants to have on his audience. He may wish to surprise, to delight, or even to shock. He may wish to move them to some sort of action, such as voting for a particular candidate in an election. The writer may simply want to impart new information, or he may want to interpret a particular subject convincingly. If he lacks enough data to achieve his intended effect on the audience, he may have to do more research before he writes. After he has gathered enough information the writer chooses the *persona* (per-so'-nah) or role he will play before the audience. The *persona* is a stance which establishes the relationship between writer and audience. The *persona* reflects the writer's degree of knowledge, the degree of directness in his approach to the audience, and his attitude toward the audience. In the passages on self-defense, canoes, and family relationships, the writers all spoke as experts.

A writer's *persona* may reflect less than expert knowledge of a subject. Although the author of the following excerpt holds strong opinions, he speaks only from limited personal experience. He is not an expert. Note the phrases in italics:

The counseling system couldn't save our marriage because it was directed toward saving the individual, and identifying individual needs. It was not directed at helping clients fulfill the primary commitment of their lives. *In my own case*, there were six lives involved. My wife was the only unhappy person. Her individual needs conflicted with the rest, so she left. She satisfied only one need, her own. That does not make good mathematical sense nor good human sense. Life is not just a matter of self-fulfillment, *at least not to me.* I recognize that one cannot force someone to be married, to continue a relationship; but we owe it to ourselves, to our children, and to our society to do better in family relationships. *I would hate to think that* future generations might view commitment and responsibility, marriage and the family, as an optional kind of thing. At what price should a person buy self-fulfillment?

A second feature of the writer's *persona* is the degree of directness employed in the communication. In informal, direct writing the writer chooses the first-person pronouns "I," "me," and "my." He may also address his audience directly, using "you" and "your." (In this book, instructions are informal and direct: the reader is addressed as "you.")

In formal writing such as essays, articles, and academic papers, the writer conventionally uses the third person rather than the informal first person. Instead of saying, "I think Hamlet's idea of honor begins to change in the second act of the play," the formal writer omits "I think" and writes: "Hamlet's idea of honor begins to change in the second act of the play." In addition to signaling a more formal style, leaving out phrases like "I think" adds a ring of authority. Instead of expressing a personal viewpoint, sentences in the third person are assertive statements.

Finally, a writer's *persona* also reflects his attitudes toward the subject and the audience. In writing—as in speech—attitudes influence word choice almost automatically. A single idea can be expressed in a variety of ways; the same person or action can be described from various perspectives. Consider the following example. A married man is having an affair with his next-door neighbor. A writer might describe this man and his activities in different ways:

Harry cheats on his wife.
Harry has an open marriage.
Harry has a little honey on the side.

In each case Harry is doing the same thing—but in each sentence the language reflects a different attitude toward Harry's behavior. The first sentence clearly expresses disapproval of Harry's actions. The second is moderately approving of his lifestyle. The third sentence gives his behavior a label that some people find attractive and positive.

Exercise: Analyzing the writer's attitude toward subject and audience

In each item in this exercise a writer describes essentially the same condition, person, or action three times. Each time he changes his attitude. When the writer refers to a third-person subject (he, she, or it), he is disapproving. When he uses the second person (you), he is moderately approving. When he speaks of himself, he uses the pronoun "I" and speaks very approvingly. In each item, write a word or phrase in the blank space that fits the attitude indicated in the parenthesis. Use the completed sentences as clues.

Example

He's in a rut. (disapproving)
You are a creature of habit. (moderately approving)
I am consistent. (very approving)

a. Her house is a mess.
   Your house is cluttered.
   My house looks _____. (approving)

b. He _____. (disapproving)
   You exaggerate.
   I am in charge of public relations.

c. He's broke.
   You are in _____. (moderately disapproving)
   I am temporarily over-extended at the bank.

d. He is getting _____. (disapproving)
   You are middle-aged.
   I am in my prime.

e. He _____. (disapproving)
   You speak loudly.
   I make myself heard.

f. He is losing his hair.
   You have a _____. (moderately approving)
   I look like Telly Savalas.

g. She _____. (disapproving)
   You urge.
   I make periodic suggestions.

h. She's a nosy busybody.
   You _____. (moderately approving)
   I share my know-how with my friends.

i. He is tactless.
   You _____. (moderately disapproving)
   I am upfront and honest.

j. He is a _____. (disapproving)
   You are a heavy drinker.
   I am a connoisseur of fine wines (and bourbon and Scotch and German beer).

(Adapted from a feature in *Harper's*)

Exercise: Analyzing the writer's persona

Read the following selection and write a paragraph describing the *persona* chosen by this writer. In the paragraph, answer the following questions:

1. What effect does the writer intend to have on the reader?
2. How knowledgeable about his subject does the writer claim to be?
3. How directly does the writer express himself?
4. What attitude does the writer take toward his subject?
5. What attitude does he take toward his audience?

I shall give no detailed explanation of Domino rules here, assuming that anyone who has played so much as one game thinks himself an expert; at least, my average challenger seems to be so inclined. I shall, however, happily list those components I have found most valuable in a lifetime of unbroken Domino successes:

. . . Play rapidly against those who ponder or hesitate; conversely, slow down against those who love slam-bang action. This is easier than it sounds: while your slow opponent is pondering, *you* have the opportunity to ponder the various potential options without appearing to. Thus, when he plays, you snap back so quickly he thinks he's pitted against a computer. This gives him no breathing room; no sooner has he made his difficult choice than he's forced to think out yet another difficult decision. It helps to say periodically—quietly, and with a touch of solicitation—"Do you pass?" as if to indicate he faces an impossible situation, or soon will. Against the action-loving foe, on the other hand, *never* say a mumbling word during those long silences while you pretend to ponder: do not answer his questions, the telephone, or a small child's pitiful cry for help. *Do nothing* to assist time's slow passage. Even after you select the rock to be played, pause with your arm in mid-air, purse your lips thoughtfully, and then place it *ever* so slowly and gently down. (Larry L. King, "The Only Game In Town," *Texas Monthly*)

Review

Every writer writes for a reason. The reason for writing may come from the audience, or from a particular situation, or from the writer himself. The situation, the characteristics of his audience, and his own knowledge, attitudes, and intention affect the writer's preliminary decisions. A writer's preliminary decisions reflect his answers to the following questions:

What is the writing situation?
What is the reason for writing?
Who are the audience?
What are their assumptions about the subject?
How much do they know about the subject?
How do they feel about the subject?
Do their language skills enable them to understand the material?
How do they feel about the writer?
What effect does the writer intend to have on the reader?
How knowledgeable about his subject does the writer claim to be?
How directly does the writer express himself?
What attitude does the writer take toward his subject?
What attitude does the writer take toward his audience?

These preliminary decisions determine the writer's *persona*, his choice of words, and other features of writing that will be discussed in later chapters.

Asking questions and making decisions

Exercise: Analyzing other writers' decisions

In this exercise you will analyze the ways in which five writers have met the demands of various writing situations. Ask yourself the questions listed above, then write a paragraph describing how each author has identified the audience and pursued his intention.

a. West Germany is a modern, extremely well-organized country, which makes travel easy for the tourist. The trains run on time; offices and shops stay open during the lunch hour; and everybody keeps appointments. Cleanliness is a virtue practiced everywhere—from the vast railway stations of the great cities to the spotless *Pensionen* of the smallest villages.

Travel is so simple that it's a delight. There is always a train, plane or bus that will take you exactly where you want to go. And if you are touring Germany by car, you should have little trouble finding a gas station with a trained mechanic who can repair whatever has gone wrong. The German superhighways, the *Autobahnen,* are superb, and the country lanes are a delight.

Americans usually feel very much at home in the Federal Republic. Aside from the difference of language, daily life in Germany seems very similar to that of the United States. There is no problem of getting used to spicy food, unusual mealtimes or perplexing local habits. There is no country in Europe, with the exception of Britain, where the American will find customs so familiar and travel so easy. (*The Holiday Guide to West Germany*)

b. In water emergencies, even well-trained rescuers should remember the slogan, "reach, throw, row, go." If possible, the rescuer should reach out and extend one arm toward the victim, maintaining his weight on the deck or shore, either lying down or slanting backwards. A pole or towel or deck chair can be extended toward the victim if he is beyond arm's reach. If the victim is farther away, a line, ring buoy, spare tire, or any buoyant object can be thrown to him. The victim at a distance of three to fifty yards can receive a thrown support and cling to it more quickly than a rescuer can swim to him. A victim who is beyond throwing range should be reached by boat if possible. In moving water the current may carry the victim away from the rescuer so swiftly that overtaking the drowning person will be very difficult without a boat. Only if all other methods are impossible should a rescuer enter the water to rescue the victim. Securing a drowning victim and bringing him to shore usually involves contact with a struggling, extremely frightened person, who heeds only the urge to seize and climb up on anything that comes within his grasp. The rescuer can be most effective if he can use his energy to provide a means of flotation for the victim, and pull him to shore without having to fight off and control a thrashing person whose actions might endanger both of them. Don't plunge into a rescue. Take a few seconds to think: "Reach, throw, row"; and only if absolutely necessary, "go."

c. I do not know whether it has been a problem or a blessing that through fate's decree we have had but one child. I confess that we have spent more time on Ethel than we could possibly have given her if the stork had been more generous. I have seen households with two or more children, and found them a little too noisy for my taste. I do my work at home, and see a great deal of Ethel; but if she had had brothers or sisters I must have sought an office or an attic at least a mile away. As it is, Ethel's nearness is no disturbance, but an inexpressible delight; the sound of her voice in the other rooms, even her occasional invasion of mine, stimulates and refreshes me; and I consider myself fortunate that I am permitted to do my work not in the chaos of the city, but to the quiet accompaniment of such happy growth. (Will Durant, *The Pleasures of Philosophy*)

d. Lead is one of the most pernicious of all pollutants emitted by automobiles. People with more than about 0.5 parts per million of lead in their blood show visible signs of lead poisoning: constipation, headaches, anemia, and emaciation at low levels of exposure; paralysis, blindness, insanity, and finally death at higher levels. In addition, lead can cause sterility, miscarriage, stillbirths, infant mortality, and mental retardation of offspring. There are no obvious effects of lead when it is present in the blood at concentrations less than 0.5 parts per million; but there are undoubtedly small yet important effects due to low-level exposure. Little medical research has been performed on these sub-threshold exposures, so we really don't know the extent of the danger over long periods. The concentration of lead in the air we breathe has increased several-fold in the last three decades, as the use of gasoline-powered motor vehicles has grown. The average city dweller in the United States now has 0.17 parts per million of lead in his blood. The amount is increasing yearly.

Lead as an air pollutant is totally unnecessary. Lead compounds are added to gasoline to cheaply and artificially improve octane rating. For approximately 2 cents per gallon (for the average driver, $14 per year) increase in the price of gasoline, the petroleum industry could modify refining techniques to increase the octane rating, thereby removing the necessity for lead additives. How many people will suffer from lead poisoning before this occurs? (Garret De Bell, ed., *The Environmental Handbook*)

e. After many years of struggle we have reached a plateau of trust together, and these trustful feelings allow us to take risks with each other and ourselves. I also feel less hung up about traditional roles of male and female, because through our openness and the resulting intimacy I have learned that my husband has many of the same weak feelings, fragile feelings, that previously I thought were female—just as he has learned that I have certain strengths he doesn't have. This kind of relationship provides a unique opportunity, I feel, for self-exploration and deep understanding about oneself and one's mate. I think the crucial thing here is time, to build up one's feelings of confidence and trust and comfort and kindness, and time also to foster a special atmosphere that seems to be a combination of closeness and openness which teaches one the confidence to begin to explore, search, and grow.

I want to stress that at this point in my life, knowing all the things now I didn't know when I got married, I would again choose monogamy, not for the sake of the children or the family, but for myself, and my husband. I don't prescribe my choice for everyone. I just feel—I have tasted love and it is good. (Women's Health Collective, *Our Bodies, Our Selves*)

Exercise: Making decisions about writers, subjects, and audiences

This exercise is a series of events or *contexts*. For each context three possible writers are presented—each of whom would respond differently. Taking the role of each writer, summarize the decisions each would make about subject, audience, intention, and *persona*.

Example

Context: Residential fire; Writers:

Newspaper reporter
Audience—newspaper readers interested in disasters
Subject—this fire and other recent, local residential fires
Intention—to persuade readers that safety inspection codes ought to be enforced
Persona—semi-expert witness

Insurance investigator
Audience—company supervisor
Subject—the cause of this fire
Intention—to discover how much the company owes the home owner
Persona—expert professional

Home owner
Audience—friend in another town
Subject—details of the fire
Intention—to share the terrifying experience, and elicit sympathy
Persona—nonprofessional participant

a.   Context: Premiere of a new Hollywood film
      Writers: Film critic
               Financial investor in the film
               Viewer

b.   Context: An off-shore oilspill
      Writers: Newspaper reporter
               Oil company's public relations writer
               Conservationist

c.   Context: Sex crime
      Writers: Medical researcher
               Novelist
               College Student

d.   Context: Discovery of a new abortion procedure
      Writers: Congressman
               Biologist
               Pregnant woman

e.   Context: A robbery
      Writers: Policeman
               Prison psychologist
               Victim

2 Complete expression

Objectives

Effective communication requires complete expression, which helps the reader understand the message precisely and fully. To achieve complete expression the writer uses both general, inclusive terms, and terms that are specific and particular. Inclusive terms introduce and summarize his ideas. Particular and specific terms explain his general statements, back up his assertions, and justify his opinions.

In this chapter you will learn to distinguish levels of inclusiveness, and recognize patterns of inclusive and particular terms in single paragraphs. By asking questions about these patterns you will learn to evaluate the completeness of expression in the writing of others and to achieve it in your own.

Inclusive and particular terms

The way we use language reflects the human ability to think about broad categories of experiences, objects, and events as well as specific instances of these categories. For example, when a word like "party" is used alone in a sentence you usually react positively, because "party" refers to a broad range of festivities: "Would you like to hear about a party?" Adding modifiers changes and restricts a term's meaning: "Would you like to hear all about the charming tea party Aunt Ann gave?" Maybe not. "Would you like to hear about a party where they took drugs?" Your ideas about the party, already altered by the clause "where they took drugs," might change even more if the term "drugs" were replaced by "peyote," "heroin," or some

16

other particular term. By modification or replacement the writer can vary the range of his reference and his effect upon the reader. He can replace "party" with "hayride," "picnic," "orgy," or "wake"; or he can add modifying terms, writing about "little brother's birthday party" or a "Halloween party," and create a different response in the reader each time.

As the examples above indicate, the writer may do two things to make an inclusive expression more particular. When using the first method he replaces an inclusive term with a more particular one that is a sub-category of the original (drugs—peyote). When using the second method the writer adds extra terms to modify and limit the inclusive term and make the image more vivid:

plant
the plant
the large plant
the large lavender-leafed plant
the large lavender-leafed plant in the hanging basket
the large lavender-leafed plant with violet blooms in the hanging basket

Degrees of inclusiveness

Words vary in their degree of inclusiveness. A term such as "thief" is less inclusive, for example, than the term "criminal," but more inclusive than terms like "pickpocket" or "rustler." Degrees of inclusiveness can be diagrammed in vertical ladders:

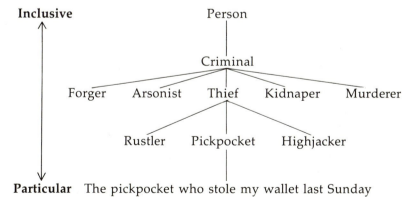

Inclusive

Person

Criminal

Forger   Arsonist   Thief   Kidnaper   Murderer

Rustler   Pickpocket   Highjacker

Particular   The pickpocket who stole my wallet last Sunday

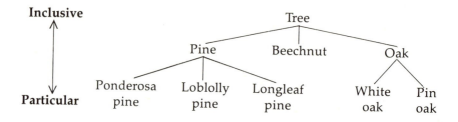

We could draw many different inclusive-to-particular diagrams for a single word, because each word has a number
of constituent ideas which make up its full meaning. The
word "desks," for example, could be placed in a pattern
under the more inclusive term "wood products" or in a
pattern headed by "furniture":

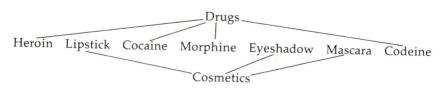

Exercises: Identifying inclusive and particular terms

1. Divide the terms in each of the following lists into two
groups, so that the members of each group have something
in common. Label each group with an appropriate inclusive
term.

Example

a. silver, copper, linen, iron, cotton, nylon
b. sweater, earring, blouse, bracelet, slacks, necklace
c. tulip, cinnamon, ginger, rose, nutmeg
d. football, pie, soccer, tennis, cake, creampuff
e. pine, coffee, spruce, fir, tea, lemonade
2. Circle the more inclusive or general term in each of the
following pairs.

Example: (shellfish)/ shrimp

a. dessert / pie   f. conflict / World War II
b. music / concerto   g. automobile / sedan
c. *Tom Sawyer* / novel   h. school / kindergarten
d. rifle / weapon   i. infant / person
e. gold / metal   j. cow / animal

3. Underline the inclusive terms in the five sentences that follow and then rewrite the sentences, substituting more particular terms for the inclusive ones you have underlined. Be imaginative!

Example
Original sentence: There was a severe <u>disturbance</u> at an <u>institution</u> in the <u>spring</u>.
Rewrite: There was a riot at Jackson Prison on May 23.

a. Convicts, armed with weapons, took some of the prison personnel hostage.
b. For the better part of a year, he had a disease.
c. A member of her family had one extramarital relationship after another and finally disappeared with a dining room employee of a hotel in one of our larger midwestern cities.
d. Rejected by the military because of an impairment of her vision, the woman became an employee of an east coast newspaper.
e. The broadcast reported that a car had overturned on the freeway north of town.

4. Use the following terms in sentences, adding modifiers to make the original term specific.

Example
Term: *contest;* sentence: The annual athletic *contest* between the soccer teams of Stanford and UCLA took place on March 24.

figure   food   building   music   office   contest

Inclusive-particular patterns

 A good paragraph or longer composition has a pattern of related inclusive and particular terms. Inclusive terms introduce and summarize major ideas. Particular terms demonstrate or support the statements made in more inclusive terms. In the following paragraph, written for people who want to lose weight, you can spot at least two patterns of inclusive and particular terms:

Although some of the advertised weight-loss devices are as harmless as they are useless, other highly touted products pose a real risk. In 1970, after four years of fighting in the courts, the Food and Drug Administration finally obtained a permanent injunction against the sale of Relaxicizor, an electronic gizmo intended to stimulate the muscles. A parade of witnesses testified that the machine could induce miscarriage, damage the heart, and aggravate illnesses such as ulcers, hernias, varicose veins and epilepsy. In 1974 the FDA seized and condemned the Love Legs Instant Shaper, a rubber stocking device that supposedly caused "fat-flushing perspiration which flushes out fatty globules." But after medical testimony, the court found that "perspiration has no effect on fat cells or fatty globules under the skin of the thighs." The FDA also showed that performing the prescribed exercises while wearing the Love Legs could impede blood flow and worsen circulatory problems, and could even cause thrombophlebitis. Similar charges have been leveled against various types of body wraps—cloths soaked in epsom salts and wrapped around a fat section of the body.

The inclusive term "weight-loss devices" introduces the topic of the paragraph. The inclusive term "real risk" introduces the author's major idea about his topic: he will not merely describe a variety of weight-loss devices, but will demonstrate that they pose dangers to people's health. Both these general terms appear at the beginning of the paragraph; the particular terms and phrases which illustrate them occur later. The relationships between inclusive and particular terms in this paragraph may be illustrated by diagrams:

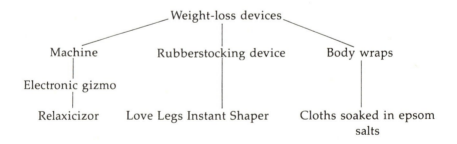

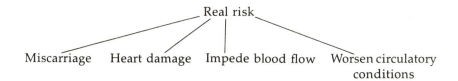

Real risk

Miscarriage   Heart damage   Impede blood flow   Worsen circulatory
conditions

Exercise: Identifying inclusive-particular patterns in paragraphs

Read the two following paragraphs. In each paragraph two general or inclusive phrases have been underlined. One serves as the heading for a diagram of related terms in the paragraph. Use the other phrase as the heading for a second diagram. Complete the diagram.

a. The Finnish people are something special. They are individualistic. The residents of the Finnish town of Kuopio have earned a reputation for being the most stubborn of all. As one resident explained to me, "When traffic lights were installed here, people driving cars refused to obey them. It was simply not in their nature to let a mechanical device tell them what to do."

Finnish people

Residents of Kuopio

People driving cars   One resident

b. A floor plan of the set for the play *Hedda Gabler* marked with the movements of the characters makes it obvious that certain places or objects are associated with certain moods of the characters. It is clear enough that Hedda brings out the pistols whenever she is frustrated and in a "killing" mood. It is less obvious, perhaps, that she goes to the stove to warm herself— she is an unusually "cold" woman—only when she wants to hear the "warming" experiences of some other person; or that she goes to the glass doors and looks out only when she longs to escape the confinement of her life. Similarly, she moves into the small back room, which is peculiarly her own, and which is dominated, significantly, by a portrait of her father, General Gabler, only when she is retreating into herself, withdrawing from circumstances that do not suit her and that she can no longer control. In this way parts of the stage and the objects on it become associated with certain emotions and attitudes; a movement to one of these places or the handling of a certain prop gives a clue to what is occurring in the character's mind. Hedda's physical location often suggests her psychic or emotional location. (Alvin B. Kernan, *Character and Conflict*)

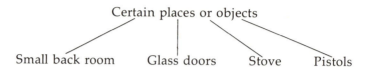

Certain places or objects

Small back room   Glass doors   Stove   Pistols

Complete expression and audience needs

As shown in the preceding exercises, writers use inclusive terms to introduce and summarize, and they use particular terms to illustrate and support their more general statements. Inclusive terms are effective for introducing and summarizing because, being more general, they provide reference points of common knowledge between writer and reader. Because the writer's subject may be difficult or technical, he needs a way to ease his audience into it, to bring them to the level of knowledge they need in order to understand his ideas completely. To achieve this "movement" of the audience, the writer carefully builds a ladder of inclusive and particular terms that will lead from some concept shared by both reader and writer to some new idea that the writer wants to explain. The difficulty of both the initial and final concepts will, of course, vary with different writers, different audiences, and different writing situations. A freshman's essay on *King Lear*, for example, will not reach the same level of difficulty or complexity as an article on *King Lear* written by a professional literary critic.

Completeness of expression is crucial in fulfilling the writer's purpose: an argument is unlikely to convince an audience or move it to action unless the assertions are supported and the opinions justified. The writing will remain ineffective unless the writer includes enough detail to convince his readers that what he says is accurate. Academic writing especially demands that student writers demonstrate a familiarity with facts, data, and background information, and that they link this particular information to inclusive theories and concepts. Whatever the discipline—history, psychology, mathematics, philosophy, biochemistry—complete expression is a means to effective writing.

To evaluate the completeness of expression in his own writing—or in the work of another writer—the student can ask the following questions:

1. Are there inclusive key terms for the main ideas?
2. Are there particular terms to supply supporting detail?
3. Could diagrams or ladders of related inclusive and particular terms be drawn?
4. Would these ladders cover a broad enough range of inclusiveness to convince the readers?

Brochures sent out by two conservation groups demonstrate the importance of providing sufficient support for assertions. The intention of each group is to solicit donations from readers believed to have an interest in preserving natural resources. The first is a letter from the president and regional vice president of the Sierra Club to the members. The second is a pamphlet from the Texas Chapter of The Nature Conservancy addressed to members of a variety of conservation organizations. As you read these selections, begin to evaluate them by applying the four questions listed above.

Selection 1

Dear Fellow Sierra Club Member:

As a resident of the Southern plains, you must be very proud of the accomplishments of the Sierra Club in your area, and concerned about maintaining a vigorous effort on our many ongoing projects. Some of these projects include:

—protection of the Illinois River in Arkansas and Oklahoma from residential and industrial development by seeking wild and scenic river designation

—study of sites in Kansas and Oklahoma for a tall grass prairie, an ecosystem presently unrepresented in the National Park System

—inclusion of the lower canyons of the Rio Grande in the Wild and Scenic River System to protect their stark beauty.

We are increasingly seeking ways the Sierra Club can promote environmental education. We are well behind the country in this respect; witness the woeful attitudes and values held by legislators and administrators. Training workshops and an environmental education network are in our plans.

Success in these and many other vital efforts will take both time and funding. If you have meant to give your time, but have not had the opportunity, may we ask for your support in the form of a contribution? As you know, we have managed to hold the line on dues increases, but continuing inflation requires that we supplement that source of income, or—as a last resort—diminish our program. And a smaller program means less wilderness, fewer wild rivers, and dirtier air and water for our descendants.

Chapters in the four states have worked together on the region's environmental problems. These efforts require both funds for our basic legislative efforts and deductible gifts that can be used for education, research, and litigation. Your contribution is significant in maintaining a vigorous Southern plains program. Please respond as your personal commitment indicates.

Thank you for your help.

Discussion of Selection 1

Several diagrams could illustrate the patterns of related terms in this letter:

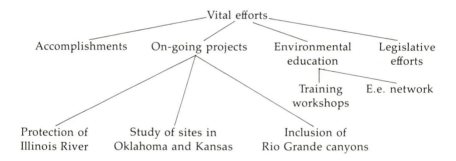

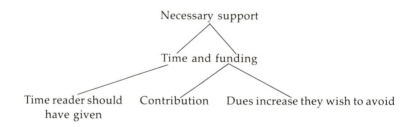

The map accompanying this letter supplies additional particulars to explain the phrase "on-going projects."

Although for the most part this letter succeeds in using particular terms to explain inclusive terms, there are a few places where the explanations are inadequate. The first clause of sentence two, paragraph two, "We are well behind the country in this respect," is difficult to understand because it offers no explanation of "this respect," and the second clause in that sentence, "witness the woeful attitudes and values held by legislators and administrators," fails to make the meaning of the first clause more particular. This sentence falls short of complete expression.

Selection 2

The Nature Conservancy
A Bold Organization Protecting a Delicate Balance
A Reason for Being
The rationale for the existence of The Nature Conservancy is simple and straightforward. Without natural land, there cannot be life—as one is diminished, so is the quality of the other, for life and land are inseparably linked. Yet every day, more and more of our precious wild resources are being sacrificed to unplanned and thoughtless development. The damage done is easy to see, but the long range effects are less perceptible. While we might only miss the rushing of a trout stream or the waving of prairie grasses, we truly suffer the consequences of silted streams and arid dustbowls. We know now that when our streams and prairies are destroyed, they are irreplaceable and future damage from flood and erosion are the prices we all pay.
The Nature Conservancy believes the time for mindless destruction is past. We must be responsible to the land and the delicate balance it harbors. We must act now. We need your help. We ask you to join us.

Idealism with Clout
The Nature Conservancy is a single purpose organization whose resources and talents are directed solely to the preservation of ecologically significant natural land. The Conservancy assigns the highest priority to land that supports rare or endangered species, contains unique beauty and performs irreplaceable ecological functions.
As an organization, we share all the idealism of other conservation groups. But we've added an extra dimension, a highly sophisticated business ability that enables us to work with extraordinary efficiency and speed. The organization is staffed by business men and women, attorneys, finance and real estate people, as well as

those with sales and marketing experience. We are represented by land experts such as biologists, planners, foresters, and ecologists. We have been joined by over 20,000 concerned members of the public. And *everyone* is committed to one central goal—the physical acquisition and preservation of land.

A Record of Results

Since its inception in 1950, The Nature Conservancy has protected nearly 750,000 acres of forest, swamp, marshland, prairies, mountains, and beaches in roughly 1,350 separate projects throughout the United States. The Conservancy retains ownership of the majority of its preserves, although selected land acquisitions are conveyed to other public or private conservation groups or educational institutions for ownership and management.

We Ask You to Join Us.
We Ask You to Let It Be.

To carry on this vital work, we need public support. In fact, we rely on it. Because all lands are acquired through purchase with funds raised privately, through donations by concerned individuals and organizations, and through cooperative programs with other public and private conservation agencies.

Join us and become part of an informed and effective volunteer network that acts to preserve the land. Naturally, you will be privy to information about our work and our progress. You'll receive our publications, and if you join at the $25 level or above, we'll send you our Preserve Directory at no cost. The Directory identifies, locates and describes every land conservation project completed by TNC since its inception.

We ask you to join us. We ask you to let it be.

Membership dues, gifts of funds, securities, and land are all tax-deductible to the limit prescribed by law. The Nature Conservancy is a publicly supported charitable organization exempt from taxation under Section 501 (c) (3) of the Internal Revenue Code.

Discussion of Selection 2

Although some of the most inclusive terms of The Nature Conservancy's brochure are illustrated by more particular terms, the writing is not specific enough for the reader to test the assertions. The following diagrams represent some of the patterns of related terms in this passage:

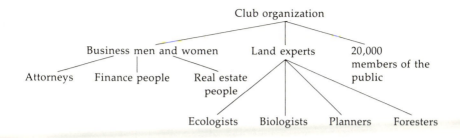

Club organization

Business men and women   Land experts   20,000 members of the public

Attorneys   Finance people   Real estate people

Ecologists   Biologists   Planners   Foresters

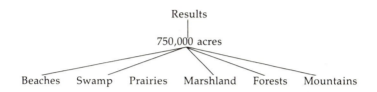

Results

750,000 acres

Beaches   Swamp   Prairies   Marshland   Forests   Mountains

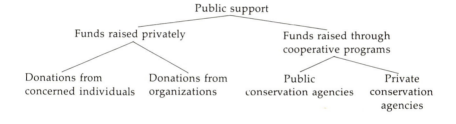

Public support

Funds raised privately   Funds raised through cooperative programs

Donations from concerned individuals   Donations from organizations   Public conservation agencies   Private conservation agencies

Precious wild resources

Rushing trout stream   Waving prairie grasses

Damage from unplanned development

Silted streams   Arid dust bowls

This club claims to be working with "land experts" such as "biologists," "ecologists," etc. The names of particular experts in these fields are needed to convince the audience. Similarly, prospective donors would want to know exact locations and brief histories of some of the group's projects, and the names of affiliated conservation agencies. While the presentation of this letter is appealing, the writing asserts but does not support, and the reader does not have enough evidence to make a well-informed decision about the group.

Review

Writers need both inclusive and particular terms to express their ideas fully. "Inclusive" and "particular" are relative terms that describe the referential capacity of different words. "Inclusive" terms suggest larger numbers of objects and broader concepts, such as "tree," "virtue," or "mammal." "Particular" terms suggest fewer objects, more narrowly-defined concepts, and sub-categories of inclusive terms, such as "cypress," "sincerity," and "wolverine."

Writers use inclusive terms to introduce and summarize topics and ideas; they use more particular terms to explain or support them. Writing may be made more particular either by replacing an inclusive term with a more limited, particular term, or by adding modifiers to restrict the meaning of the inclusive term.

Paragraphs (as well as longer compositions) should have patterns of related inclusive and particular terms to convey the writer's ideas fully and convincingly. Different writers, audiences, and writing situations will require different levels of particularity to achieve completeness and effectiveness.

The following questions evaluate completeness of expression:

1. Are there inclusive key terms for the main ideas?
2. Are there particular terms to supply supporting detail?
3. Could diagrams or ladders of related inclusive and particular terms be drawn?
4. Would these ladders cover a broad enough range of inclusiveness to convince the reader?

Asking questions and making decisions

Exercises: Evaluating the use of inclusive and particular terms

Some of the paragraphs that follow have too many broad, general terms. Others have many specific, particular terms, but lack inclusive terms that express the main idea. At least one of these paragraphs is moderately acceptable.

1. Write a two- or three-sentence evaluation of each paragraph, based on your answers to the questions listed above. State what problems (if any) you find, and make suggestions for improving the paragraph.
2. Revise one paragraph that is too general and one that is too specific.

Exa.nple: An American art history exam contained the following question:

What comment does Grant Wood's painting, "American Gothic," make about the "Gothic revival style" that was so popular in architecture, furniture, fabrics, and all the decorative arts in the nineteenth century?

Grant Wood, "American Gothic" (Courtesy of the Art Institute of Chicago)

One student's answer, which is very detailed, is given below:

The three-tined pitchfork in the man's hand points straight up. His concessions to the occasion are few: a suit coat and a tiny gold collar button on the collarless shirt. His shirt is vertically striped. His house and barn have bat-and-board construction so the up-and-down lines are emphasized. The gable has a church window at its center. A fancy curtain hangs inside, delicate and patterned. A pot with three prongs of "mother-in-law's tongue" contrasts with a large-leafed plant in a bigger pot on the porch. Her apron is patterned with tiny dots and circles and trimmed with rick-rack. A cameo brooch trims her neat white collar. He looks straight out at the viewer and at the painter, but she looks off to her left, a single curving strand of hair dangling behind her. Flat-felled seaming up the center and across the middle of the chest divides his overalls into two high pockets and seems to repeat the shape of the pitchfork. Grant Wood painted the picture. The title of the painting is "American Gothic."

Evaluation: The writer has used many particular terms in describing the picture, but there are no inclusive terms to indicate what he thinks the picture says about "the Gothic revival style." It would be hard to make a ladder illustrating the relationship between inclusive and particular terms.

Rewritten version

In "American Gothic" Grant Wood showed that the essential qualities of the Gothic revival style were marginally compatible with the strict character of rural America. The Gothic revival style was flamboyant and escapist, a nostalgic and romantic assertion that in America any man could be a prince and any woman a princess if only they worked hard enough. But the struggle to achieve success in the American farmlands required rigidity of purpose, determination, and temperance that hardly allowed the excess and frivolity of the fabled medieval Gothic world. In place of the monarch's scepter, the farmer holds a utilitarian pitchfork. Everything about this farmer-prince is severely vertical: his striped but collarless shirt, his plain bat-and-board construction buildings, his unadorned black suit coat worn over overalls whose pattern repeats the design of the pitchfork. The single frill allowed in his "castle" is a simple Gothic-arch window. His consort offers only a modest contrast. She wears a cameo brooch at the collar of her high-necked black dress, but she hardly resembles the goddess on the cameo; only a small, regular geometric pattern of dots and circles and a little rick-rack trim decorate her apron. She probably chose the patterned curtain that hangs behind the Gothic window. Achieving their modest success has allowed them the luxury of having their portrait painted, but the qualities required to attain their status have denied them the lavish and ornate freedom of the class of nobles the Gothic revival style claimed to re-create.

Follow the instructions given above for evaluating all of these six paragraphs and for rewriting one which is too general and one which is too specific.

a. Going to therapy sessions has helped me a lot. Once I worried about the problems of life and my past and future. But in the sessions we handled all my problems and worries. This experience has changed my whole outlook on everything and has made a new person out of me.

b. When new activities are introduced from another country, local characteristics and customs impose a pattern of their own on the new activity. Golf, which originated in Scotland, has become a favorite game in many nations. In Scotland the game is played on pastures where sheep may still graze. In the United States, any sheep on the course had better drive his own electric golf cart. The courses there are not pastures; the spirit of American life shows up in the artificially created and maintained greens. In Japan, the equipment is standard and international rules are observed, but the players' attitudes are different. The ritual baths, drinks, food, and awarding of prizes to all players after the game give the Scotsman's game a Far East flavor.

c. The stove, refrigerator, and sink are built into a U-shaped set of cabinets. The table is located only four feet to the right of the counter area in a cozy nook with a large window so that stove-to-table time is a matter of seconds. The freezer is only steps away to the left of the U-shaped food preparation area. Bins for staples and cabinets for canned goods are against the wall across from the U-shaped area, leaving a handy traffic path between. The cook can move easily to reach anything he or she needs in only a few steps.

d. Serving on a jury is an honor for a citizen. Most people figure it looks good for them to sit up there in a jury box. They think other people look up to them if they do it, and naturally they realize that another person's very life might rest in their hands in some cases. Democracy couldn't function if people didn't serve on juries and people couldn't get a fair trial; so a person should not feel resentful if he or she is called for jury duty, because it is an honor.

e. A bureaucracy may have power because of strong public support.

A bureau may have so much support that even a President would be unwilling to challenge it. A bureau may also have support from its clientele. The larger the number of persons who receive something from the bureau, the more power it will have. Because Congress often lacks the expertise to solve technical problems, a bureau's policies and procedure may go unchallenged for years.

f. In July, at the beginning of the 1975–76 fiscal year, sanitation workers in New York City had gone on strike to protest Mayor Beame's firing of three hundred fellow workers. Mayor Beame dismissed 2,000 firefighters. The city had a proposed debt of 650 million dollars. The State of New York authorized 330 million dollars. Mayor Beame offered cutbacks in services, salaries, and improvements. The Municipal Assistance Corporation was formed. Big Mac was able to sell 650 million dollars' worth of bonds. Banks loaned 250 million dollars to the city, which gave it enough money to last through August.

Exercise: Evaluating inclusive-particular patterns

Read the following passage, written by a student, and examine the pattern of related inclusive and particular terms. Write a paragraph evaluating the completeness of expression. Support your opinion by citing general, inclusive terms used by the writer and particular terms supplied to back up his ideas.

Room 328, Wiess College, is an oversized rat-hole, a mess, hardly fit to live in. First of all, you enter through a sagging door which you close lightly behind you so it doesn't fall off the hinges. To your right is a concrete wall that seems to have collected about six coats of paint. All along this wall you see remnants of what seems to have been a pillow fight, where bricks were used instead of pillows. To the rear of the room you see what are supposed to be bunk beds. Beyond this you see three sets of shades which are stationary because the spring on the roller has broken. The left wall, which seems to have gotten only about two coats of paint, is covered with gold handles which open doors and drawers. The paint job, which has been carbon-dated, is cracking in such a way that it looks like a hunk of Swiss cheese right there on the wall. The paint job on the drawers is so good you can't tell whether the chest belongs in an antique shop or modern art gallery. The desks in the room are similar to one which Napolean might have used, and the air conditioner could be mistaken for the first one Don Fedders ever made.

The occupants have tried hard to improve the room, although because the room is classified strictly as a "freshman" room the college limits the improvements they can make. Somewhere the two obtained a carpet which normally wouldn't be fit for the dogs' house. The carpet does look better than the floor, which had an inch-and-a-half of old wax and exactly thirteen missing tiles. To distract attention from the paint job, the pair have put up bulletin boards and several posters in various places. For instance, one bulletin board about three feet by four covers an area just big enough to give the impression that the cracking was caused by hammering the board to the wall. The other board and two posters cover the major area of cracking and peeling, but only serve to brighten the "rat-hole" to a point where it is halfway livable. (Chuck Avants, student)

Exercise: Making decisions about complete expression

Follow either set of instructions.

1. Go to a coffee shop, cafeteria, or your college dining hall, and carefully observe some eaters. There are many kinds of eaters. Select one person who has a manner of eating that interests you, and describe the eater and his style of eating in a paragraph of 150 to 300 words. Be as complete as you can, using inclusive terms to label the style of eating and particular terms to describe the eater in action. For example, if you're describing a "gulper," explain how bites of cheeseburger go down so fast they hardly require a pause in his non-stop talk with his buddy. Your intended audience is a friend at another college.

2. Pick a spot on campus where many people will be walking by, and observe the people who pass. Select a walker whose manner of walking interests you and note the details of his or her walk that make it distinctive. Note the size of the step, the slant of the body, the speed, the attitudes the walk conveys, and any other outstanding features. Describe the walker in a paragraph of 150 to 300 words, using inclusive terms to label the style of walking and particular terms to illustrate your labels. Make your description as complete as possible. Your intended audience is a friend at another college.

3 The thesis sentence

Objectives

The idea of writing as a free flow of self-expression, a gushing of spontaneous creativity, has romantic appeal. However, such writing often goes nowhere because it lacks direction; it has no sense of completeness or purpose, and thus both writer and reader never quite know where they are. To avoid this floundering, the decisive writer always constructs a thesis to guide his writing.

In this chapter you will learn how to formulate a viable thesis about your topic and how to give your thesis and topic sentences the clarity and accuracy needed for decisive, definitive, and complete writing.

The thesis and the topic sentence

A thesis is a concise statement of what any particular piece of writing is all about; it is a capsule summary of the writer's main assertion. The thesis is a product of the writer's preliminary decisions about the writing situation, the audience, and his own intentions. It also guides the writer's later decisions, determining what points will be made in the writing, the amount of detail to be included, and the order the discussion will follow. Thus the thesis functions as an organizing principle, ensuring coherence and continuity, and making writing easier for the writer and reading more pleasurable to the audience. In formulating his thesis, the writer must answer these questions:

1. What part of my topic is my audience interested in? How should I limit my topic?
2. What question(s) does my audience—or the writing situation—require me to answer?
3. How much do I know about the topic? How much more do I have to find out, to conduct my discussion intelligently?
4. What effect do I intend to have on the audience?

Thesis sentences state the topic, and a major idea about the topic, that will be discussed in a paragraph or an entire essay. Thesis sentences get to the heart of the matter. They present the writer's main response to the central question in the writing situation. If the assignment asks "What were the causes of the Civil War?", the student may summarize his reply in the thesis: "The clash between the economic interests of the industrial North and the agricultural South caused the Civil War." If the question is "What roles do women play in Thornton Wilder's *The Skin of Our Teeth*?", the student might construct the following thesis: "The female roles in *The Skin of Our Teeth* contrast 'woman as mother-homemaker' with 'woman as mistress.' " A thesis sentence is inclusive. It conveys more than a particular detail of information. *"The Skin of Our Teeth* was first produced in 1942" might appear in an introduction to an essay on the play, but it would not serve as a thesis.

The thesis—which governs an essay, a chapter, or some longer piece of written material—usually has a counterpart in each paragraph, unless the paragraph is very brief. This counterpart is called the topic sentence, and it too has a topic and a controlling idea, both of which are developed in the paragraph. The only significant difference between a thesis and a topic sentence is one of scale. Usually the words and phrases of a topic sentence are less inclusive than those in the thesis sentence. The questions used for evaluating thesis sentences in this chapter may also be applied to topic sentences.

Limiting a topic

Confronted with a topic the writer must first determine the limits of that topic. He may limit it by selecting part of a general topic. For example, he may restrict the scope of *television detectives* by deciding to discuss one particular television detective. A second way to limit a topic is to add modifiers which make it less inclusive and more particular. The broad topic of *television detectives* might be restricted by choosing to write about *British television detectives* or *television detectives who have physical handicaps*.

Exercises: Limiting a topic

1. Use both methods discussed above—substitution of a particular term for an inclusive term, and modification of an inclusive term—to convert the following broad subjects into feasible writing topics.

Example

Topic	*Substitution*	*Modification*
college athletics	swimming at UCLA	junior college athletics in 1978
a. pollution	_____	_____
b. television	_____	_____
c. education	_____	_____
d. violence	_____	_____

2. Choose *one* of the topics listed above and create ten limited topics, using both substitution and modification.

Choosing a controlling idea

After limiting his topic, the writer adds a *controlling idea* to complete the thesis. Remember this equation, which is the basis for all thesis sentences:

THESIS = LIMITED TOPIC + CONTROLLING IDEA

A thesis, whose function is to organize the writing, must have both a topic and an idea about that topic. "Lead-based paints are a health hazard to children" is a thesis. "There is a problem with paint today" is not an adequate thesis, because although it has a topic ("a problem with paint") it lacks a controlling idea. This sentence does not indicate whether the writer will go on to discuss why there is a problem with paint, the results of the problem with paint, or solutions to the problem with paint. Without a controlling idea a topic never becomes a thesis, and cannot govern the writer's decisions.

To guide the essay effectively the controlling idea must, like the topic itself, be limited or focused. This narrowing process allows the controlling idea to determine what information will be included in the essay. The thesis sentence, *The new Panther is a fine car,* has a limited topic (new Panther) and a controlling idea (fine car), but it does little to suggest the scope or structure of the discussion. A revision of this sentence would be more useful: *The new Panther is efficient in both design and operation.* Here, the key term *efficient* suggests that the discussion will focus on efficiency and will not include issues such as the beauty of the new Panther or its snob appeal. The phrase *design and operation* further specifies or narrows the content of the discussion, and it also indicates the order to be followed: *design* features will be covered first, and the Panther's efficient *operation* will be explained next.

Exercise: Focusing the controlling idea

Revise the following thesis sentences, supplying a more particular key word or phrase for the controlling idea.

Example: The first week of school was quite an experience.

Revision: The first week of school was a long series of frustrations from my arrival on campus to my last class.

a. Clint Eastwood's movies are exciting.
   Revision: _____

b. Undetected vision disabilities in grade-school children cause many problems.
   Revision: _____

c. Participation in college athletics builds character.
   Revision: _____

d. Barbecuing a steak is an art.
   Revision: _____

e. Professional tennis is popular.
   Revision: _____

f. A Volkswagen is a better car than a Buick.
   Revision: _____

Exercise: Joining limited topics and focused ideas

For each of the ten limited topics you created in Part 2 of the exercise on limiting a topic (p.36), make up an actual thesis sentence joining your limited topic with a *focused* controlling idea.

Example
Topic: television shows
Limited topic: daytime soap operas
Thesis sentence: Daytime soap operas supply city viewers with a substitute for the neighborhood gossip of small towns.

Evaluating thesis sentences

The first thesis sentence you come up with might not be the best one for your paper. Spending a little more time to evaluate your thesis will pay off by making your writing task easier and saving you time later on in the writing process. A clear, well-defined, and accurate thesis guides you effectively by reducing the choices you make as you write. Finally, it will help you produce an essay that interests the reader, an essay that contains only relevant information.

Viability

Effective thesis sentences can be evaluated by their viability, clarity, and accuracy. Viability literally means the capacity to live, which may seem a surprising concept to apply to a thesis sentence. In what sense, we may ask, does a thesis sentence or any sentence "live"? Clearly a sentence is not an organism in which biochemical reactions occur, but people have traditionally thought of language as "living." Speaking as a person speaks, the sentence, poem, novel, or essay "lives," as a person lives, through a capacity to convey its message to readers.

But no topic and no speaker will please all audiences everywhere. Different audiences have different interests, and so over a period of time or simply through a change of audience, the viability of a thesis may change. A sermon whose thesis thrilled and inspired the first congregation that heard it may bore a group of students who read it in a college textbook. In 1925, during the Scopes "monkey trial" when a young biology teacher was being tried for teaching the theory of evolution in a Tennessee public school, a thesis expressing an idea about evolution would have aroused the interest of most readers. Today only scientists who have a professional interest in theories of biological change, or fundamentalist church groups, would still find the subject controversial and engaging. Thus the viability of a thesis sentence depends on the interests of the writer and his audience, the writing situation, and the general intellectual climate of the times.

All of the following thesis sentences have lost the capacity to interest contemporary readers. They are boring, self-evident, overworked, and therefore no longer viable:

1. Christmas has become commercialized.
2. Cold weather inconveniences everyone.
3. Being married is not easy.

The following revised versions of these add *life* to the original ideas:

1. Department store Santas have formed a union to bargain for better pay and insurance against biters.
2. New meteorological evidence shows that Americans should expect progressively colder winters over the next century.
3. Marriages between people under eighteen are twice as likely to end in divorce as marriages between people over 25.

A viable thesis must be "living," and it must also be suitable in scope, given the limits (in length or in time) imposed by the writing situation or assignment. A five-page paper will not permit detailed explanation of all Newton's intellectual and scientific achievements; but you might intelligently discuss his discovery of calculus. Similarly, do not attempt a full explanation of the causes of the decline and fall of the Roman Empire in the space of four pages. Instead, explain the results of a particular battle with the invading barbarians. When forming your thesis, beware of using the words "all," "every," "never," or "none": these usually obligate the writer to discuss much more than the assignment length allows.

In addition to audience appeal and appropriate scope, a third factor in the viability of a thesis is information—how much is currently available to the writer, and how much he must (or can) obtain before beginning to write. It might be impossible for an undergraduate to write an intelligent assessment of a new surgical technique—he may lack the necessary medical background. In some cases a trip to the library can yield the required information. In other cases, however, the writer must admit that an especially ambitious or difficult project is beyond his means; he may not be able to learn enough about the topic or the needed information may not be available. In formulating a thesis, always choose a topic appropriate to your background and your sources of information.

There are three questions you should ask, to check the viability of your proposed thesis:

1. Is this thesis so commonplace that the audience will not pay attention to it? Will it interest my audience?
2. Can this thesis be adequately discussed in the time and length assigned?
3. Do I know, or can I find out, enough to develop this thesis?

Exercise: Evaluating viability

Use the three questions listed above to evaluate the viability of these thesis sentences. The writer is planning an essay of 750 words (three typed pages) for a class assignment, and he has available the resources of a college library.

Example
Thesis sentence: Brick-making is one of the oldest activities of man, and is with us still.

Evaluation: Too broad; could not be written in 750 words.

a. Many children are spoiled by their grandparents.
b. Printing has a long and complex history, during which it has brought about cultural and social reforms.
c. "Clear-cutting" forest areas produces simplified and more vulnerable ecosystems.
d. Television has affected American life.
e. Child abuse is reaching epidemic proportions in American cities.

Clarity

After the writer has chosen a limited topic, decided upon a

controlling idea, and checked his thesis for viability, he must communicate his thesis to the reader in clear and effective language. He has two goals in phrasing the all-important thesis sentence:

(a) to make his topic clear to the reader,
(b) to emphasize his controlling idea.

The writer achieves these goals through *syntax*—the relationship between words, phrases, and clauses within a sentence. The following discussion demonstrates how syntax can heighten the impact of a thesis sentence.

The words describing your topic should be the subject of the thesis sentence. If your topic is *tax reform*, your thesis sentence might read:

Tax reform has become the central issue in American politics.

Reversing the order of the phrases will confuse the reader:

American politics is primarily concerned with *tax reform*.

Here the subject of the sentence is *American politics*, and the reader might assume—with good reason—that your topic is current political concerns, rather than tax reform.

The controlling idea is the writer's particular message about his topic; obviously, he does not want his readers to miss this idea. To emphasize the controlling idea and make sure the audience gets his message, the writer places the controlling idea in that part of his thesis sentence controlled by the main verb (the predicate of the sentence). Suppose a writer has decided that the World Health Organization has done a good job of preventing disease. He writes the thesis:

The World Health Organization, which has undertaken significant programs to reduce communicable diseases in underdeveloped countries, is part of the United Nations.

Readers naturally assume that the most important part of a writer's message will occur in the predicate of a sentence. The sentence as it now stands exhibits the following structure:

Subject	Relative clause	Predicate
The W.H.O.	which has undertaken . . .	is part of . . .

Obviously no one would write a paper to prove that the W.H.O. is part of the United Nations. The writer has mistakenly placed his controlling idea within a relative clause, which is understood to be less important than the independent clause. To create the appropriate emphasis, the writer must revise his sentence by moving his controlling idea to the predicate of the independent clause:

The World Health Organization, which is part of the United Nations, has undertaken significant programs to reduce communicable diseases in underdeveloped countries.

Thesis sentences containing several ideas strung together cause similar problems for the reader; it is impossible to decide which are the important points on the first reading. In the following sentence more important and less important ideas are not adequately differentiated:

(1) [Purchasing a used car can lower the costs of transportation] and (2) [new cars depreciate very rapidly the first few years] and (3) [it can be difficult to recognize used cars that have something wrong with them that will cost money to fix] but (4) [some older cars like the smaller Thunderbird and the '70–'73 Cougars have a fairly high resale value.]

The first step in revising this sentence is to decide which clause is the most important and how the other ideas relate to that clause. Economy seems to be the most important idea, because cost comes up in every clause: "lower the costs," "depreciate," "will cost money," and "high resale value." Of these, the idea of reducing costs seems most important, making the first clause the best choice for the dominant clause of the thesis: "purchasing a used car can lower the costs of transportation." In order for this assertion of the first clause to be true, the second clause (new cars depreciate very rapidly the first few years) must be an accurate statement, so the second is logically necessary for the first. The third clause is an exception to the first clause, because unanticipated repair costs can immediately drive up the cost of owning the used car. The fourth clause is an exception to the second clause, because the high resale value of a few models seems to show that the generalization about rapid depreciation is not true in all cases.

These relationships between statements—logical condition, assertion, and exception—can be expressed through a syntactic pattern shown by pointers: Because (of) X, Y (is true), although Z and although V. Using this pattern to revise the original thesis produces:

Because new cars depreciate very rapidly the first few years, purchasing a used car can lower the costs of transportation, although it can be difficult to recognize used cars that will need repairs and a few older cars like the small Thunderbird and the '70–'73 Cougars have a fairly high resale value.

Even though this is a fairly long thesis, most readers will understand after the first reading that your intention is to explain why purchasing a used car can lower the cost of transportation.

The following questions may be used to check the clarity of thesis sentences:

1. Is the topic clear—does it appear as the subject of the independent clause?
2. Is the controlling idea properly emphasized—does it appear in the predicate of the independent clause?

Exercise: Evaluating clarity

Use the questions listed above to check the clarity of the following thesis sentences. If necessary, revise them to make them clearer.

a. *Macbeth,* which shows how evil affects man, is a play by Shakespeare.
b. Where can you find more recreational facilities than in Houston?
c. Freezing temperatures have arrived and pruned trees provide little shelter and are not comfortable and so birds will hasten away on their migration route.
d. Change is an important part of city life and would be exciting if you could cope with it, which I cannot.
e. There is something important about physical fitness.
f. Pope Julius's successor was Leo X, and Leo X was the eldest surviving son of Lorenzo de' Medici, and Leo X brought to their high point the classical and secular tastes of the Renaissance papacy, and Leo X was irresponsible in his concern for the well-being of the Church across the continent

because he drained money off to pay for his building campaign and his art works.

Accuracy

Careful grammatical construction and precise terms are crucial in thesis sentences. Relationships between subjects and verbs and between pronouns and their antecedents must be clear and exact. In the following sentence, prepositional phrases meant to add information and clarify the message fail to do so; they merely confuse the sentence and the reader:

With popular Christian instruction numerous other matters of doctrine and devotion are covered, like by treatises and occasional sermons touching on religious views.

Here, the precise meanings of the prepositional phrases are obscure. "With" usually means "by means of," but it can also mean "accompanying," or "at the moment of," or "in regard to." Which of these meanings does "with" seem to have in this sentence? "Like" and "by" also lack clear meaning here.

In order to make this sentence communicate successfully with the reader, the writer must decide upon the exact and limited topic and use the words describing it as the subject. Then he must decide upon his controlling idea and make it the predicate. To this basic sentence structure he can add prepositional phrases which supply more detail. An accurate and precise thesis sentence results:

Treatises and sermons taught matters of doctrine and devotion during the Middle Ages.

You can check for the accuracy of a thesis sentence by asking the following questions:

1. Are the words precise and exact?
2. Are the grammatical constructions clear, correct, and easy to understand?

Exercise: Evaluating accuracy

Check the following thesis sentences for accuracy, using the questions listed above. Revise three of them to improve accuracy.

a. Elementary teachers will be helped by computers if they function as they should.
b. "Star Wars" is a really far out science fiction movie.
c. Compared with other languages, English confuses you by things in it.
d. Our accomplishments in space are out of this world with all the efforts increasing.
e. Campaign and election laws aren't too good.
f. The invasion of Canada in 1775 by the American rebels was one of the great strategic mistakes of the Revolution.

Review

A well-formulated thesis is a great help to the writer: it guides the writing process, giving coherence and continuity to the composition. To produce a good thesis the writer must be absolutely clear about his subject, his audience, and his intention in writing. A thesis consists of a limited topic and a focused, controlling idea. To test the effectiveness of your thesis sentence, ask the following questions:

Viability
1. Is this thesis so commonplace that the audience will not pay attention to it? Will it interest my audience?
2. Can this thesis be adequately discussed in the time and length assigned?
3. Do I know, or can I find out, enough to develop this thesis?

Clarity
4. Is the topic clear—does it appear as the subject of the independent clause?
5. Is the controlling idea properly emphasized—does it appear in the predicate of the independent clause?

Accuracy
6. Are the words precise and exact?
7. Are the grammatical constructions clear, correct, and easy to understand?

Asking questions and making decisions
Exercise: Evaluating thesis sentences

Ask the seven questions to evaluate the following sentences.

Consider each as a thesis for a five-page essay. Write an evaluation of each sentence, and revise those that need improvement.

a. There is a problem with nutrition and junk food today.
b. Importing and exporting goods or trading has been important in the history of man.
c. The booming sales in men's grooming products show the definition of masculinity has changed.
d. It is long past time for the Federal Communication Commission to repeal its outmoded and impractical rule prohibiting CB operators from "talking skip," communicating with stations more than one hundred and fifty miles away.
e. Much of the best photography of the past generation has concerned itself with giving permanent form to a fleeting moment of experience.
f. The Western world's main job in the years ahead will be to cut back overambitious efforts to achieve an ever-rising standard of living.
g. Courts-martial of Marine Corps drill instructors for training abuses have tripled since November despite new rules aimed at more supervision and less maltreatment of recruits and it shows that these rules are not working but is it the drill instructors' faults.
h. Racial discrimination in the rental of apartments is still widespread in Manhattan, New York's prime real estate market.
i. What do you think about the idea that fresh disclosures about the death of President John F. Kennedy do not warrant a reopening of public investigations?
j. Recent furniture designs are proportioned more for spacious Mediterranean castles than for small apartments.
k. With the students assaulted karate should be taught in high schools.
l. The problems with Indian land have been the result of racist government policies.
m. That we want people liking us is clearly to be seen in the desire most people have to receive Valentines even if they're older.
n. With all the Arabs living in Israel it is going to be a movement for equal rights with the Jewish citizens.

4 Coherence

Objectives

An effective paragraph contains only relevant facts and ideas, arranged in the clearest possible order. By close attention to ordering strategies, and by the deliberate repetition of key words and sentence structures, the writer produces coherent paragraphs. Well-chosen transitions between paragraphs contribute to unity. This chapter shows you how to choose ordering strategies for your paragraphs, and how to achieve coherence and unity in your writing.

Coherence

"Coherence" comes from two Latin words meaning "together" and "to stick"; in coherent writing the parts "stick together" naturally or logically to form a unified and understandable whole. "Coherence" in a paragraph means that all the parts work together to express the writer's intention and to communicate that intention to the reader. Carefully constructed patterns of inclusive and particular terms (see Chapter 3) help to arrange relevant material in an intelligible order, thus contributing to the coherence of paragraphs. There are other writing strategies that help achieve coherence.

Coherent writing is clearly the result of decision-making. A writer who does not have a definite idea of his audience's needs, who does not have a thesis or a complete sense of his intention—in short, an *indecisive* writer—is rarely coherent. The elements of his paragraphs will not stick together, and his audience will be confused—or totally lost. To achieve coherence, the writer asks these questions:

1. Does the topic require ordering in time or space—or will logical relationships between ideas determine the order of the writing?
2. What are the correct logical relationships between sentences in a paragraph or between paragraphs in a passage?
3. What writing strategies work best to make these relationships clear to the reader?
4. Can coherence be increased through repetition of key words and sentence structures?

The exercises in this chapter give you practice in ordering paragraphs to achieve maximum coherence.

Coherence through space order and time order

The writer's purpose determines the strategies that will most effectively create coherence in his composition. If his main question concerns location in space, the writer will describe objects in a way that stresses position, or order in space. If a crew of scientists were digging up the site of an ancient city, they would write a report describing the buildings and objects found. They probably would organize the report according to the locations of these buildings. For example, they might begin with all the evidences of structures in one quarter of the site and then move on to describe an adjacent quarter, and so on. Adverbial phrases and clauses in the sentences would make these locations easy for the reader to visualize: "at the southern boundary," "fifty feet to the east," "where the west wall joins the temple garden," and so forth.

If the writer's main question concerns occurrence in time, he will choose time order, telling which events happen first, which follow, and which occur last. Processes and procedures are often described in this order. In writing about the procedures for joining the Army, a writer would begin with the recruit's first application and end with his being sworn into the service. Such order is characterized by adverbial constructions that show time order: "First," "in one week," "after he reported to the induction center," and "finally." Whenever the primary purpose is to describe or to narrate (tell a story), order in space and/or order in time is likely to be the strategy that creates coherence in the paragraph or composition.

Exercise: Recognizing patterns of space order

1. Circle the pointers (words and phrases) which help the reader to see the space order of the scene.

A street carnival easily draws people to its festive atmosphere and unusual attractions. With one end of the street left open for the crowd to come and go, the rest of the space is happily jammed with people and booths. On one side of the street a ferris wheel, bordered with flashing lights, carries customers high up the circle and down. Across the way, a spinning rocket thrusts its riders into a delirium of thrills and fears. At the far end of the street, a merry-go-round attracts the younger children. Set between these rides are booths of all descriptions: a wheel of fortune, a ball toss game, a palm-reader, jars of beans that defy guessing powers—and, of course, the food stands tempting passersby with ice-cream, hot dogs, and cotton candy.

2. The author of the paragraph below neglected to supply pointers indicating space order. Fill in the blanks with words or phrases that help the reader to imagine the scene:

It was plain to Dr. Moore that this would be a busy day, for twelve patients already crowded his waiting room. _____, the happy Smith teenager giggled over a comic book and_____there was the tonsillectomy case he needed to schedule for Tuesday. _____, Mrs. Clark was back for more coddling and another bottle of "sugar pills." Beside her the Warner infant, who needed to be hospitalized, whined and squirmed in his mother's lap. _____ both Allen boys sat glumly, as though near relapse. _____ Mrs. Slocomb waited hesitantly for her husband's pathology report.

Exercise: Recognizing patterns of time order

Pointers indicating time order are most effective when they are placed at the beginning of a sentence. In the following paragraph the writer has used time pointers, but he has not placed them effectively. Circle the pointers that indicate time order and then rewrite the paragraph, shifting these markers to the beginning of the sentence. The rewritten sentences should focus the reader's attention on a series of events beginning in November of 1911 and ending in November of 1912.

The Scott expedition began their southern sledge journey toward the pole in November of 1911. Delayed by bad weather, they reached the pole, where they found that they had been beaten by Amundsen. Sickness, insufficiency of food, and severe weather made traveling very slow on the return journey. Petty Officer Edgar Evans died under the strain on February 17. Captain L.E.G. Oates, who was too ill to travel farther, walked out into a blizzard a month later, hoping by his sacrifice to save his companions. But the weather prevented their advancing much farther. The party pitched their final camp four days later. Scott made the last entry in his diary on March 29: "Everyday we have been ready to start for our depot 11 miles away but outside the door of the tent it remains a scene of whirling drift. . . . We shall stick it out to the end, but we are getting weaker, of course, and the end cannot be far. It seems a pity but I do not think I can write any more." Their bodies were found in their small tent by a search party on November 12, seven-and-a-half months later.

Coherence through logical order

Writing arranged by space or time reflects a natural order. The writer describing a scene or telling a story knows, almost by intuition, which detail to give first, second, and so on. In most writing, however, the material is not so easily organized; the writer must first decide which logical relationships exist between his ideas and then must find words and phrases to express these relationships adequately. Usually he establishes the paragraph's central logical relationship in his topic sentence. The rest of the paragraph is devoted to working out this logical relationship. The following chart shows a number of logical relationships and their corresponding pointers, words or phrases which call the reader's attention to the appropriate relationship.

Nature of relationship	Possible signals or pointers
Addition to or elaboration of earlier statement	In addition, moreover, also, furthermore, likewise, similarly
Example of earlier statement	For example, thus, for instance, as an illustration

Contradiction of earlier statement	On the contrary, in contrast, however, on the other hand, but, notwithstanding
Concession	Although, while, even though, in spite of
Cause-effect	Consequently, since, as a result, hence, therefore, thus
Summary	In summary, in short, in conclusion
Series	First, second, finally

Exercise: Recognizing logical relations

Determine a logical relationship between each pair of sentences below. Write down the type of relationship and then choose an appropriate connective from the chart above—or supply one of your own.

a. Government spending in the past year was less than usual. _____, taxes will be lowered.
b. I hate cough medicine. _____, I know I have to take it.
c. Buster is rude to everyone. _____, he interrupts any conversation whenever he has something to say.
d. George likes spicy food. _____, Muriel likes bland food. _____, it is hard to plan a menu that both will enjoy.
e. There are many problems in the world. _____, there is the problem of overpopulation. _____, there is the problem of poverty. _____, there is the problem of pollution. _____, there is man's unwillingness to act in order to solve his problems.
f. That ends my tale of woe. _____, I would like to say that money can't buy happiness.
g. A knowledge of typing comes in handy for many things. _____, when one writes a term paper, he should be able to type it. _____, if one writes letters to important dignitaries, he should type them.
h. Stress can produce a variety of unhealthy effects. _____, consider the results of stress on blood pressure and respiratory rates.

Coherence through repetition

In addition to the use of pointers, the writer can strengthen the coherence of his composition by repeating key phrases and syntactic patterns within sentences. He must decide on the key word or phrase of the paragraph; often this key term is the subject of the thesis sentence. Repeating it focuses the reader's attention and adds force to the entire passage. Similarly, repeating syntactic patterns increases coherence by stressing certain relationships.

Exercises: Recognizing repetition of key words

1. *Circle* the words in the paragraph below which first appear in the thesis sentence and are then deliberately repeated. Why is this repetition effective? What other strategies for coherence has the writer used?

Large cities are always places of great contrast. For example, the decaying slums sorely in need of rehabilitation contrast with the newly built or carefully maintained apartment houses and residential neighborhoods. Also, in large cities some of the people are rude and alienated, while others are highly civilized and courteous. In addition, in some areas of large cities excellent public transportation is available while other areas are forgotten. Perhaps the only salvation for our large cities is specific steps to raise the morale and mutual concern of all citizens so that they feel the benefits of the city should belong to all its inhabitants.

2. What is the subject of the following paragraph? Although the key term appears only once, how many substitutes for it can you find? Replace half of these with the key term, writing it in above the substitutes. Read the paragraph again; notice the increase in emphasis and coherence gained through repetition.

The cockroaches that inhabit many apartments are parasites almost impossible to exterminate completely. Some 170 million years older than the dinosaur, this bug, with its five eyes and six legs, can hide in the dark for weeks without food or water. Whenever a new poison for these pests is created, some of the insects quickly become immune. And in one year, a female of this species can have 35,000 offspring. This, coupled with the fact that there are, at last count, 55 kinds of them in U.S., makes us hope only to control the pest and probably never to eliminate it completely.

Exercise: Recognizing repetition of syntactic patterns

In the following paragraph, how many times is the syntactic pattern "noun + should have + verb" repeated? What is the subject noun in each of these repeated patterns?

By rights New York should have destroyed itself long ago, from panic or fire or rioting or failure of some vital supply line in its circulatory system or from some deep labyrinthine short circuit. Long ago the city should have experienced an insoluble traffic snarl at some impossible bottleneck. It should have perished of hunger when food lines failed for a few days. It should have been wiped out by a plague starting in its slums or carried by ships' rats. It should have been overwhelmed by the sea that licks at it on every side. The workers in its myriad cells should have succumbed to nerves, from the fearful pall of smoke-fog that drifts over every few days from Jersey, blotting out all light at noon and leaving the high offices suspended, men groping and depressed, and the sense of the world's end. (E. B. White, "Here Is New York")

The author of this passage has used repetition to reinforce his central idea of impending destruction, with an accumulation of words which refer to doom—*destroyed, perished, wiped out, overwhelmed, succumbed.* These strengthen the reader's understanding of the author's thesis. Moreover, placing these verbs in the syntactic pattern "should have _____" increases in the reader's mind the probability of such destruction, and contributes to coherence by setting up a constant rhythm.

Paragraphs like E. B. White's on New York are rare. Usually writers employ repetition more moderately, for several good reasons. First, writers seldom hope to achieve just one effect—they seek many. Second, excessive repetition can be monotonous. Repetition builds a series of reinforcing experiences for the reader and thereby adds to intensity; but the overuse of repetition bores him, destroying the effect of the writing. There are other trade-offs involved in repetition: repeating a single word or pattern of syntax adds emphasis to the writing and allows the reader to remember key terms; but the price is a loss of the variety given by synonyms and contrasting syntax. The writer must decide with care about repetition, if he is to elicit the response he seeks from the reader.

Coherence through transition

Most writing, of course, is longer than one paragraph. But the qualities of an effective paragraph—well-defined purpose expressed in a clear topic sentence, enough specific detail, and coherence—mark all good expository and argumentative prose. How do you know when to change to a new paragraph? It is wise to do so with any shift in the exact topic or the controlling idea. In the following series of paragraphs, the writer observes these conventions in his introduction to an analysis of love.

We will accept variety in almost anything, from roses and religions to politics and poetry. But when it comes to love, each of us believes we know the real thing, and we are reluctant to accept other notions. We disparage other people's experiences by calling them infatuations, mere sexual flings, unrealistic affairs.

For thousands of years writers and philosophers have debated the nature of love. Many recognized that there are different kinds of love, but few accepted them all as legitimate. Instead each writer argues that his own concept of love is the best. C.S. Lewis thought that true love must be unselfish and altruistic, as did sociologist Pitirim Sorokin. Stendhal, by contrast, took the view that love is passionate and ecstatic. Others think that "real" love must be wedded to the Protestant ethic, forging a relationship that is mutually beneficial and productive. Definitions of love range from sexual lust to an excess of friendship.

The ancient Greeks and Romans were more tolerant. They had a variety of words for different and, to them, equally valid types of love. But today the concept has rigidified; most of us believe that there is only one true kind of love. We measure each relationship against this ideal in terms of degree or quantity. Does Tom love me more than Tim does? Do you love me as much as I love you? Do I love you enough? Such comparisons also assume that love comes in fixed amounts—the more I give to you, the less I have for anyone else; if you don't give me everything, you don't love me enough.

"There is hardly any activity, any enterprise, which is started with such tremendous hopes and expectations, and yet which fails so regularly, as love," wrote Erich Fromm. I think that part of the reason for this failure rate is that too often people are speaking different languages when they speak of love. The problem is not *how much* love they feel, but *which kind*. The way to have a mutually satisfying love affair is not to find a partner who loves "in the right amount," but one who shares the same approach to loving, the same definition of love.

My research explored the literature of love and the experiences of ordinary lovers in order to distinguish these approaches. . . . Empirically I found three primary types of love, none of which could be reduced to the others, and a variety of secondary types that proved to be combinations of the basic three. (John Alan Lee, "The Styles of Loving," *Psychology Today*)

Lee shifts paragraphs whenever his topic or his controlling idea changes. When he moves from paragraph one to paragraph two his controlling idea, disagreement over the nature of love, remains the same; but his topic shifts from contemporary persons to writers and philosophers of the past. In paragraph three he changes both topic and idea, contrasting ancient tolerance for different types of love to modern insistence on only one type. In paragraph four he chooses "the failure of love" as his topic and his idea about that topic is that this failure results from differences in the definition of love. In the last paragraph Lee's topic becomes his own research, and his idea is the discovery of three primary types or definitions of love and a variety of secondary types.

Review

Coherence in writing is the result of ordering strategies that draw similar elements into clearly defined relationships. One of these strategies is the direction imposed by the thesis sentence and its counterpart in paragraphs, the topic sentence. The thesis and topic sentences help the writer to distinguish between essential material and irrelevant material which should be left out. These sentences also contribute to coherence by setting the scope of the paragraph, letting the writer know what he must provide for complete expression, and guiding the reader's expectations. The inclusive concepts and particulars included in a paragraph are held together by a network of pointers that work together to structure the paragraph. Clearly defined relationships between paragraphs work in a similar way to structure the entire composition. To sum up, the writer's primary ordering strategies are the thesis or topic sentence; the pattern of related inclusive and particular terms; and the order—order in space, order in time, or logical order—that determines the sequence of sentences within paragraphs and paragraphs within the composition. Careful repetition of key terms and syntactic patterns also produces a unified and thoroughly coherent composition.

To evaluate coherence, the writer asks the following questions:

1. Is there an apparent order, either natural (time or space) or logical, imposed by the writer?

2. Are there enough appropriate pointers to make this order clear to the reader?
3. Has the writer used repetition of key terms and syntactic patterns to create emphasis and additional coherence?

Asking questions and making decisions

Exercise: Evaluating coherence in paragraphs

Use the questions listed above to evaluate the coherence of the following paragraphs. Then rewrite the paragraphs, supplying pointers to clarify order and logical relationships.

a. The essence of man is man thinking, and to understand thought one must understand Aristotle. Seventeen hundred years after his death, he greatly influenced the Renaissance. Eighteen hundred years after he died, scientists studying anatomy had to start with Aristotle's concepts. After 22 centuries, a group of mathematicians trying to refine logic started with Aristotle. His influence on art and literature has been as pervasive as on logic and science: Leonardo da Vinci and Michaelangelo worked within Aristotle's concept of the human figure. Even today, many literary and art critics use Aristotle's system of analysis.

b. Senator Robertson's campaign was planned to expose him to important income and ethnic groups all across the country. In the Eastern states he met with steel workers and labor leaders, industrialists and financiers. In the Southern states he conferred with lumber company representatives and representatives from small rural co-operatives. His travels took him to meet with chiefs of the movie industry, land developers, and Pacific fishing interests. The farmers and dairymen held talks with him to explain their plans for reforming the Department of Agriculture.

c. People who study patterns of birth, death, and migration in human populations do not use a "generation life table" as often as the biologists and ecologists who study most animal populations. A generation life table follows a cohort, which is a group of individuals born in the same year, throughout their lives. Consider the life history of 100,000 people all born in 1900. The generation life table would tell how many of that group died each year. Before the researcher could complete the table, he would have to wait until nearly all of the original cohort had died. In our rapidly changing society the conditions that affect mortality have varied so much since 1900 that the generation life table for the 1900 cohort might not be useful in predicting the experience of later cohorts. The table might be obsolete almost before it was completed. Population biologists who study animals that live only a few weeks, months or years find the generation life table useful, because the table covers a short period of time in which significant changes in the causes of mortality are not likely· to occur or, if they occur, can be documented and analyzed. Consider the life history of a population of spruce budworms whose life cycle is about one year. By studying the conditions that influence the survival rates of these pests in each of several succeeding years, scientists have been able to identify changing conditions that result in an economically destructive outbreak of the pest, damaging millions of dollars worth of timber. Scientists can now predict when a plague of spruce budworms will appear, allowing timber companies to take action against these pests at the most effective time.

Exercise: Evaluating coherence in a composition

Read this student's explanation of Cubism as illustrated in the paintings of Picasso.
1. Go back and identify the ways in which she has created coherence and unity.
2. Write a paragraph evaluating the coherence and unity of this sample, using the questions in the preceding exercise.

Cubism, a major movement in modern art best known in the work of the great artist Pablo Picasso, pointed to a major cultural change taking place in Western Europe. Cubism implied that "art can be other than the actual object in space." This movement, which began with Picasso in 1907, can be illustrated with his work and can be divided into roughly three periods: the first, Early Phase from c.1907 to 1909; the second or Analytic Phase from c.1912 to 1920.

Picasso's first cubist painting of the Early Phase, "Les Demoiselles d'Avignon," c.1900–1907, was an essential step forward in the evolution of twentieth-century art. His technique in this painting is characterized by great economy of means. For instance, Picasso uses the merest lines to define the facial features, breasts, and arms of his female figures; flat tones approximating flesh color delineate the sharp planes that create the body's contours. Yet, there is nothing flimsy about the female figures; they have massive solidity and elemental strength. The distorted sculptural and primitive quality of the female figures reflects Picasso's interest in oceanic and primitive art. Finally, the negative space lifts up to the surface plane with its agressive colors of pinks and blues, thereby uniting with the figures and pulling the whole composition into the front picture plane.

In the Analytic Phase from 1909 to 1912, Picasso breaks down his objects and figures into fragmentary parts. For example, in Picasso's "Portrait of Ambroise Vollard" c.1909–1910, the color contrasts and surface textures that were so important in "Les Demoiselles d'Avignon" have now been reduced to a minimum. Picasso has used a monochromatic blue color scheme so as not to interfere with the design. The canvas is broken down into areas that resemble cubes or prisms. Picasso has transferred the inner world of Ambroise Vollard with all its component parts onto the canvas, and the composition now explodes and Ambroise Vollard appears destroyed and unrecognizable.

Finally, in the Synthetic Phase of c.1912 to 1920, Picasso now builds up and brings together his forms to create a new object. He plays with what is art and what is reality. His "Three Musicians," c.1921, represents a summing up of his new artistic style. Here, in a retrospective glance, two figures from an earlier period in his career reappear. Dazzling color has also reappeared and it dances across the surface of the painting in a mixed pattern of circles, triangles and squares. A dreamy mood and a strong personal fantasy are apparent in this work. The painting is fitted together with pieces that resemble a patchwork quilt, but nevertheless the figures of the three musicians come through bright and clear.

Cubism was a revolution. It was the spirit of the times as well as the spirit of the artist that compelled Picasso to break down and dissect the inner and outer world and then to put it back together in a new way. It was a declaration of independence from the cultural and artistic heritage of the past. The viewer was now compelled to look at his art in a new way. For instance, the distortions of the face and figure, along with Picasso's placement of the figures, forced the viewer into sorting out his optical expression and experience as best he could. Picasso's cubism asks the viewer to abandon his preconceived ideas of form, to forget natural appearance altogether and to look at the fragments that make up his figures as pure forms in themselves. (Georgia Harbour, student)

Exercise: Creating a coherent composition

Write an explanation of your behavior in a certain situation: supply the background, your own feelings and the reactions of the other people involved, and the immediate consequences of your actions. Make the following decisions *before* writing:

1. Who is my audience, and what is my intention?

2. What details must I include to carry out that intention and ensure complete expression—a balance of inclusive and particular terms?
3. What is my thesis? What order in my material will best develop this thesis?
4. What strategies should I use to create coherence?
5. How should my paragraphs be divided?

5 Comparison

Often, a writer's preliminary decisions commit him to answering a question that requires comparison—an assessment of similarities and differences. The writer may need to determine whether Harvard's medical school is harder to get into than Yale's, or whether the Red Sox are better than the Pirates this season.

Comparison is a tool, a set of options and techniques, that helps to implement certain preliminary decisions. In making decisions about his audience, the writer forms an intention toward them (Chapter 1). If he chooses to explain something, his purpose is exposition—the setting forth of an idea, event, or process. An expository writer usually uses comparison (a) to explain the unfamiliar or (b) to examine similarities and differences between two or more subjects. A writer using comparison to explain the unfamiliar might, for example, compare the English game of cricket to American baseball. In this kind of comparison the reader's knowledge of baseball provides a basis for his understanding of something new, cricket. But an expository writer might want to examine equally familiar (or unfamiliar) topics. He might compare the social attitudes of two novelists, the grading habits of two history professors, or the job opportunities of two different professions.

When the writer has decided to persuade his audience to hold an opinion or to take some action, his purpose is argumentation. The argumentative writer—who is more interested in "selling" his idea, his product, or his candidate than in "explaining" something—will use comparison to prove that one idea (or product or candidate) is better than the others. He might, for example, assess the differences between two presidential candidates in order to demonstrate the vast superiority of one of them.

Whether his intention is to explain or to persuade, the writer must be clearly aware of the major question he wishes to answer in order to organize his comparison carefully. In this chapter you will learn how to write effective comparisons. You will learn to choose points of comparison and patterns of organization. You will also practice writing sentence patterns that give force and coherence to comparisons.

Using comparison

Choosing bases of comparison

A thesis usually offers a response to a major question about a topic. Every major question that calls for comparison implies subordinate questions that the writer must answer for the audience. Nearly always there is at least one key term in the thesis which gives a clue to these subordinate questions. In the question "Is Harvard's medical school harder to get into than Yale's?" the key term is "harder." What makes one school "harder" to get into? Does one require a higher undergraduate gradepoint average than the other? Does one have a more complex process of admission, with more interviews, examinations, and procedures than the other? Do more people seek admission and fail in one school than in the other? Does the process take longer at one than at the other? Any questions that help define the meaning of the key term are subordinate questions that the writer must answer. These questions become the *bases of comparison* (*bases* is the plural of *basis*), and supply the structural elements for the comparison—and for the writing. Without organized bases of comparison, a paragraph or an essay will degenerate into a rambling, ineffectual, and usually disjointed series of sentences.

The writer must also think about which questions will fit his audience's needs and serve his own purpose in writing. These questions vary according to the particular writing situation, as illustrated by the following example.

Two candidates, Smith and Brown, are running in a congressional primary election. The state political committee of the party wants to launch a successful campaign, so it hires a political analyst to compare the two candidates' potentials. In his report the analyst would choose bases of comparison that answer the questions implied by "potential," questions he believes the committee wants answered and that his own professional expertise tells him are important: How much money could each of the candidates supply for his or her own campaign? Would one be better able to secure large donations from wealthy contributors? What attitudes do large interest groups such as organized labor or big business have toward each of these candidates? Does the public already know one candidate better than the other?

In contrast, a writer preparing an informational brochure for a civic group like the League of Women Voters would choose bases of comparison that answer a different set of questions about Smith and Brown: What sort of previous political experience do the candidates have? What educational qualifications? What are their personal characters? What plans do they have to benefit the voters? What principles of government do they support? The bases chosen for a comparison reflect the writer's analysis of his audience's needs, his subject, and his intention.

Exercises: Choosing bases of comparison

1. Consider each of the following situations, giving special attention to the needs of the audience. Write at least three questions that might guide the writer in choosing bases of comparison.

   Example: A young woman with a limited income wants to take up an outdoor sport and has asked you to compare water-skiing and snow-skiing.

   Possible questions: How much does the equipment cost? How much do lessons cost? What traveling expenses are involved? How much do lodging and meals cost?

   a. Help a family of five (two adults, one 14-year-old boy, and twin 8-year-old girls) decide between two vacation sites for a two-week trip.

   b. Help a friend entering college avoid disappointment by

explaining how your expectations of college differed from the actual experience.

c. Convince your team-mates that their annual award for Realistic Treatment of Professional Sports in Film should be given to movie A instead of movie B.

d. I want to support a liberal senator. How can I tell a liberal legislator from a conservative one?

2. Read the following paragraphs. Then write a brief analysis of each, answering these questions:

1. What two topics are being compared?
2. What are the bases of comparison? (What subordinate questions are being answered?)
3. Are these bases the same for each topic?
4. If not, how does this influence the paragraph's effectiveness?

Example

It is more important for a man to have a college education than for a woman. If a man lacks a college education he cannot get a good job, and statistics reveal that a male college graduate can earn $100,000 more than the nongraduate. This is ample proof that if a man wants to provide for his family, he'll need a diploma. Furthermore, women who go to college usually get married, and then their education is wasted.

Evaluation: The topics being compared are the importance of a college education for a man and for a woman. The bases are not the same for both. The bases for a man are: ability to get a job, lifetime earning capacity, and ability to provide for a family. The basis for a woman is future marital status. The reader cannot judge the conclusions easily, since the writer never talks about the effect of education on a woman's ability to get a job, total earnings, or ability to provide for a family.

a. Chicago just can't equal Atlanta. In Chicago the weather is really bad—cold and damp in winter and steamy in summer. And then there's a lot of racial trouble in Chicago as well as too much union control. On the other hand, Atlanta offers ample work opportunities, a wide variety of recreational activities, and an outstanding theater.

b. The poems of Walt Whitman and Emily Dickinson, two nineteenth-century American poets, differ in tone, treatment of subject matter, and form. Whitman celebrates the bonds of community, approves the complex variety of human nature, and yearns to be one with all he perceives. Dickinson expresses a sense of isolation, fears the contradictions of human emotions, and is keenly aware of her inability to commune with other people and with nature. Whitman writes poems that catalog his world and his society, whereas Dickinson concentrates on describing a single perception or experience. Whitman's poems employ free verse and often extend for many pages; Dickinson's poems distill ideas in brief controlled stanzas.

c. In contrast to the mystery movies of the forties, the crime movies of the sixties emphasized visual violence. The exploding face of the small-town victim in *Bonnie and Clyde* introduced a flood of close-ups of maimed and ever more spectacularly dying persons throughout the decade as Dirty Harry, Matt Helm, and 007 did their work. In the Sherlock Holmes movies of the forties the viewer barely saw enough to know a crime had been committed. After a glimpse of the victim's foot the camera switched to study Holmes' face as he pondered the significance of clues and figured out the criminal's next move. Whether such change reflected a change in the viewing public's interest is uncertain.

Organizing comparisons

Once the writer has chosen the bases of his comparison, he must select a pattern of organization for his writing. There are two common patterns for organizing comparisons. The writer who follows the first of these considers his topics in sequential order, examining one topic fully before proceeding to a complete treatment of the second. In comparing two biology teachers, the writer who follows this "A then B" pattern would complete a discussion of Professor A's lecture habits, grading habits, and attitude toward attendance before turning to an equivalent discussion of Professor B. This pattern of organizing comparisons has several benefits. It allows the writer to create emphasis through the accumulation of detail (see Chapter 4), and also to gain persuasive force by saving the statement of his preference (Professor B is better than Professor A) for the final, climactic section of the writing. In this pattern of organization, emphasis falls on the two topics themselves (Professors A and B) rather than on the bases of comparison (lecture habits, etc.).

Although the writer who uses this "A then B" pattern gains emphasis and persuasive force, he risks losing coherence. To avoid this he must structure his details carefully, covering the same bases of comparison in the same order (called parallel order) for both A and B. To strengthen coherence in this pattern, the writer needs a clear pivot point, a point at which the focus of the discussion shifts from A to B. This pivot is usually signaled by words like "but," "however," "on the other hand," "in the case of." Other devices that strengthen coherence, especially repetition of key terms and sentence patterns (see Chapter 4), help to unify the "A then B" pattern.

An outline of this pattern of organizing comparisons would look like this:

Topic A Rock concert audience

Basis 1 Kinds of experiences they value
Basis 2 Relationship with performers
Basis 3 Attitudes toward each other

Pivot (In contrast, . . .)

Topic B Folk concert audience

Basis 1 Kinds of experiences they value
Basis 2 Relationship with performers
Basis 3 Attitudes toward each other

More effective in many situations, especially for the beginning writer, is the second comparison pattern, in which the two topics are considered simultaneously, point by point. Rather than devoting an entire block of his composition to A, and then another to B, the writer considers both A and B in one sentence, or in pairs of sentences. Here the *bases* of comparison are dominant and create the order of the passage. Notice the difference in the two patterns below:

"A then B" pattern	*"Point by point" pattern*
A. Rock concert audience	A. Experiences valued
1. Experiences valued	1. Rock concert audience
2. Relationship with performers	2. Folk concert audience
3. Attitudes toward each other	B. Relationship with performers
Pivot	1. Rock concert audience

B. Folk concert audience
  1. Experiences valued
  2. Relationship with per-
     formers
  3. Attitudes toward each
     other

2. Folk concert audience

C. Attitudes toward each
  other
  1. Rock concert audience
  2. Folk concert audience

One very common version of the "point by point" pattern presents similarities first and differences second. All the bases on which the two topics are alike are treated first, and all the bases on which they differ follow afterward. If, in the example above, the kinds of experience the audiences value are similar, this point might be discussed first. Then, attention would turn to those points on which they differ. Although some people think of this pattern as a third comparison pattern, it is really a common form of the "point by point" pattern.

Exercise: Identifying patterns of organization

Answer these questions about each of the following para-graphs:

1. What pattern of organization is used?
2. Is the pattern used consistently?
3. If the "A then B" pattern was used, where is the pivot?
4. How was coherence achieved? Mention specific devices used.

a. The new house proved to be an improvement over the walk-up apartment. Whereas the small, crowded apartment had oppressed and hampered their spirits, the new, more spacious house seemed to release their dreams and their painting began again. And the noises which had been so jangling and abrasive—sirens, traffic, and the El—were now replaced by children's voices, the neigh-borhood dogs' woofing, and bird songs. Most important, the light which had been so fogged and filtered by the city's narrow streets and polluted air now warmed every corner of the open and airy house, and even spilled into the paintings now in progress.

b. Inflation has drastically reduced the power of the dollar since 1967. In September of 1967, Mrs. John Q. Public outfitted John Jr. for school, purchasing school shoes for $9.95, shirts and Levi's for $3.99 a piece, and a very nice sweater for $14.95. At the grocery, she bought a Thanksgiving turkey for 39¢ a pound and five pounds of sugar for 79¢. Then she drove home in her new '98 Oldsmobile which had cost $4,350 and ran on 28.9¢ a gallon gasoline. However, when September 1977 rolled around Mrs. Public had problems. John Jr.'s shoes ran $24.95, his Levi's cost $7.99 a pair, and shirts were hard to find, even at $13.95 a piece. He did without a new sweater! At Minimax, turkey was still the best buy but now sold for 79¢ per pound while the sugar now cost $1.79. Loading these purchases into her new car (another Olds but this time the tag was $8,970), Mrs. Public was relieved to see a gas station open where she could fill up for only 59.9¢ per gallon. Where would it end?

Exercises: Choosing comparison patterns

1. Choose a set of topics from the list below. Next, select a hypothetical audience and decide what questions you would want to answer about the topic for that particular audience, and choose three appropriate bases of comparison. Formulate a strong thesis sentence and write a paragraph of 150 words, using the organizational pattern "A then B."
2. Choose a second set of topics and follow the instructions above, but this time use the "point by point" pattern to construct your paragraph.

Topic sets:
Two movies
Two rock groups
Two schools you have attended
Two food styles (soul food vs. Italian food—or any other combination)
Two math (or science, English, etc.) courses
Two styles of art (architecture, painting, jazz, etc.)
Two television performers
Two hobbies
Two related life forms (two kinds of beetles, mushrooms, etc.)

Exercise: Identifying extended patterns of organization

After reading each of the two essays that follow, answer these questions:
1. What pattern of organization is used?
2. If "A then B" is used, where is the pivot?
3. What devices are used to achieve coherence?

a. *Two Ways of Going Away*

In the last year I have witnessed two funerals that should have been much the same—both buried old people, both were fundamentalist in religious attitude, and both used similar music and ritual. But in fact, one was an experience of anguish and the other truly a source of assurance.

At the first, an old man was buried who had been irresponsible to an extent, irascible and largely untouched by social niceties—including habits of church attendance. Thus, when the minister spoke of the promise of God's justice it fell a bit ominously on our ears, and the plaintive songs describing those jasper walls and pearly gates seemed far-fetched. The sighs and tears of a family who had never opened themselves to this man while he lived, somehow said more of guilt than grief. The whole experience seemed to wound rather than heal.

In almost total contrast was the funeral of an old woman, resolute in her faith and in her religious disciplines for 91 years. When the wavering tenor proclaimed her a new citizen of that celestial city, it seemed only the just culmination of years of conviction. And the family sat bound in total certainty that what they had known of her and had been to her had been full and sufficient. There was a tearful reminder of parting, but no sense of apology. As she was lowered into the ground, the mourners seemed somehow assured that there was, after all, a plan and a justice in life.

b. *History in the Movies*

Movie-makers, like other artists, are often motivated by the desire to provide a lasting image of a historical period or event. John Wayne and Jan Troell share this intention but to achieve their goal they use very different cinematic techniques, representing different theories of how a movie influences an audience.

The plot of Wayne's *The Alamo* is carefully composed to heighten the significance of the concluding battle and enhance the moral character of every Texan leader. Early scenes stress the crucial importance of delaying the advancing Mexican army so that Sam Houston can train his troops. Minor preliminary brawls are followed by skirmishes and night raids, which build up to a final epic battle. Small scenes are given to each Texan leader to show his noble moral commitment to the battle. Bowie is committed to avenging the death of his family, who fell victim to plague while fleeing the Mexican advance. Crockett speaks of the sentiment he feels when he hears the word "republic." Travis devotes his life to buying time for General Houston. All find their highest personal values coincide with the common good.

The plot of Troell's *The Emigrants* has juxtaposed scenes whose relationships the viewer must pretty much figure out for himself. A man hurts his leg clearing boulders from a field; a young woman flirts with a suitor; the same woman suddenly has two children; a young boy lets his wooden clogs float down a stream. Only as the viewer pieces together the incidents do the themes of population pressure, starvation, and religous intolerance and the effects of empirical observation and experimentation in the period emerge. When they do and if they do, the viewer's sense of historical forces is vivid and experiential rather than abstract and theoretical. This insistence on daily domestic events gives the viewer a nonheroic perspective on the pioneer Swedes who frequently wipe their noses, fall sick, suffer lice, scurvy, diarrhea, recurring infections, and impairment from brutal punishment. The only character who talks of divine providence is a self-proclaimed minister whose opinions, such as his belief that once they reach America God will make all the true-believers speak English without studying the language, look foolish if not pathetic.

Wayne's film uses dialogue in two different ways. Sometimes the talk advances the action, but most of the time action stops for talk. The camera zooms in on a character who delivers a soliloquy on the meaning of the term "republic," Mexican contempt for individualism, the role of women in revolution, the meaning of the land to a patriot, or the obligation of a leader to his men. Troell's film uses dialogue quite differently. Like his use of scenes, the function of his dialogue is to force the viewer-hearer into deducing what went before and finding a meaning in obscure phrases, poorly recorded. When values do enter into a discussion between his characters, the speeches are essential to the situation rather than commentaries on it. For example, when the protagonist's wife appears to be dying during the voyage to America, he asks her forgiveness for having made the journey, pleading that he only wanted a better life for them. His defense is a natural part of the emotional situation between them.

Wayne and Troell both want to influence their viewers, but Wayne tries to accomplish this by organizing scenes and using dialogue to interpret them for viewers. Troell refuses to deliver an overt interpretation for his audience, apparently believing that the most powerful interpretation is the one the viewer derives from his own reasoning processes. Troell's interpretive work is implicit in his choice of details.

Using sentence structure in comparison

Readers are familiar with a number of sentence patterns conventionally used to present contrasts and comparisons.

The decisive writer uses these familiar sentence structures to emphasize his comparisons. In most of these patterns key terms point out the comparison:

1. Although _____, _____.
2. _____, whereas _____.
3. Unlike _____, _____.
4. _____, but _____.
5. _____; on the other hand, _____.
6. _____; however, _____.
7. Not only _____, but also _____.
8. Then _____; now _____.
9. Any repetition of sentence patterns, deviating to show contrast.

Exercise: Identifying sentence structure

Circle the words in the following sentences that stress comparison. Then, use the same patterns to structure sentences of your own.

a. Maritime law is not a *corpus juris* (an independent body of law); but Justice Robert H. Jackson of the United States Supreme Court emphasized its international character in an opinion he wrote in 1953.

b. Although the Creek and Cherokee tribes allowed unmarried persons to have sexual relationships, illegitimate pregnancy brought severe punishment for the woman.

c. Unlike lymphatic leukemia, which affects the lymph nodes, myeloid leukemia is primarily a disease of the bone marrow.

d. Not only did the tributary of the Hermus river bring necessary water for the people of Sardis, it also carried gold-bearing sand that provided an important source of wealth for the city.

e. In most states, a "lynching" is the execution of an individual accused or convicted of a crime without due process of law, by three or more persons; however, in a few states the law requires that to be a "lynching" (rather than a "murder") the victim must have been in the hands of a peace officer before being seized by the mob.

f. The people of Lozère no longer cultivate rye and chestnuts, whereas they plant more and more potatoes each year.

g. Not only did David Livingstone open up the southern half of the African continent, he also shook the conscience of the civilized world by disclosing what he called "the running sore of Africa," the slave trade.

h. We want students to be able to complete their education as rapidly as possible; on the other hand, we do not want the University to lose money by operating a full summer program for only a few students.

i. The donor could influence the choice of subject for a stained glass window, but the finished design was essentially the personal creation of the master glazier, who was an artist in his own right.

j. He denied the bodily resurrection of the dead; however, he affirmed the immortality of the soul.

k. Formerly a public man needed a private secretary as a barrier between himself and the public; now he has a press secretary to keep him in the public eye.

Combining dominant and subordinate comparisons

An expository essay uses comparison to illustrate the similarities and differences between two topics or things. In the following essay, the student writer explains how the American and Soviet systems solve three basic economic questions in very different ways. The contrast in methods stems from basic differences in economic and social ideology. Two kinds of comparison are involved in this writing task: (a) a comparison of the different ideologies, and (b) a comparison of the economic mechanisms used to solve the three questions: what to produce, how to produce, and for whom to produce. The writer decided the reader needed to grasp the relevant ideological differences first, in order to follow the subsequent discussion of how such principles influence the economy. As a result, the first comparison becomes a *subordinate* part of the essay, functioning to introduce and define the two systems of thought. To ensure clarity, and to place emphasis on the two systems of thought, the writer chose the "A then B" pattern for his introduction. The second comparison—of specific economic mechanisms—is the dominant one and organizes the main body of the writing. For this comparison, the writer chose the "point by point" pattern of organization, showing how each system answers a specific question according to its ideological stance on resource allocation, operational and decision-making mechanisms, and social priorities. The distinction between dominant and subordinate comparisons becomes an important device for organizing the writing.

In the sample essay that follows, identify in the text the organizational patterns noted in the margin.

Introduction   Every economy must solve three basic problems: what to produce, how to produce, and for whom to produce. Two widely disparate ways of solving these problems are exemplified by the American capitalist system and the Soviet socialist system. Because of widely divergent ideologies, the Soviet and American economies base their answers to the fundamental economic questions (what to produce, how to produce, and for whom) on different resource allocation mechanisms, different operational and decision-making mechanisms, and different social priorities.

A then B: Principles of Marxist doctrine   To understand these mechanisms one must first look to their respective ideologies. Soviet socialist ideology is based on the writings of Karl Marx. While Marx's doctrine encompasses many different areas, his major contribution to economics is his Labor Theory of Value, which advocates state ownership of all capital and resources, and implies that capital and resources cost nothing in a socialist society. Marx's Labor Theory of Value proposes that the value of a good is equal only to the value of the labor used to produce the good. According to Marx, capital in itself adds nothing to the value of a good. For example, the value of a car would be the accumulated wages of all the workers who made or worked on any of the parts of the automobile. The capital used to make the car, such as a blast furnace, a paint sprayer, a mining tool, or any other machine used in its construction, would not add any value to the car. A direct implication of the Labor Theory of Value is that capital and natural resources are costless. Furthermore the state, and hence the people, own all capital and resources, so obviously they need not pay for them. In this way a socialist society avoids the dangers of rich capitalists and land owners who charge high prices for capital.

Pivot of introductory comparison   The U. S. capitalist principles are the complete opposite. Although capitalism has no official system of thought, it does have an outlook which evolved over many centuries and is based on

A then B: Principles of capitalist economy   these tenets: (1) ownership and arbitrary disposition of private property is an inalienable right, (2) capital and natural resources are worth whatever you can get for them, and (3) every individual is worth what he can produce, whether with his labor or with his

Thesis   capital. The ideological differences between Marxism and capitalism foster different ways of managing resources, different ways of answering the three basic questions of what, how, and for whom.

Point by point Basis 1: What to produce (Soviet)   The first basic question is what to produce. In the Soviet Union, since all productive resources are owned by the state, the state decides what to produce. The state works through a Central Economic Committee. It is the Committee's job to set the output targets for virtually everything produced in the Soviet Union. The Central Committee's criterion for its output targets is the betterment of the society as a whole. What constitutes betterment is subject to change as conditions change. In general, the Committee has the power to pick production targets arbitrarily. The Central Committee's actual mechanism for resource management is the Five-Year Plan. The Five-Year Plan sets broad goals and targets to be achieved in the next five years. Because the Five-Year Plans are very broad in scope and relatively long-term by nature, they don't specify actual target details. The details are left to the One-Year Plans. One-Year Plans operate within the scope of the broader and more general Five-Year Plans, but are much more detailed about who will produce what and how much. Every year the old One-Year Plan is reviewed to see how successfully it furthered the goals of the encompassing Five-Year Plan, and a new One-Year Plan is drawn up that tries to avoid mistakes made in previous ones. After a One-Year Plan is completed, output targets are distributed to the individual plant managers. The manager must then attempt to produce the target quantity and comply with any other restrictions placed on him.

Basis 1: What to produce (U.S.)   On the other hand, what is to be produced in the United States is decided mostly by a feedback process, based on a pricing system. Information on what to produce is passed indirectly from the consumer to the producer by means of the pricing mechanism. For instance, consider the case where not enough bologna is being manufactured; people are lining up to buy bologna because there is not enough to go around. Two automatic mechanisms would come into play. First, some people would want the available bologna more than others, so they would bid up the price until the excess customers were driven away. Second, the new higher price of bologna would induce suppliers to make more bologna, since now they could cover the costs of additional labor and capital with the added revenues from the bologna. The increased supply would then drive down the price, though probably not as low as the original price. In the end, more bologna would be produced, though probably at a higher price, reflecting the added costs of producing more bologna. At that time people would be content to buy just as much bologna as was being produced, at the new price. In general, in a capitalist society the quantities produced are determined by the pricing mechanism.

Basis 2: How to produce   The next basic question is how to produce. This involves asking how much labor to use; how much capital to use; and what technology to use. Most importantly, one must decide what criteria to use in answering the preceding questions.

(Soviet)   In the Soviet Union these three questions are resolved by the Central Planning Committee. Included in the One-Year Plans are specific quantities of labor and capital that each enterprise should use in achieving its output target. The manager is obliged to stick to these quantities. The Committee also decides the technology to be used. The Central Committee's method for evaluating quantities of labor and capital is as follows. After it has decided what it wants to produce, it starts matching up available resources with appropriate manufacturers. It decides how much new investment is needed to achieve targets, and what resources to apply. It decides how much of the national product can be diverted to consumer goods, and sets wages accordingly. This match-up of resources and targets is a complicated business, and involves solving dozens of simultaneous equations.

(U.S.)   By comparison, how to produce in the U.S. system is decided by individual firms. The main criterion is cost. A firm will look at the current price of all resources. It will choose the resources which can produce what the firm wants at the lowest cost. Hence the manager answers the questions of how much labor, how much capital and what technology by looking respectively at the labor wage, the interest rate, and the labor-capital ratio of a technology.

Basis 3: For whom to produce (Soviet)   The last basic question is for whom to produce. This question is a matter of priorities. In the Soviet Union the people who control the priorities, the Central Planning Committee, place a high value on growth and industrialization. The consumer is of secondary importance. In the U.S. the consumer sets the priorities, so naturally he places himself at the top of the list of priorities.

(U.S.)

Conclusion   In conclusion, the Russian economy is characterized by commands passed down from the top (Central Planning Committee). The U.S. economy is characterized by commands passed up from the bottom (the consumer). As we have seen, these two points of view lead to very different answers to the three basic economic questions: What to produce, how to produce, and for whom to produce. (Charles Arnold, student)

Review

An effective comparison must have a clear purpose. The following questions clarify the writer's purpose and organize his comparison.

1. What major question(s) does this comparison attempt to answer?
2. What is the key term in this major question, and what subordinate questions does it imply?
3. Why does the audience want this question answered?
4. What bases of comparison meet the audience's needs and fulfill the writer's intention?

Once the bases or points of comparison have been chosen, the writer may choose one of two patterns of organization. He may use "A then B," treating each of two (or more) topics fully, first one (A), then the other (B). The bases of comparison should be discussed in *parallel* order, and the pivot point marked to indicate the change from one subject to another.

All About A

　　Basis 1
　　Basis 2
　　Basis 3

Pivot

All About B

　　Basis 1
　　Basis 2
　　Basis 3

The other pattern compares both topics, point by point:
Basis 1

　　Topic A
　　Topic B

Basis 2

　　Topic A
　　Topic B

Basis 3

　　Topic A
　　Topic B

In a common variation of the "point by point" pattern, the writer first discusses points of similarity and then deals with points in which the two topics differ. Single paragraphs or entire essays may be organized according to these patterns. The "A then B" pattern gives the reader an integrated and complete view of each topic. The "point by point" pattern emphasizes contrasts between the topics. Special sentence patterns emphasize comparisons. Comparisons may be either dominant or subordinate in an essay, and they may be used to persuade or to explain.

Asking questions and making decisions

Exercise: Evaluating student essays

You now have a good idea of the questions behind a writer's decisions when planning comparisons. Read the two student essays that follow: one is expository, the other is argumentative. *Write at least one page* about each essay, in which you evaluate it as an example of comparative writing. Support your opinions by reference to specific points in each essay.

Expository comparison

"Fair and Foul on the Western Frontier"

"Home on the Range"

Home, home on the range,
Where the deer and the antelope play;
Where seldom is heard a discouraging word
And the skies are not cloudy all day.

Where the air is so pure, the zephyrs so free,
The breezes so balmy and light
That I would not exchange my home on the range
For all the cities so bright.

How often at night when the heavens are bright
With the light of the glittering stars,
Have I stood here amazed and asked as I gazed
If their glory exceeds that of ours.

"Starving to Death on a Government Claim"
My name is Tom Hight, an old bach'lor I am,
You'll find me out West in the country of fame;
You'll find me out West on an elegant plan,
A-starving to death on my government claim.

Chorus: Hurrah for Greer County! The land of the free,
           The land of the bedbug, grasshopper and flea;
           I'll sing of its praises, I'll tell of its fame,
           While starving to death on my government claim.

   . . .

How happy I am when I crawl into bed,
A rattlesnake hisses a tune at my head.
A gay little centipede, all without fear,
Crawls over my pillow and into my ear.

   . . .

Goodbye to Greer county where blizzards arise,
Where the sun never sinks and the flea never dies,
And the wind never ceases but always remains
Till it starves us all out on our government claims.
(Songs reported by John A. and Alan Lomax, *Folk Song U.S.A.*)

Although the most famous western movies like "How the West Was Won" have preserved the optimistic songs of the pioneers, a second tradition of lament, discontent, and ironic disenchantment existed in American folksongs and ballads of the nineteenth century. These two traditions recorded very different impressions of the frontier experience. The positive tradition included such songs as "Sacramento," "Black Eyed Susie," "Bound for the Promised Land," and "Home on the Range." The hard-life tradition included "The State of Arkansas," "The Boll Weevil," "Goin' Down the Road Feelin' Bad," and "Starving to Death on a Government Claim." Contrasted in these two traditions are landscape, animal life, suitability of the land for human habitation, and approximation to an ideal. The differences between these two traditions can readily be seen in "Home on the Range" and "Starving to Death on a Government Claim."

A true paradise delights the cowboy in "Home on the Range." The country is the home of deer and antelope; the sky is cloudless; the air is pure; and the breezes are "balmy and light." Man is happy here. He feels no discouragement, and not only would he refuse to exchange his home for "all the cities," he wonders if his range-land home isn't more glorious than the heavens themselves. The rhymes emphasize the similarity of "play" and "all day," "light" and "bright," "stars" and "ours." The repetition of the word "home" in "Home, home on the range," intensifies our sense of the singer's satisfaction and oneness with the land.

In contrast, an infernal mockery of the ideal runs through Tom Hight's song, "Starving to Death on a Government Claim." Tom, unmarried, sings of a landscape of promise, "country of fame," where he came "on an elegant plan." But this ideal has turned out to be the home of bedbugs, grasshoppers, rattlesnakes and centipedes, not deer and antelope. Tom has suffered intense discouragement, and records the disparity in promise and fulfillment. Instead of balmy zephyrs he tells of blizzards, and wind that "never ceases but always remains, till it starves us all out on our government claims."

Far from rivaling heaven, Greer County is the antithesis of the ideal, and the rhymes contrast "claim" with "fame" and "land of the free" with "grasshopper and flea." Not man, but the centipede, is "without fear"; and only death by starvation awaits those who remain on their "government claims." Throughout the song, the phrase "government claim" resonates with the dual meaning "my area of land given by the government," and the illusory, false claim to paradise made by the government to prospective settlers: "claim" as false promise negates "claim" as substantial earth. The student who searches the songbooks will find more than one hopeful frontiersman who discovered a rattlesnake hissing the tune when he answered the call to "Go West!" (Art Evans, student)

Argumentative comparison

"Wanted: A choice of Weapons"

Perhaps you have noticed that at fencing competitions the women's event is soon over and only men are allowed to fence with the saber and the epée. Women are thought to be socially unsuited and too fragile for an event in which the whole body is a target; or in which male strength is needed to handle weapons derived from those traditionally masculine activities, dueling and warfare. Such assumptions are based on subjective social attitudes rather than a realistic assessment of the physical skills needed for the sports. As new members of the University Committee on Intercollegiate Athletics, I hope you will approve our student petition to the Amateur Fencers' League. This argues for the admission of women to competitive fencing with sabers and epées, as well as with foils. It points out that the skills required in these two events are similar to those in the permissible foil fencing, and are well within the capacity of most women who now compete with foils.

The size and shape of the three weapons require similar capacity. The epée (a modern dueling sword) and the saber (an updated cavalry sword) do not in themselves differ greatly from the foil, which was originally designed as a practice weapon for the smallsword. Foils, epées, and sabers are all the same length: forty-three inches. The saber blade is more rigid than that of the epée or the foil; and it is slightly heavier, twenty-seven ounces versus seventeen-and-a-half ounces for the foil. Both the epée and the saber have a large handguard. Obviously, the similar lengths and the presence or absence of the handguard require no difference in capacity, although one would concede that the extra nine-plus ounces of the saber might tire the arm more quickly.

Epée and saber competition require no greater endurance than foil fencing: the time limit is the same. Speed and flexibility are the essential physical attributes needed in all three forms of fencing; therefore a woman's smaller physical size will often help her if she has endurance. A woman in shape for foil is prepared for saber and epée.

All motions used in the three competitions can be executed by women. The permitted foil and the banned epée are both thrusting weapons; similar skills are needed for both. Saber competition involves slash, cut, and thrust motions. The additional moves are well within a woman's capacity. Unlike baseball, which requires overhand throwing unsuitable for the joint structure of the female shoulder, saber competition does not call for any movements impeded by sexual differences in physiological structure.

Women are excluded from epée and saber competition more because these events are traditionally male than because of any female inadequacy. All three events are equally safe for both sexes, if the prescribed clothing is worn. With modern protective gear it is virtually impossible to sustain greater injuries than the bruising that occurs even in foil fencing. If women are allowed to fence in this "gentleman's" sport at all, they should be accorded the privilege granted to all men, whatever their size, strength, or social station— the privilege of a choice of weapons. (Carla McFarland, student)

Exercise: Writing comparisons

Choose one of the hypothetical situations described below. Think of a question about the situation which must be answered by a comparison. Plan and write an essay which answers this question. Write at least four paragraphs, using the first paragraph to clarify the situation and to explain your bases of comparison.

a. Situation: Two athletes play the same position
b. Situation: Two theories attempt to explain the same event
c. Situation: Two candidates seek election to the same office
d. Situation: Two campus bars compete for customers

6 *Causes and consequences*

Objectives

Preliminary decisions often commit writers to explaining causes and consequences for their audiences. Modern people want to understand why and how things happen, so that they can produce and control change. Preventing disasters and achieving goals are prime motives for concern with causes and effects. For example, after nine years of a massive worldwide campaign to eradicate smallpox, only seven persons living in a remote Ethiopian village were known to have had the disease in 1976. The elimination of this devastating disease, which killed two million people in 1967, suggests other possibilities for dramatic change and has reinforced American interest in causes and effects.

Americans are also newly aware of what unexpected results can come from products and processes of experiments in science and technology. The drug thalidomide caused hundreds of infants to be born deformed before it was found that thalidomide could alter the normal development of a baby's arms and legs before birth. The need to avoid any undesirable outcome from thousands of innovations has made Americans anxious to anticipate the full consequences of their actions, and of the interaction of components in large systems. Thus, writers often find themselves expected to discuss causes and consequences.

In academic studies, as well as in daily life, you will become involved in reasoning and writing about causes and effects. Certainly if you study history, biology, sociology, economics, or physics, you will need to know how to investigate causal relationships and to evaluate other writers' hypotheses, reasoning processes, and conclusions. In some situations an entire essay may be devoted to discovering the causes of an event; or to tracing or predicting the consequences of a particular action. In your writing you might seek to establish the causes of the Civil War, the housing crisis on campus, or the high mercury level in deep-sea fishing areas. Or, your goal might be to trace the effects of wage and price controls, the discovery of penicillin, the widespread use of oral contraceptives, or the withdrawal of U.S. forces from Vietnam. In each of these writing situations you would present the relationship you have discovered, through a process of reasoning about causes and consequences.

In other situations cause-and-effect relationships would be a subordinate part of the essay, and other organizational patterns—such as comparison—would dominate. For example, your purpose might be to compare two kinds of sound systems for your school's auditorium. Your explanation of how certain devices in one system produce effects that the other system cannot deliver might be a subordinate part of the comparison, justifying and explaining your preference for one particular system.

The writer investigating causal relationships works like a detective, first inspecting the data at hand, and then using careful inductive and deductive reasoning to build a watertight case. The objectives of this chapter are to aid you in this detective work by teaching you: the difference between inductive and deductive reasoning; how both are incorporated in reasoning about causes and consequences; how to recognize logical fallacies in cause-and-effect reasoning; the appropriate use of evidence in cause-and-effect arguments; and patterns of organization that effectively communicate the results of your investigation.

Cause-and-effect reasoning

Inductive reasoning

Most cause-and-effect reasoning begins inductively, with inspection of data and the formation of a generalization. Consider the simplest example. If you examine everyone in your classroom and see that they all have two eyes, you could conclude with assurance that "all of the people in this classroom have two eyes." In this instance your statement applies only to the people you have observed. Recalling a lifetime's experience of looking at people, you might assert that having two eyes is a characteristic of all normal people. Since the category "all normal people" includes more people than you have ever seen (or ever could see), you risk making a statement that you cannot prove by actual inspection. This shift from making an assertion about a group actually examined to making an assertion about a larger but similar group is called "making an inductive leap." The thinker or writer who makes this leap must be sure that his generalization is very likely to be true.

Now consider a more complex example. Two kinds of European butterflies, indentical in every feature except color, were long regarded as separate species. Even their designs were identical; only their coloration was not. Scientists who had observed these butterflies made an inductive generalization about the two groups: *butterflies of the first color pattern appeared in the cool spring; butterflies of the second color pattern appeared in the hot summer.* Knowing that light and temperature had been shown to induce chemical changes that affect color, these scientists formed an hypothesis that the color of the two types was the result of temperature differences. They conducted experiments to test the hypothesis. When pupae (the stage between caterpillar and adult butterfly) that ordinarily would have emerged with the summer colors were kept at a low temperature, the adult butterflies emerged with the spring coloration. But pupae that ordinarily would have emerged as the spring type did not as readily show summer coloration when kept at high temperatures. The scientists concluded that the spring type was the dominant one and that the summer type was an acquired, or more recent, development.

The first inductive generalization in this example, in italics above, is that color, temperature, and time of year were related. The hypothesis, and the testing of it, are later stages in the cause-effect reasoning. The pupae experiment to test the hypothesis can also be called inductive, for it is confirmed by inspection of evidence.

Because the first inductive generalizations are the basis

of all the reasoning that follows, and because inductive reasoning may be involved in testing the hypothesis, it is important to avoid errors in inductive reasoning. Three questions help the writer to evaluate his inductive reasoning:

1. Is the evidence representative?
   Evidence that is not typical will cause your generalization to be false when you make an inductive leap. A writer might, for example, try to draw a national portrait of all Australians based on his acquaintance with one Australian penpal. But he has no way of knowing whether his friend is typical of the other 13.5 million Australians. Because further evidence could show that another generalization is more appropriate, this kind of error is called *hasty generalization*. Sometimes the writer has the right kind of evidence, but not enough of it. This too is called hasty generalization.

2. Is the generalization based on the right kind of evidence?
   The camper who claims that water in a nearby pond is safe to drink "because it's very clear" is basing his conclusion on the wrong kind of evidence. Clear, still water can be a fine breeding ground for disease-causing microorganisms; clearness alone is the wrong kind of evidence for determining the safety of drinking water. The writer who bases his conclusion on inappropriate evidence produces an *unreliable generalization*.

3. Is the writer deliberately slanting evidence by suppressing or disguising contradictory facts?
   A writer who attacks a politician for being "soft on defense," while ignoring the politician's record of support for military appropriations bills, is dealing in half-truths or indulging in distortion. Distortion is the most difficult error to detect; for the reader can recognize it only if he happens to know or, is alert enough to seek, the information left out by the writer.

Exercise: Spotting flaws in inductive reasoning

Look for hasty generalization, unreliable generalization, and distortion in these inductive arguments. Comment on the problems (if any) you find in each passage.

Example: Did you hear about that English doctor who examined eighty patients in only three hours? Doctors don't give patients enough time under socialized medicine.

Comment: The generalization is hasty, based on only one example.

a. A mixture of equal parts of sulphur and saltpeter will always explode if placed upon a cement floor and struck with a hammer. I know this because I tried it once.

b. American troops are unfailingly courteous, generous, and respectful to civilians when they are on military duty in other countries. American forces have built many hospitals and orphanages for the people of South Vietnam. [Hint: What about the massacres of Vietnam villagers, of which some Americans were convicted?]

c. I didn't realize what the most popular soft drinks in this locality were until my son began collecting bottle tops in the park last Sunday. He got a good supply from around the refreshment stand, and he arranged them in rows on the rug when we got home. The rows came out this way: Golden Age, 58; Pinkpop, 40; Pepsi, 16; miscellaneous, 5 or fewer each.
So now I know which companies are doing the best business in soft drinks around here.

d. A generation has passed since the last grizzly bear was shot in California, so it seems safe to assume that the grizzly is extinct in that state.

e. I have been riding up and down in that elevator every day for the past ten years. Now they come around to inspect it! Hasn't it proved safe already?

f. Returning from his three-day inspection trip, Congressman Casey reported that both civilian and military morale was high, that the enemy's strength had been shattered, and that victory was at hand.

Forming a hypothesis

Once a writer has inspected his data on the events, objects, or ideas he is interested in, and has made an inductive generalization about these data, he is ready for the next step in reasoning about causes and effects: the formulation of a tentative hypothesis. The writer often uses principles and concepts from appropriate academic disciplines (mathematics, sociology, psychology, chemistry) to form this hypothesis about causes or results, as in the case of the nearly identical butterflies:

Inspection of data

$\downarrow$

Inductive generalization
(interacting with previously
known principles and concepts)

$\downarrow$

One or more tentative hypotheses

It is important to form a tentative hypothesis that is neither too vague nor too simplistic. A timid writer may feel that only an omniscient being could really identify all the possible causes and results of a particular phenomenon; the timid writer may therefore retreat to the "safety" of a very general tentative hypothesis. He will blame the Civil War on "human nature"; the rising crime rate on "evil in society"; and campus discontent on "foreign subversive plots." While these hypothesized causes may actually have some influence on the phenomena in question, they are so very general that direct causal relationships will be hard to prove. An essay attempting to demonstrate that "human nature" caused the Civil War would be full of vague explanations, instead of concrete and specific evidence.

While the timid writer's argument is so vague as to be useless, the reckless writer's faults can make him seem like a fool. Most frequently, the rash interpreter of causes and effects oversimplifies. He matches a single cause with a single effect:

Student activism is the result of beards and long hair; bad marks on standardized English tests are caused by television; coed housing arrangements would solve all student discontent on campus.

The reckless or flippant writer fails to establish a proper relationship between his evidence and his conclusions; instead of taking the time and effort to work out a logical relationship, this hasty (and lazy) writer tosses off a fast, easy, and inaccurate hypothesis.

Writers should try to be aware of large interacting systems when they create hypotheses about causes and consequences. Fostered in part by advances in physics, cybernetics, biology, and ecology, there is a growing assumption that events and processes cannot be accurately studied as isolated phenomena. This has led writers to focus on complex webs of interrelated events. Researchers, too, try to acknowledge the presence of various influences even though they focus their work on just one of them. When a physician or medical researcher studies, for example, only one variable—how often a particular drug is administered—he or she will design the experiment to control for a variety of social, psychological, and biological factors that might influence the results.

Three questions can be used to identify (and to avoid) major faults in the tentative hypothesis:

1. Does the writer ignore the possibility of multiple causes for a particular situation or event?

Example

What can you expect? Of course the boy turned out to be a thief. His grandfather spent two years in the state pen.

Young Brian didn't become a thief merely because his grandfather had a criminal record. There were probably many reasons why Brian turned to crime—his grandfather's example may or may not have been one of them.

2. Does the writer rely merely on succession in time as proof that the first event causes a second event?

Example

Yesterday I ate two lobsters. Today I got sick. Lobsters make you sick.

This kind of simplification substitutes a temporal relationship for a proven causal relationship. When the writer assumes a causal relation only because one event follows another in time, logicians call his error in reasoning a *post hoc, ergo propter hoc* fallacy, literally: "after this, therefore because of this." *Post hoc* is a special case of ignoring multiple causes.

3. Does the writer depend upon a faulty comparison, or false analogy, to support his assertion of cause or effect?

Example

Even as a tiny child Mary looked like a carbon copy of her mother.

I've never known a mother and a daughter so alike in face, figure, voice, talents, and temperament. Mary's mother has always been a modest, moral, dignified person, so I can't believe these wild stories I've been hearing about Mary.

The validity of all analogies depends on whether the known points of resemblance necessarily indicate a resemblance in other, unknown points of comparison. Two things may be similar in some ways, but that does not guarantee that they are similar in all other ways. The author of the passage about Mary has failed to realize that a similar appearance does not necessitate similarities in character. Certain key points of difference may outweigh any similarities, and destroy the logical weight of the comparison. The author of the following passage has recognized an important differ-ence between Mary and her mother, that outweighs their similarities: Although Mary is a mirror-image of her mother, she has always had an insatiable desire to be the center of attention. Lately, this need for attention has led to bizarre behavior quite different from her mother's.

Exercise: Spotting logical fallacies

Test the following statements for (1) failure to recognize multiple causes, (2) the *post hoc, ergo propter hoc* fallacy, and (3) faulty analogy. Some of the statements contain no errors. Evaluate each passage in a sentence or two.

a. War is the incubator of poetry and drama. After the Persian wars came the great Greek dramas. After the victory over the Armada came Marlowe, Shakespeare, and Ben Jonson. After the Napo-leonic Wars came Shelley, Byron, and Keats. After World War I came T. S. Eliot.

b. The high cost of living is due to the exorbitant demands of the unions. There would be no need for manufacturers to raise their prices if the workers weren't constantly demanding higher and higher pay.

c. The rise in the number of men being treated by psychologists for impotence is due to the clamor for women's rights and women's aggressive behavior.

d. Mrs. Smith's death is no accident, and the logical suspect is her husband. Her husband's three previous wives all drowned in the bathtub as she did; all were heavily insured, as she was. Mr. Smith has fled to Europe, the insurance money in his fist, with his typist, leaving Mrs. Smith's soggy remains behind.

e. "I ask gentlemen, sir, what means this martial array, if its purpose be not to force us to submission? Can gentlemen assign any other possible motive for it? Has Great Britain any enemy in this quarter of the world, to call for all this accumulation of navies and armies? No, sir, she has none. They are meant for us; they can be meant for no other." (Patrick Henry, 1775)

f. Rogers is a jinx. He was riding the South Main bus the other day when it hit a truck pulling out from a construction site. He was in a train wreck at an amusement park three years ago when three people were seriously injured. Only yesterday he made a deposit at University State Bank, and before midnight the bank was afire. I'm glad he's your roommate, not mine.

g. All the more violent forms of athletics require physical courage; so does war. Athletics teaches discipline; so does war. Athletics requires quick thought; so does war. Athletics develops the will to win; so does war. If we approve athletics as a training for life, we must approve war.

h. In six Latin American countries where the United States has given financial aid to the government in power, military coups have overthrown the ruling party. Clearly we must stop sending money to Latin American countries, because it causes rebellion, disrupts the national life, and prolongs institutional instability in the southern hemisphere.

i. Unwittingly, American parents destine their sons to become great football players when they give them effeminate or unusual names. The boy named Milton Plum, Darryl Lamonica, Dante Pastorini, or Bob Lilly, has no choice but to prove his masculinity to the world by excelling in the most violent sport.

j. Forty-five percent of the inmates of the regional mental institution have been heavy drinkers. It follows that alcoholism is one cause, if not the leading cause, of mental illness in the U.S. today. [Which way should the causal arrows be drawn? Do people drink because they are mentally ill? Or do they become mentally ill because they drink?]

Testing the hypothesis

The third step in cause-and-effect reasoning is testing the tentative hypothesis. Sometimes the writer will conduct an empirical test, just like the scientists who were interested in the effects of temperature on the coloration of *Araschnia* butterflies. In some cases, especially when the writer is making predictions rather than searching for causes, he will apply logical principles, without any additional experiments to reach his conclusions.

The logical application of principles to information or data is called deductive reasoning—the kind of reasoning that made Sherlock Holmes famous. Deductive reasoning moves from principles, or premises, to conclusions about evidence. Reasoning that moves from premises to conclusions is called deductive reasoning even when the writer presents his conclusions first, and then explains the principles that led him to these conclusions. It is the order of thinking, rather than the order of writing, that makes an argument inductive or deductive.

In deductive reasoning the most inclusive statement is called the major premise. The statement that refers specifically to the evidence at hand is called the minor premise. The third statement is the conclusion:

Major premise
Minor premise
Conclusion

These three statements together form a *syllogism*. The most famous of all syllogisms is probably:

All men are mortal
Socrates is a man
Therefore, Socrates is mortal

In this syllogism, as in all others, the major premise presents a principle, the minor premise gives specific data, and the conclusion is the result of applying the premise to the evidence. There are rules of logic that can help you construct and test syllogisms; you can find them in any logic text.

So far in this chapter, cause-and-effect reasoning has been described by the following pattern of steps:

Inspection of data
↓
Inductive generalization
(interacting with previously
known principles and concepts)
↓
One or more
tentative hypotheses
↓

Deductive reasoning
(or experimenting)
↓
Conclusions

A few cases will illustrate the process of cause-and-effect reasoning.

Case 1

Suppose you are an academic counselor and an outstanding senior student, Lee Dickinson, has made very high grades the first three years of school. In early December of Lee's fourth year, you receive reports about Lee's performance in several classes. After checking Lee's file and the reports, you make an inductive generalization: Lee's grades have gone down ten to fifteen points in every class; a significant change can be seen in this student's performance. Why has this change occurred? Several tentative hypotheses can be constructed from the comments in the reports. One instructor commented: "Several of Lee's friends in this class belong to a group that is into drugs. I'm afraid Lee may be going along with the crowd." Another wrote: "Although I replaced Mr. Baynes as Anthropology instructor only a few weeks ago, I recognize the kind of student Lee is: one of those brilliant kids who think they're too good to be bothered with work." The sociology instructor noted: "See if there's a crisis. This student seems extremely depressed." Implicit in these remarks are several syllogisms:

1. Major premise: Some members of this group take drugs
   Minor premise: Lee seems to belong to the group
   Conclusion: Lee may be taking drugs
2. Major premise: Students who refuse to do their work are brilliant but conceited
   Minor premise: Lee has refused to do classwork
   Conclusion: Lee is brilliant but conceited
3. Major Premise: People who are depressed and uninvolved in their work are often people who are going through a crisis
   Minor Premise: Lee seems depressed and doesn't do assignments
   Conclusion: Lee may have experienced a crisis.

The tentative hypotheses suggested to you are that this student is on drugs, is brilliant but conceited, or is experiencing a crisis. You evaluate the major premises of these arguments and decide that on the basis of your past experience with this student, hypothesis two is not worth testing. In your interview with Lee you seek a personal explanation, and you try to find out whether Lee is closely associated with known drug users, and whether there has been some sort of crisis. Lee admits that during her mother's illness it seemed necessary to take a job as a short-order cook in an all-night café and that lack of sleep, little time for study, and small improvement in her mother's condition have made the future seem bleak. There is rarely time to see friends in the group who are on drugs. You discard the first hypothesis and begin to work with the student on financial aid, calling in a social worker to assist the family. In writing up your report on Lee, you explain this student's behavior on psychological principles.

Case 2

Suppose you are taking a chemistry course and that you and twenty other students are performing the same laboratory experiment. Everything goes well for all of you until the last step in the experiment, when the expected reaction does not happen. After talking with the other students in the lab, you conclude (by inductive reasoning) that the problem originated somewhere in the last step of the experiment. Next, you recall that slow or incomplete reactions occur if a reagent (reacting substance) is oxidized. Thus, deductive reasoning contributes to the formation of the hypothesis. Your thinking would continue, in order to check whether the reagent could have been oxidized. You recall a principle of unequal expansion that is related to oxidation. Changes in temperature may allow air containing oxygen to enter a partially full bottle, when unequal expansion of the bottle and the stopper has destroyed the airtight seal. Oxidation of the reagent would follow. This reagent came from an old, half-full bottle kept in the lab for several months. Therefore, this reagent may have been exposed to air and may have become oxidized. You form a tentative hypothesis that the reagent added in that step is responsible for the failure of the reaction. You form that hypothesis on the basis of your deductive reasoning just described.

As a limited test of your hypothesis you would obtain new, fresh supplies of the reagent and begin the laboratory work over again. If the new reagent worked well, you could explain your first failure in the laboratory report, using deductive reasoning and offering your successful experiment as partial proof of your explanation.

In a fascinating book, Robert Pirsig shows how all these elements of cause-and-effect reasoning may be varied with increasing rigor, complexity, and completeness in the full-dress scientific method. He illustrates his points with problems of motorcycle maintenance:

> Two kinds of logic are used, inductive and deductive. Inductive inferences start with observations of the machine and arrive at general conclusions. For example, if the cycle goes over a bump and the engine misfires, and then goes over another bump and the engine misfires, and then goes over another bump and the engine misfires, and then goes over a long smooth stretch of road and there is no misfiring, and then goes over a fourth bump and the engine misfires again, one can logically conclude that the misfiring is caused by the bumps. This is induction: reasoning from particular experiences to general truths.
>
> Deductive inferences do the reverse. They start with general knowledge and predict a specific observation. For example, if, from reading the hierarchy of facts about the machine, the mechanic knows the horn of the cycle is powered exclusively by electricity from the battery, then he can logically infer that if the battery is dead the horn will not work. That is deduction.
>
> Solution of problems too complicated for common sense to solve is achieved by long strings of mixed inductive and deductive inferences that weave back and forth between the observed machine and the mental hierarchy of the machine found in manuals. The correct program for this interweaving is formalized as scientific method. . . .
>
> In Part One of formal scientific method, which is the statement of the problem, the main skill is in stating absolutely no more than you are positive you know. It is much better to enter a statement "Solve Problem: Why doesn't cycle work?" which sounds dumb but is correct, than to enter a statement "Solve Problem: What is wrong with the electrical system?" when you don't absolutely know the trouble is in the electrical system. What you should state is "Solve Problem: What is wrong with

cycle?'' and then state as the first entry of Part Two: "Hypothesis Number One: The trouble is in the electrical system." You think of as many hypotheses as you can, then you design experiments to test them to see which are true and which are false.

This careful approach to the beginning questions keeps you from taking a major wrong turn which might cause you weeks of extra work or can even hang you up completely. Scientific questions often have a surface appearance of dumbness for this reason. They are asked in order to prevent dumb mistakes later on.

Part Three, that part of formal scientific method called experimentation, is sometimes thought of by romantics as all of science itself because that's the only part with much visual surface. They see lots of test tubes and bizarre equipment and people running around making discoveries. They do not see the experiment as part of a larger intellectual process and so they often confuse experiments with demonstrations, which look the same. A man conducting a gee-whiz science show with fifty thousand dollars' worth of Frankenstein equipment is not doing anything scientific if he knows beforehand what the results of his efforts are going to be. A motorcycle mechanic, on the other hand, who honks to see if the battery works is informally conducting a true scientific experiment. He is testing a hypothesis by putting the question to nature. The TV scientist who mutters sadly, "The experiment is a failure; we have failed to achieve what we had hoped for," is suffering mainly from a bad scriptwriter. An experiment is never a failure solely because it fails to achieve predicted results. An experiment is a failure only when it also fails adequately to test the hypothesis in question, when the data it produces don't prove anything one way or another.

Skill at this point consists of using experiments that test only the hypothesis in question, nothing less, nothing more. If the horn honks, and the mechanic concludes that the whole electrical system is working, he is in deep trouble. He has reached an illogical conclusion. The honking horn only tells him that the battery and horn are working. To design an experiment properly he has to think very rigidly in terms of what directly causes what. This you know from the hierarchy. The horn doesn't make the cycle go. Neither does the battery, except in a very indirect way. The point at which the electrical system directly causes the engine to fire is at the spark plugs, and if you don't test here, at the output of the electrical system, you will never really know whether the failure is electrical or not.

To test properly, the mechanic removes the plug and lays it against the engine so that the base around the plug is electrically grounded, kicks the starter lever and watches the spark-plug gap for a blue spark. If there isn't any, he can conclude one of two things: (a) there is an electrical failure or (b) his experiment is sloppy. If he is experienced he will try it a few more times, checking connections, trying every way he can think to get that plug to fire. Then, if he can't get it to fire, he finally concludes that (a) is correct, there's an electrical failure, and the experiment is over. He has proved that his hypothesis is correct.

In the final category—conclusions—skill lies in stating no more than the experiment has proved. It hasn't proved that when he fixes the electrical system the motorcycle will start. There may be other things wrong. But he does know that the motorcycle isn't going to run until the electrical system is working and he sets up the next formal question: "Solve Problem: what is wrong with the electrical system?"

He then sets up hypotheses for these and tests them. By asking the right question and choosing the right tests and drawing the right conclusions the mechanic works his way down the echelons of the motorcycle hierarchy until he has found the exact specific cause or causes of the engine failure, and then he changes them so that they no longer cause the failure. (Robert Pirsig, *Zen and the Art of Motorcycle Maintenance*)

Review

Inspecting the evidence

1. Is your evidence representative?
   Do you have enough evidence to know whether a particular case is representative? Avoid *hasty generalization.*
2. Is the generalization based on the right kind of evidence? Avoid *unreliable generalization.*
3. Is there any contrary evidence that has not been acknowledged? Avoid *distortion.*

Evaluating the hypothesis

1. Is the hypothesis too general or vague?
2. Is the hypothesis simplistic? Does it fail to recognize multiple causes?
3. Does the hypothesis involve a *post hoc* error?
4. Does the hypothesis rely on a faulty comparison or faulty analogy?

Testing the causal reasoning

1. Are the inclusive premises clearly and logically linked to the evidence?

2. Are there any relevant principles you might have left out?
3. If you have any doubts, check a logic textbook for deductive fallacies like double negative premises.

Asking questions and making decisions

Exercise: Evaluating cause-and-effect writing

The following passages are from student essays on the probable effects of a single cause: ratification of the Equal Rights Amendment, which guarantees equal civil rights for women. Most of these writing samples contain reasoning errors. Use the questions and concepts learned in this chapter to measure the strengths and the weaknesses of these examples, and write one or two sentences about each.

Example

Woman's role today is that of the homemaker, wife, and mother. She is not expected to go out and work to support the family. There is even some pressure to keep her at home and off the job market. She is expected to keep the house clean, the children well fed and well behaved. If a woman wants to work, however, she can. But there is no pressure on her to bring home a larger salary. Untrained for highly-skilled jobs, women are not given the chance to be employed as men are. Expected to be politically conscious, a woman is not expected to be politically active.

With the passage of the Equal Rights Amendment, the possible roles for men will have changed. They will have the right to stay home. But men will not take advantage of this new freedom. Rather they will keep on trying to provide for their families. And they may lose their jobs as more skilled women enter the job market. The freedoms men gain will be offset by competing with women in fields where before they have competed only with other men. Men will be able to get traditionally female jobs such as nurse, secretary, or typist. In these jobs, they will be pressured to achieve success above their women co-workers. Just as when the Woman's Suffrage Amendment was passed, little effect will be felt on men.

With the passage of the Equal Rights Amendment, men's roles won't change. They will still be working, providing, and administering. They won't face social pressure with the Equal Rights Amendment. They will face job competition. Men won't be pressured to keep the family united. And men won't gain the role of homemaker.

Women will gain a new role as provider for the family. Women

Margin annotations:

Generalization is too broad

Why? Causal steps missing

Contradicts above

Contradicts previous statement

Contradicts previous paragraph

Causal principles for last two consequences not explained

Why? Causal principle not explained will be expected to fulfill a man's role as well as a woman's. They will be expected to succeed in the careers they choose. Women will also have to keep their role as housekeeper. They will have to keep a clean house and handle the bills as well.

Evaluation: Several unjustified consequences are predicted; the writer doesn't supply any sociological or logical principles to support the predictions. Some causal steps are omitted; the reader doesn't know exactly why the predicted changes occur. There are many contradictions.

a. The ERA will eliminate the few remaining laws which call for greater punishment of women than of men. As an example, there is a statute in one state allowing women to be committed for up to three years in the reformatory for offenses such as "drug using" and "habitual intoxication," although men cannot be sentenced to more than 30 days for drunkenness. Laws like these, that discriminate on grounds of sex, would be nullified by the enactment of the ERA.

b. Women won't be affected by ratification of the ERA. Women are passive and submissive and no law will change that. When 2001 rolls around, women will still be getting out ring around the collar, because that is what really matters to them anyway.

c. Ratification of the ERA will bring thousands of unimaginable changes in the lives of U.S. citizens. The amendment is short, and it is widely felt that women already have their rights in most matters. But what starts out small can end up big. It will be just like a rock or a little stream. A stream can start out as no more than a trickle, and end up like the Mississippi River. A single rock sets off an avalanche. By the end of the century, women will run everything and men will just be slaves.

d. Once the right to be treated equally by department store credit departments, automobile companies, and other credit-lenders is assured, more women will begin to apply for credit. As job opportunities are provided, earning power and the credit eligibility will increase. In turn women will be able to borrow more, invest more, save more, and play a fuller part in the economy of the country. The number of persons who can contribute to the strength of the country, theoretically, will nearly double.

e. The ERA will not undermine the traditional family like most anti-ERAs claim. Changes in the family are due to developments in American capitalism which take more and more functions away from the family.

Second, conditions for women workers will change radically with the passage of the amendment. Women will no longer be considered replacements for men in the job market. Previous "protective legislation" has denied women extra income and promotional opportunities. Federal laws stipulate overtime pay after a certain number of hours' work per week. Various state laws and union agreements go further, by requiring overtime pay after a certain number of hours per day and for work on Saturday and Sunday. Such existing legislation places the two sexes in separate categories, with the result that women receive less salary. With the adoption of ERA such laws will have no force, and women will create increased competition among sectors of the working class.

f. The Equal Rights Amendment will result in unemployment for thousands of men. The big companies will lay off men who have held jobs for years and hire women, who are cheaper labor. Gangs of unemployed men will form, and there will no doubt be riots, with attacks on women who have taken away jobs.

g. [These paragraphs follow paragraphs on women's role in the military.]

It will be very interesting to see what new rights and laws the Gay Liberation Movement will demand under the Equal Rights Amendment. Probably they will want all anti-homosexual rules and regulations in the Armed Forces off the books. An intriguing conjecture will be, how much has society changed its views and how will the Archie Bunker segment resist change in laws relating to homosexuals? At this time it is almost impossible to speculate on what changes, if any, might come about in the laws affecting homosexuals, if the ERA is ratified.

Great changes, though, will certainly come about in many other areas if the ERA is ratified. The new laws growing out of the old sexually-biased laws will probably not have to go through courts, but will be changed by federal and state governments in the two-year period stated in Section three of the Twenty-seventh Amendment. These two years, between the ratification of the ERA and the time that the ERA goes into effect, should be ample time for clearly reshaping sexist laws to give men and women equality and the same legal rights. Without a doubt, though, some of these revised laws will be brought to court after the two-year period is over. Some states won't comply, and will discriminate against men or continue to discriminate against women.

h. The immediate effect of the Equal Rights Amendment (ERA) will be the complete legal equality of women, resulting at once in increased opportunity, protection, and benefits for them. Women will be legally entitled to the same opportunities as men in (1) education, (2) business, (3) retirement benefits, and (4) legal punishment.

Passage of the ERA will give women a better chance to further their formal education. At present college admissions give men an advantage over women. In the fall of 1968, only eighteen percent of the men entering public four-year colleges had high-school grade averages of B-plus or better, while 41 percent of freshmen women had attained such grades. An admissions brochure from one state university says: "Admission of women on the Freshmen level will be restricted to those who are especially well qualified." No such requirement is made for men. Stricter requirements for women, purely because they are women, put them at a disadvantage compared with men. The ERA would outlaw such discriminatory requirements, thus assuring equal educational opportunities for women.

Organizing cause-and-effect

Writing that explores causes and consequences may be organized in several ways. Although writing that involves cause-and-effect reasoning will always be influenced by the kinds of reasoning used, the writing structure will not always follow the reasoning pattern step by step. There are several patterns of organization for an essay on causes and consequences.

First, of course, you may choose to order your essay according to the reasoning pattern described in this chapter:

Pattern 1

A. Description of events or data, leading to a generalization

B. Hypothesis of probable cause(s) or consequence(s)

C. Reasoning that justifies hypothesis, applying principles or giving test results

Example

A. Many shrimp and tiny marine creatures have died in the bay where a new chemical plant is permitted to discharge hot water after use in a chemical process.

B. The temperature of the effluent (which is rigorously tested for purity) has raised the temperature in the bay around the discharge outlet to one higher than the small crustaceans can tolerate.

C. Results of tests show that: (1) the temperature of the water around the discharge outlet is X degrees; (2) shrimp perish at X minus 10 degrees; (3) no other occurrence is known that would introduce toxic substances or destructive conditions in the bay.

D. Conclusion

D. Therefore it appears that the temperature change resulting from the effluent being discharged is having a lethal effect on some marine life.

A second possibility begins with the principles:

Pattern 2

A. Review of principles, concepts, or theories that you intend to apply (justification if necessary)

B. Evidence or data you have collected

C. Discussion of how this evidence should be interpreted by these principles

D. Conclusion

Example

A. Theory about the psychological interaction of families in which one member remains obese (very fat) for a long period of time

B. Case history of the Brown family, taken from interviews

C. Interpretation of the mother's jealousy and explanation of why the daughter is obese

D. Recommendation for counseling for this family

A third possibility offers the conclusion first. In Part B of this pattern the writer describes the events in the cause-and-effect process rather than the reasoning process he may have used in thinking about the topic.

Pattern 3

A. Conclusion

B. Description of the causal process, showing principles involved in each step

Example

A. Prediction of the conditions five years in the future in the fifth ward of City X: few jobs, few businesses, high crime rate, etc.

B. Explanation of process of deterioration that began in the late fifties, identification of factors that accelerated the process: buildings not eligible for improvement loans because they did not meet building code requirements, etc.

Pattern 4 describes causal actions in complex systems:

Pattern 4	*Example*
A. Description of events to be explained	A. Situation at old urban high school
B. Analysis of system into kinds of processes involved (such as different kinds of chemical reactions or different social processes); principles related to each process	B. Social, economic, educational, political processes affecting student learning and teacher morale
C. Review of major causes or consequences	C. Review of major causal factors

It is usually helpful to review the degrees and kind of relationships (C) between various processes. Some will be partly independent of the others; some will be tightly related. A kind of verbal model of the complex system can be especially useful at this point in the essay, which will probably be fairly long because of the complexity of the system described.

A fifth pattern demonstrates analogy:

Pattern 5	*Example*
A. Brief description of evidence or data to be explained	A. Stalactites, thin tubes of calcium carbonate and other minerals hanging from a horizontal structure above a void
B. Description of analogous process	B. Description of action of malted milk poured through soda straw and left to dry, suspended from the top Repetition builds tip of straw with dried remains of malted milk
C. Explanation of the process as it applies to the evidence in A	C. Process of accumulation of particles moving very slowly in solution along a tubular structure; minerals form thin layer at tip of tube before solvent drops into the void, yielding a growing stalactite

A sixth possibility for organizing cause-and-effect writing is dubbed "the butler pattern" (the nickname comes from detective stories in which the private eye or police detective declares, after eliminating all the other suspects, "The butler did it.") In this the writer lists what he considers to be all possible causes or consequences, then eliminates all but the true one. The problem with this pattern of organization is that he must be sure to list the true cause or effect in the original array of possible causes or effects; unless this is done, the elimination of all the hypotheses but one will not yield the right conclusion:

Pattern 6	*Example*
A. Possible causes or con-sequences	A. Possible causes for the loosen-ing of floor tiles in a commercial building: seepage of water through a crack in the floor slab; incorrect kind of adhesive (glue); chemical reaction be-tween floor wax now used and original adhesive; heat from pipes embedded in floor; etc.
B. Inspection, discussion, and rejection of all but one	B. Consideration and elimination of all but the use of the wrong kind of adhesive when the floor was originally installed (records can no longer be found)
C. Conclusion	C. Conclusion that the floor was installed with the wrong kind of adhesive

Why so many organization patterns for writing about causes and results? First, a writer can have many kinds of audience, with different levels of knowledge about the topic and different needs. The organization pattern used in ex-plaining causes and effects can strongly affect the reader's ability to understand the causal process. If you have had some experience using laboratory manuals in a physics or chemistry class, you will recall that the information about the principles or reactions involved in the experiment are in a separate section of the manual, called "Background of Theory," and the successive steps of the experiment are labeled "Procedure." This division makes it easy to carry out the experiment. If the theory and the procedure were written up together, it would be harder to see what to do next at any given point. But this division of theory and procedure also makes it harder to understand theoretically what is happening in each step; and it takes careful thinking to relate these two sections as you write the discussion section of your laboratory report.

Your readers, also, will be influenced by the way you organize your cause-and-effect writing, and they will have different needs and expectations. If you are writing a paper about a process, to show you have understood certain concepts studied in class, the second pattern may be most advantageous. Pattern two allows you to review the concepts or principles first; right away the instructor will see you have understood the essential ideas he or she has emphasized. Further, the instructor is already familiar with these principles, and presenting them in a separate section will not hamper the grasp of the process you intend to explain. On the other hand if you are writing for an audience unfamiliar with the topic, to help them identify a certain process, you will choose another pattern of organization. Pattern three would tie the explanation to the sequence of events in the process, and indicate the principles involved in each step. This pattern would be suitable for explaining the course of a disease, or the process of developing film to new photography students.

You may find your readers understand a process more rapidly if you can refer to a process already familiar to them. In such a situation, Pattern five would be a useful way of organizing your essay. The sixth pattern, "the butler pattern," creates suspense for an audience you wish to entertain, and it is also useful when you must report on several hypotheses that have been examined. Before you begin writing, review your preliminary decisions and choose a pattern of organization that suits your audience, your subject, and your intention.

Exercise: Choosing patterns of organization

Explain to each of the following writers what pattern of organization would be best.

a. The writer is a student writing for a political science professor on the physical effects from 1945–1970 (not the political effects) of the two atomic bombs that were dropped on Japan.

b. The writer is a newspaper reporter preparing for his readers a feature story about how excessive use of nitrogen fertilizer can cause birth defects. (The nitrogen gets into rivers, and pregnant women drink water containing the nitrogen compound.)

c. The writer is reporting on the durability and rust-proof quality of four paints tested for use in a company plant. The paints have different chemical properties and composition. The audience is the head of the building and maintenance section of the company.

d. The writer is predicting the development of a section of town for a group of businessmen who are thinking of investing a large amount of money in the area.

e. A student writer is preparing a paper for a sociology class on the growth of early Christian groups during the first hundred years after Christ's death.

f. A college student wants to write a brief explanation of the expansion theory of the universe for his twelve-year-old brother, who already knows how raisins in cake batter move apart from each other during baking. (hint: raisins = galaxies)

Exercises: Explaining causes and predicting consequences

1. Select an event in the last ten years that you personally judge to have been important. You might choose the Vietnam War or some aspect of it, Watergate, the landing on the moon, the civil rights movement; the availability of citizen-band radios or small calculators, or some other technical achievement; the appearance of some social theory or system such as transactional analysis or behavioral modification techniques. Next, make a list of things that you believe happened because of that event. Be specific. How did the event affect you personally? How did it affect your friends, your family, your community? Do not list vague generalities: "It made people more honest," or "It made me aware of ethical standards." Write down specific instances: "We decided to draft an ethics code for members of the student senate." Select from your list three to five of the of the most important results, and write an essay explaining to a specific audience the way this event brought about these results, discussing the cause-effect process that was at work in each case.

2. Select a problem that you consider worth solving. Think carefully about the problem, and decide what questions you should ask about its causes. Consider several instances of this problem, and make one or more inductive generalizations. Create hypotheses about the problem's causes. Test these hypotheses by logical reasoning or by practical experiments. Formulate your conclusions. Decide what person or group can help solve this problem, and address your essay to the person who can tackle the job. Choose the organization pattern that best suits your subject, your situation, and your audience. Check your thesis, plan an outline, and write an essay of four to six pages on your topic.

7 *Analysis and definition*

Before a writer begins to write, he decides what questions he wishes to answer about a topic. Often he decides to answer questions of "what," "what kind," or "what parts": "What is art nouveau?" "What kind of book is *Gravity's Rainbow?*" or "Does this mental illness have stages?" Students are often asked to write papers and essay tests that answer such questions. This chapter will help you (1) to see that similar processes serve to answer all of these questions, (2) to evaluate essays that answer such questions, and (3) to apply these processes in your own writing.

The writer's perspective

When a writer is asked a question about "what," "what kind," or "what parts," he usually forms an answer based on ideas and feelings already familiar to him. Because each writer has his own background of experience, education, and culture, each one's answers reflect his personal perspective. Suppose, for example, that an artist, a canoeist, and a geologist were invited to a spot along a rushing mountain river and were asked to answer the question "What do you see here?" The artist might see in the scene an impressionistic rendering of light playing upon rapids. The canoeist might focus on the Class IV rapid and consider the challenge of running it. The geologist might view the river as a strong force rapidly cutting through the stream bed. Each visitor describes the scene from a perspective that reflects his personal background. The artist's perspective is rooted in familiar ideas about the reflection of light and its effects on

105

an audience, and the techniques that can magnify these effects. The canoeist's mental framework includes facts about current flow, the danger of certain rock configurations, and the national standards for classifying rapids. The geologist's perception includes ideas about the characteristics of different rocks, patterns of change in rock surfaces, and water speed.

An individual may have more than one perspective, or way of interpreting his experience: quite possibly the geologist enjoys, and could write about, both canoeing and painting. The writer must decide, therefore, which perspective will best suit his purpose, because the one he chooses will set the emphases in his writing and will provide the framework for the development of his topic.

Even when a topic is assigned, the student must still decide what perspective his professor expects. The student who answers the question "What kind of book is *Roots?*" by writing "a paperback," is clearly not choosing a framework acceptable to his literature teacher. In writing about *Roots* he must decide whether to interpret this book according to historical accounts of slavery; or according to the tradition of novels about the South, works by Faulkner and others; or according to the tradition of novels by black authors such as Ralph Ellison, James Baldwin, and others; or according to some other perspective. If the student compares the events in *Roots* to historical accounts of slavery, he will be concerned with whether they are representative of the experiences of people known to have lived then, rather than with the structure of the novel or its effect on readers.

The student who answered the question "What kind of book is *Roots?*" by identifying it as a "black novel" or "a novel written by a black writer," would emphasize other things. He might consider how most novels by blacks stress a black person's loss of identity when interacting with white society. The writer might compare *Roots* with several other novels that are also concerned with the black person's experience in American society.

If the student looked at *Roots* as one of many American novels about the South, he might see that *Roots* emphasizes the consequences of sexual relationships forced on black women, like many of these novels, but that it takes a different view of the problem. Further, *Roots* has no redeeming white characters who champion black rights. Because it controls direction and emphasis, choice of perspective is the most important preliminary for an essay that answers questions of "what," "what kind," or "what parts?"

Exercise: Predicting perspectives

In this exercise, predict what aspects of the situation each professional's perspective is likely to include.

Sample situation: New uniforms proposed for the Navy are being evaluated. The following individuals weigh various factors as they view the garment samples:

An accountant from the General Accounting Office:	cost, depreciation, and durability
A fashion designer:	style, attractiveness of design, and fabric quality
A safety expert:	fireproofing, and potentially hazardous features
A career officer of sixteen years:	comparison with traditional uniforms

a. Members of an ecology club are at a dinner meeting in a local Oriental restaurant, whose host invites them to be seated and announces that twelve special courses have been prepared for this occasion. As the first course is placed on the table, what would you predict each of the following members to perceive?

A nutrition expert
A gourmet food editor for a magazine
A vegetarian
The director of a travel agency
A dieter following an all-protein diet
The club's program director

b. José, age 8, is having trouble in school. He spells poorly and often writes fragments instead of complete sentences. José speaks English as a second language. What would you expect each of the following people to focus on if they reviewed José's case?

The director of the bilingual teaching program
A family social worker
An educational sociologist and counselor
The director of psychological testing

c. When the state celebrated its one-hundred-and-fiftieth an-
niversary, a citizens' commission was appointed to select
from drawings and photographs a monumental piece of
sculpture for the new park across from the capitol. What
would you predict as the major concerns of the commission
members viewing the three finalist entries?

The director of the state historical association
The director of a contemporary art museum in the state's
largest city
A famous painter who works in a "realistic" style
The president of the state garden club

Using models

A writer's chosen perspective determines the elements to
be emphasized in his writing. Once that is decided, he can
choose a model showing how these elements relate to each
other and how they support his answers to the questions
"what," "what kind," or "what parts?"

The geologist at the river's edge might look more closely
at the rocks. He customarily uses systems to identify rocks—
by chemical composition, by age, by the processes that
formed them, and so on. Any one of these systems would
organize and interpret information familiar to a geologist,
and any of them would provide a model, or a unified
picture, to describe his perspective.

A writer chooses a specific model to organize the elements
that support his thesis. When a satisfactory model is not
available, he must develop one. For example, nearly all
people for thousands of years have seen something burn—
a match, a campfire, or a candle—but their models for
explaining what they were seeing changed over time. To
explain burning, Aristotle in ancient Greece used a model
that identified four elements: air, earth, fire, and water.
He believed that all physical things were mixtures of these
four elements, each of which tended to seek its own state.
When substances of the proper mixture were heated, the

fire escaped and sought its own place in the universe, just below the moon. For him, burning was not something that happened to a substance, but the emergence of an element with properties of its own.

In contrast, most chemists of the late seventeenth century accepted a model of burning proposed by Georg Ernst Stahl, who believed that three "earths" or basic materials made up all matter: vitreous, fatty, and fluid "earths." Stahl called the fatty earth *phlogiston* (flō gist'on), and claimed it was the "fire principle." When a body burned, the *phlogiston* was lost, and Stahl believed that air was needed to carry away the liberated *phlogiston,* although it did not take part in the burning. This model seemed to agree with the common perception that fire "consumed" or "burned up" matter, leaving only a small residue.

Between 1770 and 1790 Antoine Lavoisier, "the father of modern chemistry," performed many quantitative studies of the change in weight when different reactions occurred. He noticed that when sulphur or phosphorus burned, it increased in weight—a result contrary to the loss of matter suggested by the phlogiston model. Lavoisier concluded that when elements burned they absorbed oxygen, or "vital air" (a new substance identified by Joseph Priestly), leaving "non-vital air," or nitrogen, behind. In Lavoisier's model, oxygen was an active and essential part of the model of burning.

A writer needs to be aware of his own preferences in models and to consider how his preferences may differ from those of his readers. The writer's success in answering questions of "what," "what kind," or "what parts," depends on how well he helps the reader to accept his interpretive model.

Internal and external models

The model chosen to describe the relevant elements of the topic may be limited in scope to the topic, or may extend beyond the boundaries of the topic. An *internal model,* within the confines of the topic, emphasizes the topic's parts or subsystems. A model for the human body, for example, might contain the following subsytems:

Neural system	Skeletal system
Vascular system	Urinogenital system
Digestive system	Muscular system

Any of these bodily subsystems can, of course, be subdivided further; for example, the digestive system:

Mouth	Small intestine
Esophagus	Large intestine
Stomach	

Depending on the degree to which the internal model is subdivided or elaborated, it can provide an extensive approach to the topic. The model for the human body could be the basis for a one-paragraph answer in a high-school student's biology quiz, or a textbook on human physiology for medical students, depending on how completely the writer developed the subsystems.

A writer may also describe a model of a system larger than the topic he is considering. For example, the model of American novels by black authors takes in many works other than *Roots*, the topic assigned to the student in the example. A model including all American novels would be even larger. Such models can be called *external models* because they extend beyond the limits of a topic.

A writer who is concerned with the question "what parts" usually applies an internal model, one limited by the boundaries of the topic itself. An essay bearing on the component parts of a topic is usually called an analysis. The thesis sentence usually mentions, in a general way, the parts to be identified by the chosen model: "Any poker game contains three stages: the deal, the betting, and the showdown." "Mitosis (cell division) has five phases: prophase, metaphase, anaphase, telophase, and interphase." "Carcinogens (cancer-causing agents) include certain chemicals, ultraviolet light, X-radiation, and certain viral agents." "Ceramic pots may be pinch-built, poured, wheel-built, or slab-built."

Notice that in all these examples the topic of the thesis identifies the parts, or instances, or events, or items. In the first two examples, all the instances are presumed to be basically the same: all poker games, all occurrences of cell division. In the last two, the topic includes elements that are collectively known by a general term: "carcinogens" and "ceramic pots." Thus, *internal models* can serve a number of functions: they may list components, such as parts of a poker game; they may show stages in a process, such as phases in mitosis; they may describe different groups within the topic, such as ethnic groups within a population, or different kinds of cancer-producing agents. (Some textbooks on writing consider the last two thesis sentences examples of "classification," because the parts described by the model represent categories or classes of items.)

If the writer is answering the questions "what" or "what kind," as in "What is art nouveau?" or "What kind of book is *Gravity's Rainbow?*", he will probably apply an *external model* to the topic in order to locate it among other ideas, objects, or events. To answer the question, "What is art nouveau?" he must define the topic by showing in what part of what system it belongs, and how it differs from other parts of the system. In the following brief answer, in order to define art nouveau the writer applies a model describing art movements. First he identifies art nouveau as belonging to a class, international art movements, and then gives characteristics that set it apart from other art movements:

Candelabrum designed by Henry van de Velde, c. 1898–99 (Musées Royaux d'Art ed d'Histoire)

Art nouveau was an *international movement* beginning in the *1880's* and reaching its peak about *1900*. The artists of this movement reacted against the formalism of the beaux-arts style and *attempted to reform* the state of the decorative arts by creating a *new vocabulary of forms and relationships*. This vocabulary for painting, architecture, and the applied arts stressed *asymmetry* and *two-dimensional patterns*. Its *linear dynamics* idealized the motions of waves, flames, draperies or whips. The style was marked by a *strong sense of structure,* implied by constant reference to principles of natural growth such as the organic movement of vines, flowers, and branches. Its *colors* tended to be muted, and the style as a whole evoked a *mood* of luxury and mystery.

The model used by this writer to define and interpret art movements extends beyond art nouveau itself. Because the writer refers to another style, and limits the period of time in which art nouveau was active, the reader may infer that this larger scheme uses time and stylistic features to describe art movements in relation to each other. The italicized terms in the passage suggest that the model picks out these features: time of prominence (1880–1900), purpose (to reform decorative arts), ways of achieving this purpose (new vocabulary), and elements of style (principles of organization, colors, mood).

To answer the question "What sort of book is *Gravity's Rainbow?*", the writer (like the one concerned with a similar question about *Roots*) would probably use a model that refers to various kinds of American novels. Essays answering "what" or "what kind" locate one thing in relation to another, or specify the nature of the topic by describing its component parts.

Exercise: Choosing internal and external models

In this exercise you will choose internal and external models for specific topics. First, think of systems and subsystems that might describe the features or functions of the topic, and write down at least one of these internal models. Next, think of larger (external) models of which the topic might be a part.

Example: Oil well

Internal model ("What parts does a well have?"):

derrick, bit, shaft, casing, pipes, pump, engine

External model ("Of what is an oil well a part?"):
oil refining system: catalytic cracking units, *wells*, tanks

a. Hide-a-bed sofa
   internal systems:
   external systems:
b. Tennis racket
   internal systems:
   external systems:
c. Military attack on a fortified castle
   internal systems:
   external systems:
d. Religious order (of nuns or monks)
   internal systems:
   external systems:
e. Highway
   internal systems:
   external systems:

Choosing appropriate models

Models may be used to describe, interpret, or evaluate a
topic. The subsystems of the body, for example, might be
used in a textbook as a model to *describe* physiology to
nursing students, and to help them analyze how parts of
the body usually interact. A version of that model might
be used by a pathologist to determine the cause of death
and write an autopsy report. Here the doctor would look
for deviations from what he would expect to find in a
healthy body. The pathologist also knows models describing
the effects of various diseases, and he also applies these, to
help *interpret* his findings.

Models can also evaluate. A model called a stress test
measures the heart rate, and respiratory rate against work
done, and will then *evaluate* a person's physical fitness for
an exercise class, or an astronaut training program, or
medical treatment.

Some models are more useful than others in providing
an appropriate framework. A deficient model confuses the
perceptions of both the writer and the reader. For a long
time Renaissance style was commonly divided into three
stages; but certain works located in one category, baroque,

were highly incompatible with many other baroque works. Eventually, critics accepted a four-stage structure that would allow them to identify and characterize more accurately works and themes in Renaissance style.

In choosing or developing a model, the writer must follow a principle of equal and exclusive division: parts of the model at any given level must carry equal weight, and no parts may overlap. For example, a food editor should not divide pies into "fruit pies," "cream pies," and "holiday pies," because some fruit pies and some cream pies could easily be served as holiday pies.

Exercise: Checking equal and exclusive division

Examine the following models to decide whether the writers practiced equal and exclusive division. Eliminate categories that might allow overlapping.

Example

Voters in Tallaway County:
Voters over 65 years of age
Voters between 40 and 65 years of age
Voters between 21 and 29 years of age
Voters between 18 and 20 years of age
Female voters
Voters who own homes

Comment: The last two categories should be eliminated because women voters and voters who own homes would already be listed in the first four groups. Further, the model excludes voters between 30 and 39 years of age.

a. Products from orchards
of Yakima Valley:
apples
peaches
jellies and preserves
cherries
juices

b. Contemporary art:
stone sculpture
colossal sculpture
metal sculpture

acrylic painting
portrait painting
oil painting

c. Sports:
basketball
football
tennis
women's archery
sharpshooting
professional sports
archery

d. Government authority: county
   local   state
   judicial   regional

Using analysis and definition

Sometimes the questions "what," "what kind," and "what parts?" are the writer's primary concerns, his major reason for writing an essay or paper. For example, a student might write several paragraphs or several pages defining "a modern hero," "romanticism in nineteenth century painting," "nationalism in Renaissance England," "rational positivism," or "Kissinger's theory of 'detente'." Similarly, analytic examination questions and essay assignments ask students to explain "Thomas Kuhn's theory of the stages of scientific revolutions," "steps in the process of socialization," "two kinds of acquired immunity," "the structure of the human kidney," or "the stages in the urea cycle."

Analysis and definition are sometimes secondary concerns in the essay. Often the writer must define a phenomenon and identify its parts before he can explain the cause and effect. The model he chooses will affect his ability to reason about causes and effects. As long as people used a model that defined matter as "earths" and considered air an unreactive medium, they explained burning differently from modern chemists. Students should understand that an analysis of the elements involved in a causal process is helpful in explaining the process to a reader.

Analysis and definition can also be important subordinate parts of a comparison. Did you ever think why a football program lists the weight, playing position, year in school, team number, and name of each football player on both teams? If you wanted to meet one of them, you probably would not consider these the most important things to know about him. The team members are defined by these things in the program so that spectators can compare players and identify those on the field by their numbers. Spectators use programs to answer comparative questions: "Is the Blue center better than the Red center?" "Well, the Blue center weighs forty pounds more than the Red center and has two more years of experience, so he probably is stronger and better." "Do the Hawks' linemen outweigh the Cougars'?" "Only by an average of two pounds per man."

In order to use certain bases of comparison, one must define the topics by models that admit those bases. No doubt that sounds terribly obvious, but occasionally writers do make mistakes of this kind. An engineer turned in a report describing the flow rates of gases in his experimental equipment in SCFM (standard cubic feet per minute), but compared these rates with a standard test defining flow rates in pounds per hour. Obviously, the reader could reach no conclusion unless he could convert SCFM to pounds per hour.

Review

A writer's use of models to analyze, define, or otherwise interpret a topic can be evaluated by the following questions:

1. How apparent is the writer's choice of the model he uses to define the topic?
2. How well did he justify the use of that model?
3. How well did the writer compare the features of the model and the characteristics of his topic?
4. Were his explanations full enough for his intended readers?
5. If subordinate to some other controlling intention, was the analysis or definition complete and appropriate?

Asking questions and making decisions

Exercise: Evaluating analyses and definitions

The following analyses and definitions range from very poor to excellent. Use the questions above to write an evaluation of each. For those which need revision, explain what should be done.

Example

Situation: This is an answer to a law exam question telling the student to identify the legal issues in a given set of circumstances. The audience is the student's professor.

In the case of Robert Gorsch the issue is whether Gorsch has a claim of assault against the Bigger brothers. The law says that assault is unprivileged, unconsented behavior that causes another to fear bodily harm from an imminent touching. When Gorsch returned to his old neighborhood to visit his mother, the Bigger brothers approached him with drawn knives and told him to get out of town in less than an hour or they would cut him into little pieces. The Bigger brothers have no official position that would have given them any privilege to treat Gorsch in this way. Gorsch's leaving without entering to see his mother, who died a few hours later, shows that he was indeed afraid of an imminent touching and bodily harm; otherwise he would have gone in to see her.

Commentary: The model, with its conditions and definitions, is well described. He justifies the model by saying that it is the legal definition. It is applied incompletely, because the student does not tell whether Gorsch consented to the Bigger brothers' behavior. The student doesn't define an *"imminent* touching"

a. Situation: Policy manual description of an accounting procedure, for new employees.

A knowledge of straight-line depreciation is useful in answering the client's questions about what depreciation method to use. It is also useful to the auditor in the examination of the property, plant and equipment accounts, and in accounting for the expenses on income statements. Depreciation accounting is a system which aims to distribute the cost or other basic value of tangible capital assets less salvage over the estimated useful life of the unit in a systematic and rational manner. It is a system of allocation, not valuation.

Straight-line depreciation allocates the cost of the asset over its useful life and reduces the book value of the asset to zero. This method is preferable to other depreciation methods because of its simple computations and its applicability for income tax purposes. However, the yearly depreciation charge is not a good measure of the deterioration of the asset; neither does the cost of the asset less depreciation measure the value of the asset on the second-hand market, which is the resale price of the asset. However, the present definition of depreciation does not require a method of depreciation to measure either of these values. These faults can be disregarded, and the client may use the method without qualms.

To apply this method in the accounts, two measures must be made: net depreciable cost, which is the cost of the asset less the estimated salvage value at the end of the asset's life; and the estimated service life of the asset. The net depreciable life is divided by the estimated service life, which results in the yearly charge. For example, an asset costs $10,000; its estimated life is 10 years and its estimated salvage value is $500. Therefore the net depreciable cost is $9,500, and when this amount is divided by the estimated life of 10 years, it yields the yearly depreciation charge of $950. This charge is recorded on the books yearly. The expense account is debited and the reserve for depreciation is credited. The expense account is closed to the income statement at year end. The reserve accumulates yearly until the asset is sold or retired.

b. Situation: Newspaper article for the general public.

National Nutrition Week is a good time to reflect on our continuing need for nutrition information. Carrie McNutt, Ph.D., a research associate with the National Nutrition Association, has interpreted the data from several recent surveys on consumer knowledge of nutrition. According to her, Americans need to learn the Basic Four Food Groups system, "a plan that makes it easy to choose appetizing meals for the well-being of the whole family, from baby to grandparent."

The Basic Four Food Groups system makes sure you are serving well-balanced meals that provide all the necessary nutrients. The cook should plan menus to include at least the number of servings that give you the daily minimum. Indeed, most family members will need more than the 1200 to 1400 calories of the basic plan.

For each person, plan two servings of meats, fish, poultry, eggs, or cheese. Occasionally, substitute dried beans or peas for the meats. Three ounces of meat, three eggs, or three slices of cheese equal one serving and provide protein, iron, niacin, and other B vitamins.

Four servings of fruits and vegetables are needed. Be sure that one of these servings is a leafy green vegetable and that one is a citrus fruit or tomato. These choices, in ½ to 1 cup servings, will give you Vitamins A and C and provide minerals and roughage.

The third group—cereals, breads, and pasta—are important sources of B vitamins. Four servings of enriched or whole-grain breads or cereals are needed each day. A serving equals one slice of bread, one small biscuit, ½ cup potatoes or rice, ½ cup cooked cereal, or 3/4 to 1 cup flaked or puffed cereal.

Many people seem to misunderstand the value of breads and starches, and banish such foods from their diets because they think them "fattening," says NcNutt. Enriched breads and cereals contain iron and supplemental protein. Consumers' fears of obesity and heart attack, cancer, and food-related disorders have caused them to simplify their food decisions in bizarre ways. More education is needed, McNutt concludes. We never outgrow our need to know.

c. Situation: An answer to the question "What kinds of transition are used in films?", on a film-making course exam.

A transition is an interruption, or break from one scene to another, in a film. Transition techniques include cuts, fades, dissolves, wipes, gestures, songs or music, and various other means.

Cuts are abrupt changes from a shot of one scene to a shot of another scene. A cut usually makes the viewer feel rushed as he adjusts to the new information on the screen. Some cuts are humorous because they unexpectedly juxtapose contrasting images.

A fade is a slower transition, in which the first image gradually disappears and there may be a brief moment of darkness on the screen before the new image is seen. Fades, especially slow fades, are useful for showing the passage of time between scenes.

A dissolve, also called a mix, is a technique for briefly showing the old and new images at the same time. The new image is seen for a second before the old image fades away, creating a special kind of double exposure. Dissolves are good for introducing flashbacks and memories.

Other technical devices include wipes, iris-outs and iris-ins, and color splices. Wipes, where a line passes across the screen replacing an old image with a new image, are used in movies to show violent transitions, and to accelerate the hectic pace of comedy. Ingmar Bergman used moments of blank red color to link scenes in "Cries and Whispers."

Gestures, like the snapping of a magician's finger, or repeated images, can indicate the passage of time. The spinning wheels of a stage coach or railroad train suggest changes of both time and place.

Songs and sounds often signal changes in scene or mood, or let the audience know something is about to happen. Slow motion can indicate a remembered action; and a period of speeded-up jerky images can provide a laugh break between scenes. A wide variety of other devices can also be used for transitions.

d. Situation: Answer to "What was the rococo style in American painting?"

The rococo style in American painting was a minor art movement born of English rococo techniques introduced by two English painters, John Wollaston and Joseph Blackburn, who came to the colonies about the middle of the eighteenth century. Their paintings had an idyllic note, pleasing artificiality, and delicate movement. Two young native artists, John Singleton Copley in Boston and Benjamin West in Philadelphia, developed the style. Copley abandoned the artificiality of rococo scenes—shepherdesses, fawns, fanciful landscapes—in his portraits of people in day-to-day settings. His subjects appear caught in the midst of life, speaking with characteristic expressions and gestures, among their possessions. In his portrait of Mrs. Sylvanus Bourne, the lady seems to have laid down her book for a moment to make a sensible comment about the author.

The "conversation pieces" of Charles William Peale and Matthew Pratt emphasized clean luminous colors and combined realism and delicate formality, in a manner similar to the best of the English provincial rococo painters; although the Americans' art was simpler and more direct than that of the fashionable London rococo painters.

The rococo preference for simple natural forms also fostered the development of a great artist–naturalist of the period, William Bartram. Bartram's books, illustrated with his own botanical drawings and paintings, are delicate and exact in color and line, vital, graceful, and blessed with artless spontaneity.

e. Situation: Newspaper article for women.

Personal safety habits for women drivers include: (a) actions while getting into the car, (b) actions while driving, and (c) actions while getting out of the car. Before getting in you should watch for anyone lurking near where your vehicle is parked. Have your ignition key between your thumb and forefinger, ready to open the door. In the few minutes while you search your purse for the key, you could be overtaken and assaulted. If you are forced to defend yourself, let your keys protrude between your fingers and rake them across your assailant's face or drive them into his stomach. It may be a move that will set you free. Before climbing in, check the back seat to make certain no one is hiding there. It takes only a second to cast that glance every time you are about to enter the car—a second that could save your life.

When driving, lock your car doors, and if you have air conditioning roll the windows up. At least roll them up far enough to make it difficult for an intruder to reach the lock button and enter the car while you are waiting for a traffic light. Never, never pick up a hitchhiker. Use your CB, if you have one, to report motorists out of gas or to send back assistance from a garage.

When getting out of your car, scan the parking lot before you turn off your motor. Watch out for a person or persons standing in a corner, or by an area where it is dark or difficult to see. If the scene appears at all unusual, drive off. If anyone attempts to enter your car, or approaches as you park, be prepared to drive off. He isn't mistaking your car for the city bus. Before you leave, lock your car, and think ahead to the conditions of your return. Is the lot lighted? Will there be an attendant there? Is it a long walk to your car from the elevator or stairs? Thinking ahead can make returning to your car less hazardous.

f. Situation: Newspaper article for general readers.

Ash Waylon's new detective series *Delmontico* aired last night, and TV watchers weren't exactly startled by the plot. It was written according to the standard four-part, one-hour formula that prevents our watching all those commercials at once. First, an event caused a problem: Chief of Detectives Delmontico's star witness against the gang boss was bumped off by a hired killer. How would Delmontico nail the gang boss now that his star witness was gone? How would Delmontico solve the murder of the witness? Predictably, both questions could be answered together because the witness, as viewers knew, had been murdered at the command of the mob chief.

In stage two, it was complication time. The mob chief had the hit man and his daughter murdered. The dead witness's sister, a cute but naïve missionary home from the Orient, needed Delmontico's consolation: at dinner, in the park, over lunch, on the telephone. If a police detective is going to run a good department, he's got to have a lot of romantic stamina. If the viewers got bored, it wasn't the mob boss's fault. He tried to have the sister killed, but she shot the new hit man, who had already killed the first hit man and his daughter. The viewers knew what was coming next.

In the third part of the show, the "yes, but . . ." or "near solve," the questions were almost answered without the hero's genius. Another department tracked down the second hit man, hoping to make him talk; but the sister had already shot him when they arrived. Delmontico's men, assigned to tail the gang boss, lost him in traffic as he went to pick up an incriminating narcotics shipment. Delmontico and the sister had lunch together, walked in the park, and talked on the phone. The lab boys thought they had the gang boss's thumb print on a glass, but the evidence was too smudged.

Stage four, the writers let the hero earn his pay. Delmontico tried to send sister back to Denver with the witness's body for the funeral. Earlier they had eaten lunch, dinner, snacks, walked in the park and talked on the phone (remember, it's a one-hour show). He called the missionary society, and got the "missing information." Next, he figured out where the mobster chief was headed and ordered every available unit to go there. Delmontico arrived at the scene, where he could observe the mobster making the pickup, thus solving part (a) of the problem; and prevented the witness's sister from killing the mobster in revenge (after he confessed to having the witness murdered), thus solving part (b) of the problem. Bonus that proved Delmontico *really sharp*: he unmasked the sister, revealing her as the witness, who pretended to be a missionary because she feared being killed. Probably Delmontico suspected something when they had lunch, dinner, walked in the park, talked on the telephone, etc.

If this kind of thing gets on the air, why don't more of us make money writing for television? It isn't because we don't understand the formula.

g. Situation: Examination answer in a child psychology class.

Children who can't control themselves probably missed out on something when they were little. In each person's head there is a record of all his early experiences: tape recordings, like, of all those conversations and events from birth on. On one set of tapes are the parental voices of authority and loving concern, that insisted on rules and routines. When these tapes control the child's behavior he is said to be in a "Parent" ego state, where he feels, thinks, talks, and responds just as one of his parents did when he was little. A second set of tapes grows as the result of objective appraisal of what he saw, or, rational calculation. These tapes govern the "Adult" ego state. Most children have had only limited time to develop these "Adult" tapes. The child also stores up tapes of his own feelings and wishes. These tapes, which govern his "Child" ego state, record three types of attitudes: rebellious, optimistic (or pleasure-seeking) and adaptive (seeking parental approval). Children raised by hostile, unloving adults who make arbitrary, unpredictable and excessive demands on them often fail to develop successful adaptive ego tapes from their own experiences; and the inconsistent and threatening voices of the Parent tapes make it difficult for them to fall back on a Parent ego state to cope successfully with the world. Thus the pleasure-seeking and rebellious feelings dominate his child ego state, which exercises a miserable tyranny in the absence of any nurturing Parent voice and he cannot develop an adaptive role to win gratification from others. Seemingly rebellious and self-centered, a hating child in fact has no love for himself and believes the worst about himself.

Ordinary child's ego

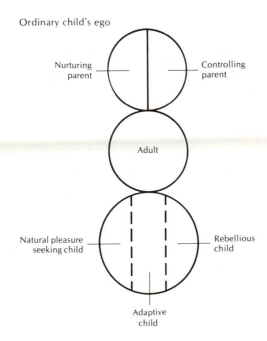

Hostile child's ego states

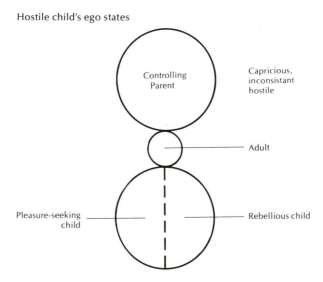

Exercise: Subordinating analysis to a dominant pattern

In this article the writer explains to newspaper readers the probable effects of winter wheat losses. He uses models to define different kinds of wheat, and to explain the market system. Assess his use of these models. Write out your evaluation.

Showers, Soviets, and American Consumers

The recent severe winter weather has caused Americans to wonder whether they will be paying more for bread next summer because of winter wheat losses. Investors are worried that if foreign demand for wheat is heavy, prices will soar and touch off a new round of inflation. Considering potential variations in supply and demand, however, Americans may safely expect no drastic rise in the price of bread, and it might even be cheaper to "let them eat cake." Even if the Soviets place another seventy million bushel order, results may not be inflationary. The decline in demand has increased the probable supply of wheat in the coming year, and that margin is likely to avert a rise in price like that of two years ago, when prices reached $6.50 a bushel after heavy foreign demands encountered a reduced supply.

The recent bad weather does threaten this year's supply somewhat. This winter three of the "Big Five" winter wheat states—Kansas, Oklahoma and Texas—had less than half their normal moisture, but the weather in Nebraska and Ohio was better. Last year we produced 1,651 million bushels of winter wheat. The December 1 crop survey of the United States Department of Agriculture (U.S.D.A) estimated that the new crop would be only 1,496 million bushels because of the drought. However, new sources suggest that the U.S.D.A. estimates of drought damage were too high and that production will exceed those estimates. Even if the weather does not improve in Kansas, Oklahoma, and Texas, where last year they produced 650 million bushels, and we assume a 50 percent loss, the total winter wheat production is not likely to be reduced to less than 1,300 million bushels. This figure is probably too low, because wheat has amazing recuperative powers, given just a little moisture. Nevertheless, no one can be sure rains will come in time, and 1,300 million bushels is probably the most pessimistic picture of supply. When the expected carry-over and other types of wheat are added up, we still can expect to begin the new year with 2,250 to 2,300 million bushels.

"Supply and demand" can be influenced not only by rains and Russians but also by the kinds of wheat produced, their uses, the times of the year and the places they are grown. Seventy-five percent of all wheat produced is winter wheat, which is harvested in late spring; twenty-five percent is planted as soon as the ground becomes workable and is harvested in late summer. Most of both crops is made up of hard wheats suitable for bread flours. Soft wheats are used for pastry products—cakes, rolls, donuts, etc. The drought has sent prices of hard wheat up by about fifteen percent, and in turn has even caused the price of soft red wheat to rise about six or seven percent. The soft wheats are mostly grown in areas where the weather has been better, so soft wheat should be in good supply. Although a little rain between now and crop time could increase the supply of hard wheat, soft wheat will surely be plentiful.

Unexpected demands by the Soviets would affect the market. The Soviets would want hard wheat used for bread flour—which will be scarcer—rather than the more plentiful soft wheat. Therefore, demand for wheat might be high and the supply a little low, a condition that could raise the price of bread flour slightly. But the price of soft wheat should remain about the same, due to ample supply and lower-than-average demand, despite the possible slight rise in demand caused by those who can substitute soft wheat for more expensive hard wheat. In other words, even if bread costs a few pennies more, you can eat cake as cheaply as ever.

8 Organizing the essay

Objectives

The decisive writer uses a relatively small number of skills, like composing and judging a thesis sentence and organizing a comparison, to make his writing serve many different purposes and influence a variety of readers. Using these basic tools of his trade, the writer can discuss anything with anyone. He can write on practical matters, like the rising cost of groceries, or more exotic topics like Balinese religious rites. He can adapt his material and his style to meet the needs of any audience—whether an old friend, a prospective employer, or an English composition teacher. In this chapter you will learn how to adapt the patterns of organization already studied, to meet the demands of various writing situations. You will learn how to choose the pattern of organization best suited to your thesis and your rhetorical purpose—your reason for discussing a particular topic with a particular audience. You have already mastered several principles of organization. Now you will learn how to analyze your thesis sentences, to find what development that they require.

Many students find organizing their material the most difficult part of essay-writing. We hope to show that you have already learned the skills necessary for this. All that remains is to combine the basic patterns of organization into coherent essays.

The thesis sentence as guide to organization

The thesis sentence, you will remember, joins a limited topic and a controlling idea:

THESIS = LIMITED TOPIC + CONTROLLING IDEA

There are only a limited number of patterns for joining the topic and its controlling idea. As you read the following list of "topic + idea" patterns, you will see they reflect the different kinds of writing strategies you have learned. In each case, the pattern relating the controlling idea to its topic suggests a pattern of development for the entire essay.

1. *Definition pattern: Topic belongs to a class; or topic = x*
   A variant of this pattern states that the topic *does not* belong to a class, or that it is *not* a true example of x.

   Examples

   The new morality is a code of unrestrained self-interest and exploitation.

   "Gothic revival" was a style of architecture, painting, and decorative arts in the United States during the nineteenth century.

   Evel Knievel is a modern American hero.

   Romeo and Juliet has a comic plot but a tragic ending.

   Contrary to popular opinion, Senator Filibuster is not a victim of circumstances.

   The writer of the first example is committed to explaining how his subject, "the new morality," belongs to a particular class (moral codes of behavior). Next he must indicate how this code differs from the rest of its class (it is a moral code based on principles commonly called vices, not virtues).

   One common strategy for writing extended definitions is to take a widely accepted definition for the class to which the topic belongs, and use it as a criterion. This strategy gives a choice of the "A then B" or the "point by point" comparison pattern. The pattern of organization for this extended definition would thus become: "The standard definition, made up of points X, Y, and Z; then all about the topic on points X, Y, and Z"; or "Point X of the standard definition, then a discussion of point X of the topic; point Y of the standard definition, then point Y of the topic; and so on." The writer has several options in choosing a definition: he may quote an authority respected by his audience; he may refer to widely accepted ideas; or he may develop a definition of his own, acceptable to his audience.

The argument of an essay that begins with the thesis sentence "Evel Knievel is a modern American hero" will depend on how the writer defines the class, "modern American heroes." This writer's definition of Evel Knievel as a hero will probably be organized according to the comparison pattern. The characteristics and accomplishments of this biking daredevil will be compared to the specified characteristics of a "modern American hero."

The thesis sentence *Romeo and Juliet* has a comic plot but a tragic ending" could also generate an essay organized according to the comparison pattern. In this case, the writer's argument would depend on what he meant by "comic plot" and "tragic ending." He might take definitions of these terms from a book of literary criticism, and then show how the plot and ending of *Romeo and Juliet* match these definitions.

Other methods of organizing a definition include cause/ and/or effect reasoning (an X is something which produces effect Y; or X is something caused by Z) and analysis into parts. The point to remember is that whenever the thesis sentence places the subject in a class, or states that the subject *is* or equals something else, the ensuing argument depends on definition.

2. *Analysis pattern: Topic = constituent parts*

Examples

Texas has four kinds of ecological systems.

The Chinese Army's "Long March" consisted of three phases.

To develop a discussion based on analysis, the writer chooses an internal model that divides the material into units and describes each of the consitutuent parts. The author of the first example would probably devote a paragraph or two to each of the four ecological systems found in Texas; the author of the second example might spend several paragraphs discussing each of the three phases of the "Long March."

3. *Time or space pattern: Topic as it occurred in time or topic as it existed in space*

Examples

Fatal injuries to drivers involved in head-on collisions at 70 mph occur in a ten-second sequence. *Time*

Cancer is most likely to be found in three areas of the lymphatic system. *Space*

The "topic in time or space" pattern is a special instance of the analysis pattern. Here, however, time or space organizes the constituent parts in relation to each other. The writer organizes his material according to the time or space pattern set up in the thesis sentence. For example, when discussing the injuries in a head-on collision he would describe the injury that occurs first and then would go on to the injuries that follow, until the ten-second sequence is complete. The writer discussing lymphatic cancer would describe each of the three areas where cancer is most likely to develop.

4. *Comparison pattern: Topic 1 in comparison to topic 2*

Examples

Kissinger's practice of personal diplomacy is similar to the tradition of negotiation employed by powerful ambassadors in the nineteenth century.

The style of the Russian gymnasts on the uneven parallel bars was more daring and flamboyant than the styles of their closest competitors.

Comparison theses nearly always demonstrate the comparative sentence patterns you practiced in Chapter 5. The middle of the essay will follow the "A then B" or "point by point" structure.

5. *Cause and/or effect pattern: Topic was caused by . . . or topic resulted in one or more effects*

Examples

A higher rate of profit increase for large corporations was caused by the imposition of wage and price controls.

Recession resulted in a wave of discriminatory firing of women workers in Japan, where equal opportunity is not ensured by law.

Cause-and-effect thesis sentences often contain the word "cause" or "result," or one of their synonyms such as "brought about," "destroyed," "modified," or "improved." The patterns of organization frequently used in cause-and-effect writing were discussed in Chapter 6. In this type of writing, your preliminary decisions, your mode of reasoning, and your available evidence will affect how you organize the essay.

6. *Interpretive generalization pattern: topic + generalization*

Examples

Martin Luther King used religious images to make his actions in Birmingham more acceptable to the clergymen he addressed in "Letter from Birmingham Jail."

Negotiations between opera societies and musicians' unions usually last four or five months.

Interpretive organization can parallel the process that led to the conclusion by presenting data first, then stating the generalization. Alternatively, interpretation can begin with a generalization based on inductive reasoning. The writer must then summarize the data that support his generalization, and offer carefully chosen examples of those data. These two patterns may be diagrammed like this:

a. *Data*
   presented,
   summarized, and
   explained
   Generalization

b. *Generalization*
   supported by
   Data
   presented,
   summarized, and
   explained

If your audience is likely to be hostile to your generalization or conclusion, it is better to explain your data before stating the generalization—unless you intend to shock them. If you believe they will be receptive to your ideas from the beginning, you may wish to begin with your generalization and follow it with supporting examples. "Those students whose parents help them with their homework show less grasp of the subject matter in examinations" is a generalization that would not surprise or disturb teachers, psychiatrists, or educational sociologists; but the writer might wish to delay stating it in an article for the *Parent and Teacher* magazine. In most writing situations, the second pattern is the more useful, as the general statement serves to introduce and interpret all the specific data that follow. This pattern is very common in expository writing.

final Exam

7. *Recommendation pattern: Topic + recommendation*   *persuasive paper*

Examples

Lead-based paints should be banned in the manufacture of children's furniture.

The job placement office at Cornell should expand its services.

American consumers should boycott imported beef, because American cattlemen are hurt by the competition of low-cost foreign beef.

Buy IBM stock because the price of shares is down.

A thesis of this pattern urges the audience to hold some opinion or take some action concerning a topic. The body of the essay would consist of paragraphs justifying the recommendation. Although such thesis sentences sometimes contain the words "because" or "since," this pattern is not necessarily a cause-and-effect pattern. The cattlemen's loss of income is not a cause of the boycott, but a circumstance to which the consumer might respond in his desire to see his countrymen receive fair compensation.

Exercise: Writing patterned sentences

Practice the seven sentence patterns by composing two thesis sentences to fit each.

1. *Definition: Topic belongs to a class; or topic = x*

Example: George S. Taylor, candidate for the Senate, is a conservative.

a. _____
b. _____

2. *Analysis: Topic = constituent parts*

Example: The three most important sectors of Michigan's economy are industry, agriculture, and mining.

a. _____
b. _____

3. *Time or space: Topic as it exists in time or occurs in space*

   Example: Don has successfully hosted television shows in Seattle, Albany, and Atlanta.

   a. _____
   b. _____

4. *Comparison: Topic 1 in comparison to topic 2*

   Example: In Thailand the demand for electric power is greater than the supply.

   a. _____
   b. _____

5. *Cause and/or effect: Topic was caused by . . . or topic resulted in one or more effects*

   Example: Use of electronic detection devices has virtually eliminated highjacking of airplanes in the United States.

   a. _____
   b. _____

6. *Interpretive generalization: Topic + generalization*

   Example: The platform of the Nationalist party is primarily concerned with controlling inflation and providing services in health and education.

   a. _____
   b. _____

7. *Recommendation: Topic + recommendation about it*

   Example: College tuition should be waived for those students who maintained an "A" average during the preceding year.

   a. _____
   b. _____

Choosing a dominant pattern of organization

Some thesis sentences seem to suggest more than one pattern of organization. Take, for example, the thesis "Mollusks are important intermediate hosts of trematode parasites that cause serious diseases in man." This suggests both pattern 6, interpretive generalization and pattern 5, cause and/or effect. Earlier, in Chapter 3, you practiced placing the most important idea of your thesis in the independent clause of the thesis sentence (see pp. 41–43). If you have checked your thesis for clarity, and have made sure that the thesis sentence expresses precisely the core of what you want to say, then the syntax of your thesis sentence will help you choose a dominant pattern of organization, or outline, for your essay. In the "mollusk" thesis, the predicate of the independent clause is "are important intermediate hosts of trematode parasites." The syntactic pattern of this predicate suggests a central concern with the idea that mollusks are *important* intermediate hosts for parasites. The second idea, that these parasites cause serious diseases in man, appears only in a modifying relative clause—a subordinate structure. This placement indicates that the second idea is less important to the writer. Following the guidelines established by his thesis sentence, he would probably devote most of his essay to examples showing the presence of parasites in mollusks. Only a small portion of the essay would describe the effects of these parasites on humans.

The writer could, however, revise the thesis sentence to make the disease-producing effect of the parasites the central idea of the predicate: "Trematode parasites, which often find intermediate hosts in mollusks, cause serious diseases in man." An essay that develops this thesis sentence would be devoted largely to a discussion or explanation of the disease-producing activity of the parasites, including a list of the specific diseases they cause. The fact that these parasites can be found in mollusks would be given in the introduction, or in a description of how the parasites enter the human body—for example, when raw or pickled shellfish is eaten.

The syntax of the thesis sentence guides the writer in his choice of an organizing pattern for the essay: ideas empha-sized by being in the independent clause of the thesis sentence provide the dominant pattern. Ideas placed in the dependent clauses of the thesis sentence suggest the minor patterns of development that will help support the major argument of the essay. Examples of subordinate and dominant patterns of organization can be seen in Chapter 5, pp. 71–74, where an "A then B" pattern of comparison is subordinate in the introduction, and a "point by point" comparison pattern dominates the body of the essay.

Exercise: Evaluating patterns of organization

The following exercise consists of a series of thesis sentences, and proposals for developing essays based on these sentences. First determine the pattern of each thesis sentence. Then decide whether the proposed method(s) of development is appropriate. If not, suggest another plan or combination of plans for developing an essay based on the thesis sentence.

Examples

1. The kind of military intervention we have witnessed in the past quarter century is a clear departure from a long and deeply-rooted tradition.   *Contrast*
(Pattern of development: ~~Definition~~)

   Evaluation: The writer apparently has mistaken the comparison pattern for the definition pattern. Although the writer uses "is" to equate "the kind of intervention" with "a clear departure," it is obvious that he really intends to contrast recent interference with the "long and deeply-rooted tradition" of the past. The proper form of development would be a comparison, probably one in time sequence.

2. College graduates of 1976 are less articulate in speech and writing than graduates of 1968. (Pattern of development: Comparison)

   Evaluation: Correct. The writer will probably compare test scores and student records of the two years in question. He might have evidence for the years in between, too. If he does, he too will probably use time order.

a. In each of the four cities where the program has been tried, completely different problems turned up. (Pattern of development: ~~Time~~)*Contrast*

b. Three ways of adjusting to widowhood can help a woman become more independent. (Pattern of development: ~~Comparison~~) *Analysis*

c. Good manners is the art of making the people with whom

we converse feel at ease. (Samuel Johnson) (Pattern of development: Definition)

d. Rather than a cold education factory, college is a friendly and stimulating place with many exciting people and activities, both inside and outside the classroom. (This writer has made a survey of the views of 30 class members.) (Pattern of development: Comparison) Contrast

e. The proposal of the Committee on Student Life consists of four recommendations for helping students to a fuller expression of their various ethnic heritages. (Pattern of development: Interpretive generalization) analysis

f. The decay of modern cities has been caused by the concentration of political power in the hands of business leaders and professional people who used city funds for the benefit of their own neighborhoods, industries, and enterprises. (Pattern of development: Cause and/or effect)

g. The Kaibob squirrel can be mistaken for the well-known grey squirrel and poses a problem of identification for naturalists. (Pattern of development: Recommendation and comparison) Contrast

h. The poetry of Edmund Spenser repeatedly describes a world whose mutability becomes proof of fixed universal purpose and complex harmony. (Pattern of development: Interpretive generalization)

i. Speed limits on freeways in open country should be abolished. (Pattern of development: Topic in space) recommendation

j. Events from 1855 to 1865 left Mary Lincoln a changed woman. (Decide for yourself the kind of evidence the writer has, and choose a pattern accordingly.) (Pattern of development: Analysis)

k. Basic research, using different approaches, was being done on the structure of DNA at four different universities during the same period in which Watson and Crick made their famous discovery. (Which ideas are emphasized by the sentence structure?) (Pattern of development: Cause and/or effect)

l. Zero Population Growth (ZPG) educates the public about the dangers of an expanding population. (Pattern of development: Time)

m. Five factors determined the outcome of the Korean War. (Pattern of development: Analysis + cause and/or effect)

n. Since the beginning of the twentieth century the sociologists' definitions of "poverty" have stayed the same, and their solutions have differed very little; but the techniques of measuring poverty have become increasingly complex. (Pattern of development: Interpretive generalizations subordinate to a comparison of three topics)

o. Child-care facilities should be provided for teachers, since there are few nurseries in this area. (Pattern of development: Cause and/or effect)

p. College differs from high school in teaching methods, homework, and tests. (Pattern of development: Interpretive generalization)

Using an outline

For a brief letter or a one-page memorandum, an outline may not be necessary. With a longer project and more information to be presented, the writer may find it hard to hold in his mind all that he wants to say. He may leave things out inadvertently; or more likely, as new thoughts occur to him, he will take off in directions he did not originally intend. With both a thesis and an outline to guide the writing, he can concentrate on each paragraph and sentence, and can check back to see exactly what comes next.

The outline is a framework that represents the dominant and subordinate organizing patterns suggested in the thesis. Each major heading, usually designated by a roman numeral, should be written out as the topic sentence for that section of the essay. Each subordinate part of that heading, usually indicated by a capital letter, corresponds to the topic sentence for a paragraph within the major section. Specific points to be made can be noted with arabic numbers under their own subheading:

I. Topic sentence for a major section of the essay
  A. Topic sentence for a subordinate part of this section
    1. Point of information supporting topic sentence A
    2. Another point of information supporting topic sentence A
  B. Topic sentence for another subordinate part of Section I
    1. Point of information or evidence for topic sentence B
    2. Another point of information or evidence for topic sentence B

II. Topic sentence for second major section of the essay
    A. . . . and so on, as in section I

An example of this structure can be seen in the following outline, which frames the essay in support of the thesis:

"New kinds of crime carried out by computer are difficult to detect and prevent." Referring to the patterns used earlier in this chapter, we can see that this thesis makes a generalization about a topic, "new kinds of crime carried out by computer." There are actually two generalizations, that the crimes are (1) difficult to prevent and (2) difficult to detect. The writer will have to do three things in this essay: (a) use specific examples to show that there are indeed new types of crime being carried out by means of the computer; (b) show why they are difficult to detect; and (c) show why they are difficult to prevent. These three obligations become the three major sections of the outline. Although some texts will tell you that any subsection must be supported by at least two examples or points, sometimes you will have only one kind of evidence or one case to illustrate a subsection.

Sample outline

Thesis: New kinds of crime carried out by computer are difficult to detect and prevent. [Interpretive generalization]

I. During the past fifteen years, new kinds of crime carried out by computer have appeared as knowledge in the field of electronics increased.
    A. Money may be located by "piggybacking"—tapping a phone line while two computers are "talking"—and then be switched to the thief's account by sending illegal instructions to the computer.
        1. Chicago case
        2. San Francisco case
    B. A thief can instruct the computer to take fractions of cents accumulated in interest by depositors, and credit the fractions to his own account: a procedure that adds up fast in a big institution.
        1. Baltimore case
        2. Miami case
    C. Altered deposit slips marked with the thief's magnetized code number were substituted in a bank so that for

several days the computer sent deposits to the thief's account, which he closed out before his disappearance: Washington, D.C. case
D. A disgruntled employee, about to be fired, programmed the company's computer to destroy all payroll records when his company number was dropped from the payroll, a revenge that cost the company thousands of dollars: Denver case
E. Valuable computer programs have been stolen and sold to rival firms.
  1. Los Angeles case
  2. St. Louis case

II. Computer crimes are difficult to trace, and often go undetected for a long time.
A. Almost all known computer crimes were discovered accidentally.
B. Auditors who check records are usually not familiar with computer intricacies, and need help from programmers, the very people who are able to commit the crimes and mislead auditors.
C. The lack of a security system often allows the crime to escape notice until the thief is gone and his tracks are well covered.

III. These crimes are difficult to prevent because the potential criminals, bright and experienced computer programmers, are the same people hired to design and maintain security systems and to use the computers in company business.
A. Employee dishonesty is the cause in a majority of computer crimes.
B. Security-system designers are familiar with individual computer systems and their weaknesses, so that the people best able to defend the computers are also the best-qualified thieves.

Students who found a simple list of topics adequate in high school often resist advice to prepare an outline before beginning their essays in college. Rather than urge our opinion further, we offer the comments of a student, in writing about his course:

"The best thing this course taught me was to make an outline with a thesis and topic sentences for the parts of the essay. I used to have to go back and rewrite big sections of my papers where I had started putting in extra material and gotten off the track. Making an outline takes about ten minutes of extra time at the beginning, but it makes the real writing go faster and cuts down time revising later, so I figure the ten minutes are more than worth it."

Exercise: Evaluating an outline

A thesis tells you what belongs in an essay, and implicitly demands certain patterns of development. It also excludes material not related to the controlling idea about the limited topic. In the following outline the writer has failed to fulfill the demands of his thesis, and has included material irrelevant to his controlling idea. Read the outline and ask yourself these questions:

1. What is the pattern of the thesis?
2. What does the writer assert or offer to prove?
3. What is promised by the thesis, but missing from the outline?
4. What changes would make the outline appropriate to the thesis?
5. What topics included in the outline are irrelevant to the thesis?
6. Are sections of equal importance given equal rank and space?
7. Given the same available material, could you suggest a *better* thesis?

Einstein's View of the Universe

Thesis: Albert Einstein's theoretical contributions to physics in our time were as great as Isaac Newton's contributions to his age.
I. In 1905 Einstein published four important papers, each containing a great discovery in physics.
   A. Special theory of relativity
   B. Mass–energy equivalence
   C. Theory of Brownian motion
   D. Photon theory of light
II. In 1916 he published his famous theory of relativity.
   A. The cornerstone of the theory is the principle of equivalence, which says that an accelerated observer will see a physical process taking place the same way as if he were not accelerated, because a gravitational field would be present, which would produce the same acceleration in the observed process.

     B. Einstein explained the laws of physics as being the laws of geometry in four dimensions.

     C. These laws are determined by the distribution of matter and energy in the universe.

     D. From the theory of relativity there developed a new doctrine of the properties of the universe, replacing Newton's cosmology.

III. Einstein's research in statistical theories produced two contributions on the nature of light.

     A. At first he dealt with the classical problems of statistical mechanics.

     B. Later he attacked problems in which quantum theory and statistical theory merged.

     C. He developed the quantum theory of a monatomic gas, which led Schrödinger to develop the theory of wave mechanics.

IV. As his fame mounted, he became an important public figure.

     A. His fame and his lucid manner of speech made him a sought-after speaker.

     B. His interest in social problems prompted him to give public speeches on social issues.

     C. He traveled widely, and visited the United States in 1921 to support the Zionist movement.

     D. He wrote a famous letter to President Franklin D. Roosevelt, pointing out the dangers of Germany's developing an atomic bomb before the U.S.

V. The arts responded to the theory of relativity.

     A. Painters began to re-examine the relation of particles and colors.

     B. Dramatists and poets were fascinated by the notion of the space–time continuum.

VI. Conclusion. Einstein's attitude toward the world, whose view of matter, space, and time he changed, can be summed up by his remark: "God is subtle, but he is not malicious."

Review

In organizing his essay, the writer makes two important decisions. First he chooses the pattern of organization appropriate to his thesis, the pattern that most closely reflects the relation of the controlling idea to the limited topic, and that fits the evidence he has. The possible patterns are:

1. Definition
2. Analysis
3. Time or space

4. Comparison
5. Cause and/or effect
6. Interpretive generalization
7. Recommendation

Next, the writer outlines the major ideas needed to fulfill the demands of his thesis and his pattern. To evaluate the outline he asks these questions:

1. Are the divisions of the outline those suggested by the structure of the thesis?
2. Are the topic sentences of the outline complete and clear enough to control subordinate parts of the essay?
3. Is anything promised in the thesis missing from the outline?
4. Are any topics in the outline unnecessary or irrelevant to the thesis?
5. Are sections of equal importance given equal rank and space?

With a complete outline, the writer is ready to begin his first draft.

Asking questions and making decisions

Exercise: Evaluating outlines

After asking the questions above, write an evaluation of each of the following outlines, commenting on how well it follows the structure implied by the thesis sentence, and how well it presents the argument of the thesis.

Example

Thesis: The effects of changing to coed residential housing would be mostly advantageous.

I. The advantages of coed residential housing would range from introducing a new kind of relationship between the sexes to teaching major lessons of life.
   A. Opportunities for daily social interaction with opposite sex exist.
   B. People mature, and learn not to fool around with other peoples' emotions.
II. A few disadvantages would result from the coed system.

A. With the temptation of women around, male students wouldn't study so hard.
B. Girls may not handle the invitations they get to go out and may study less because they were socially inexperienced.
C. Students who live in coed dorms suffer from lack of privacy.
D. Most parents don't approve of coed housing systems.

Sample Commentary
1. The thesis suggests two patterns of organization. The dominant pattern makes a generalization about the effects of coed housing, labeling them "mostly advantageous." A second pattern of cause and/or effect is subordinate to the dominant one. The writer will have to establish that the things he calls effects are actually produced by the switch to a coed system. The major divisions claim to describe all the effects of coed housing. Section I promises to show the advantageous effects; section II is supposed to show the few disadvantageous effects. No subsections appear to be given to proving that effects claimed actually result from changing to a coed system.
2. The topic sentences of the major sections do not adequately support the argument required by the thesis.
3. No definition of "advantageous" is indicated.
4. The parents' opinion is irrelevant to the question of "advantageous" outcomes. In addition, the entries under "advantages," in Section I will have to be made more particular before the audience will be convinced.

Thesis: Although modern naval warships resemble merchant ships in many respects, a naval vessel's mission requires a different design from that of a merchant ship.
I. Because any ship's purpose is to provide safe passage during a voyage, naval and merchant ships have many similarities.
    A. General design of bows, midsections and sterns
    B. Size and stability
    C. Allocation of space for sleeping and storage
II. The different functions of merchant and naval ships dictate certain differences in design.
    A. Purposes of merchant vessels require special design characteristics
        1. Plating

2. Shape of hull
3. Width
4. Speed
5. Structural reinforcement

B. Functions of naval ships require different characteristics
   1. Plating
   2. Shape of reinforcement
   3. Width
   4. Speed
   5. Structural reinforcement
   6. Construction and materials
   7. Compartments
   8. Complexity of steering mechanism

Thesis: The limitations of conventional energy forms and failure to develop new energy sources necessitate the development of nuclear energy through the construction of plants with proven designs.

I. Reserves of natural gas and other conventional fuels are being depleted.
   A. New deposits harder to find
   B. Depletion of present fuels
II. Alternative sources of energy have not been developed.
III. Careful study and planning must precede the construction of a nuclear power plant.
   A. Preliminary investigations
   B. Evaluation procedures
IV. Safety features are available for nuclear power plants.
V. Safe methods of operation can be enforced in nuclear power plants.
VI. Objections to nuclear wastes are out of date.
VII. World conference on energy usage will be held in June.
VIII. Plans to build a power plant at Allans Creek are underway.

9 Introductions and conclusions

Objectives

People communicate better if they first establish good relationships. In writing as in social life, sharing ideas and feelings is a more satisfying experience if people involved show consideration for each other's needs and interests. The writer shows his consideration for the reader by providing an introduction that suggests what is to follow. In this introduction he does several things: he introduces the general topic, defines key terms, explains his purpose, and gives clues to the organization of the rest of the essay. The writer shows his concern for the reader by making his subject as interesting and as appealing as possible. A writer must make his listeners feel comfortable and involved; otherwise he will be ignored. Most readers are too busy to waste time reading things that do not meet their needs or interests.

A good writer shows consideration for the reader in other ways, too: before writing his introduction he thinks about what he has in common with his reader, what the reader already knows about the subject, and what new aspects the reader might find most appealing.

An introduction should be of appropriate length. The introduction to a three-page paper should be one paragraph, whereas the introduction to a book might be a chapter in length.

It is not suitable to begin an introduction by forcing the reader back to the title in order to understand the text.

Beginning the essay with a pronoun that refers to the title is discourteous.

The conclusion is an equally important part of the essay. It is the writer's last word with the reader. In the conclusion the writer must briefly reemphasize the intention of the paper, refocus the reader's attention on the paper's central thesis, and reveal the implications of his judgments about this thesis.

In this chapter you will learn how to evaluate and write introductions and conclusions.

Evaluating introductions

1. *Does the introduction arouse the reader's interest in the thesis or central theme of the essay?*

   A good writer uses the introduction to link the reader's interests and the given topic. Ask yourself why the reader would be interested in your subject, and then emphasize this link in the introduction. Notice how the writer of an advertisement uses the readers' self-concern to involve them in the topic in the first few introductory sentences:

   > Find out the truth about yourself! Will your marriage be happy? Will you die young? Will you become wealthy? An astounding key to human destiny has been found in a recently deciphered scroll from ancient ruins in the Far East. Learning the numerical values of the consonants in your full name and applying a few simple mathematical formulas will let you discover the future that is yours . . .

   The example is a cheap appeal that offers the reader a set of mathematical tables and formulas to learn more about himself for "only $25." You need not be so blatant and heavy-handed, but every reader asks "What's in it for me?" Do you have new information, a better explanation, fresh solutions, or new goals to offer him? Whenever you can appeal to the reader's established interests, the job of persuasion becomes easier.

2. *Does the introduction move from the general to the particular, directing the reader's attention from a broad, general idea to a specific thesis?*

   A thesis, we said in Chapter 3, equals a limited topic + a controlling idea about the topic. In beginning the introduction, the writer may take *either* the topic *or* the idea back up the ladder of inclusiveness to a level familiar to the audience.

Example

Thesis sentence: Self-paced instruction in several innovative programs has increased the level of student comprehension and the rate of learning.

In leading up to this thesis, a writer might begin by talking about how people get the most pleasure from activities they can do at their own speed, without feeling rushed or delayed by someone else. Or else he could begin with *the controlling idea of the thesis,* which is the two major effects of the self-pacing factor: (1) increased comprehension and (2) increased rate of learning. The writer could begin his introduction by explaining the various standards for judging innovative educational programs, and then narrow the field to comprehension and rate of learning. The writer's options look something like this:

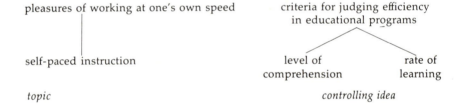

pleasures of working at one's own speed

self-paced instruction

topic

criteria for judging efficiency in educational programs

level of comprehension   rate of learning

controlling idea

Deciding where to begin on the ladder is a matter of where you have common ground, an existing point of contact with your reader. Likewise, in deciding whether the topic or the controlling idea should first be presented more inclusively, the guide is once again your preliminary decisions about the audience's knowledge and attitudes. In the example under discussion, educators might be more interested in criteria for measuring efficiency in educational programs, but students would probably respond to the pleasures of working at one's own speed. If you have a legitimate reason for writing for a particular audience, you should be able to find a point of contact with them.

It is almost too obvious to mention—but without a thesis there can be no real introduction, because there is nothing to introduce. Unless the writer has decided on his thesis, he should not try to write an introduction.

3. *Does the introduction act as a funnel to limit the topic and focus the controlling idea?*

If the writer introduces the topic at a higher level of inclusiveness than the thesis sentence, the introduction will move from general to specific as the topic is narrowed and the idea about the topic is focused. This restricting movement limits your writing obligation, and can be diagramed like this:

Introduction
Broad general statement introducing the topic (or the controlling idea) at a higher level of inclusiveness or generality than in the thesis → appeal to reader interest → definitions of unfamiliar and key terms → narrowing/focusing the topic/idea → *General statement* → introducing the idea about the topic (or the topic, —depending on which you introduced earlier) → definitions → limitations on scope of idea →

Thesis: Limited topic + controlling idea

In the following example the writer plans to write his essay about abortion, but the first few sentences are unrelated to each other and give no hint of the direction of the essay:

Abortions are not yet totally acceptable, but they are effective in reducing the world's population growth. A woman should have the right to control the course her life will take. The situations and reasons for abortion given by both married and unmarried women are quite similar . . .

The ideas presented so far by the writer are all "about" abortion, but they are unrelated:

Social acceptability
Use as population control
Personal control of one's future
Reasons for abortion
"Situations" of women who choose abortion

In the next example the writer uses a funnel, working from the broad question of population control to the thesis that abortion is an undesirable means of controlling population growth.

Population growth cannot be allowed to continue unchecked, but governments need to be selective in the methods of control they approve. Expense, effectiveness, and risk to human life must be considered in selecting methods for growth control. Abortion effectively prevents unwanted births, but the resulting expense and risk to human life make it a less desirable means of population control and a last resort for policy-makers.

Related ideas in the second example include:

Population growth must be *controlled*
Methods of *control* must be *selected* carefully
Criteria for *selection*
Measured by *criteria,* abortion not acceptable

The first example wanders around the topic; the second moves directly to narrow down the topic from the problem of population growth to the usefulness of a single method of control.

4. *Does the introduction establish the desired relationship between writer and audience?*
At the outset, a writer makes preliminary decisions about his audience and chooses his *persona,* keeping in mind his level of knowledge, his attitude toward the audience, and the demands of the situation (see Chapter 1). In writing the introduction he establishes his relationship with the reader primarily through the tone of his language. He must be consistent in his word choice, or a firm relationship will not be created. Notice the tone in this introduction to a formal letter to eight clergymen who issued a statement criticizing civil rights demonstrations:

April 16, 1963

My Dear Fellow Clergymen:
While confined here in the Birmingham city jail, I came across your recent statement calling my present activities "unwise and untimely." Seldom do I pause to answer criticism of my work and ideas. If I sought to answer all the criticisms that cross my desk, my secretaries would have little time for anything other than such correspondence in the course of the day, and I would have no time for constructive work. But since I feel that you are men of genuine good will and that your criticisms are sincerely set forth,

I want to try to answer your statement in what I hope will be patient and reasonable terms. (Martin Luther King, Jr., "Letter from Birmingham Jail" from *Why We Can't Wait*)

In this short paragraph, King says several things about himself: he is the equal of the men he addresses; they are all "fellow clergymen"; King is a busy man, an executive, with secretaries; he is devoted to constructive work and seldom answers critics; and he is going to be patient and reasonable in this letter. King also creates an identity for his audience, claiming that they are men of genuine good will who sincerely set forth their criticisms. He also classes them as critics, people with whom he would not ordinarily bother, but whose opinions he will answer because they are sincere. The tone is dignified, simple, and straightforward.

Exercise: Beginning the introduction

In this exercise you are given several writing situations. In each one there is a writer, an audience, and a thesis sentence. Imagine what preliminary decisions the writer must have made about the reader's interests and knowledge. Based on your speculations, pinpoint the common ground between writer and reader. Write the first two sentences of the introduction, establishing this point of common ground and setting the appropriate tone.

a. Situation: Writer is preparing an introductory essay for a booklet offering over two hundred wilderness trips, ranging from two days to two months, to members of a large national club.
Audience: Members of a large national conservation club
Title of essay: What Can you Expect of a Wilderness Outing?
Thesis: Your first wilderness outing promises both adventure and surprise.
First two sentences: _____

_____

b. Situation: Junior Achievement Club needs advice on selling solid stick air fresheners to homeowners. The writer, last year's club president, has been asked to write a one-page guide for this year's salespeople. Last year the club sold

more items and made more money than ever before, so the writer will speak as one who has known success.
Audience: Junior Achievement members
Thesis: The key to selling is convincing people they want your product.
First two sentences: _____
_____

_____

c. Situation: Paper for American History class. Recent class discussions have dealt with discrepancies between popular images of American heroes and their actual personalities. Writer is a sophomore college student.
Audience: History professor
Thesis: Lincoln's decision to emancipate the slaves was intended to provoke rebellion among the slaves in the South.
First two sentences: _____
_____

_____

d. Situation: Professional writer is preparing an article on Walter Cronkite for a monthly magazine. She has had three long interviews with Cronkite, who at this time is anchorman for the CBS Evening News. In 1956 he hosted the *You Are There* show, a weekly series of re-enactments in which CBS correspondents tracked down and interviewed people like Louis Pasteur, Benedict Arnold, and General Sherman. Cronkite narrated while these historical figures vaccinated patients, committed treason, plundered towns. As CBS news anchorman, Cronkite reports investigations, assassinations, coronations, launches, landings, and confrontations.
Audience: General national audience who are at least high-school graduates
Thesis: Walter Cronkite, the most trusted man in America, on a particular day interprets and reports those events that alter and illuminate our time.
First two sentences: _____
_____

_____

e. Situation: Newspaper ad for toothpaste that has a time-release breath-freshener ingredient. Writer is a professional copywriter.

Audience: Decide who the audience will be.

Thesis: Choose the headline of appeal.

First two lines of the paragraph of information in this ad (other than the thesis): _____

_____

_____

Evaluating conclusions

So far our method has been to teach you to ask questions about writing in order to evaluate its effectiveness. In the case of conclusions, this method poses problems because the appropriateness of a conclusion depends on all that came before it—the thesis the writer chose, the development pattern he adopted, and the intention he had toward his topic and his audience. Space forbids offering you eight or ten complete essays to read, in order to judge their conclusions. Instead we wish to arm you with some questions, trusting that by now you will accept their usefulness and later remember to apply them as you write and revise your own essays. Test your conclusions with the following questions:

1. *Has the writer focused the reader's attention on his central concern? Has he summarized the main points of his argument? Has he offered an apt quotation that is easy to remember?* If, after reading the conclusion, you cannot tell what the essay was about, the conclusion has failed in its most important function.

2. *Has the writer inverted the funnel structure of his introduction, moving from definite conclusions to their broader implications?* The conclusion should finish with the broadest statement of the implications of the thesis.

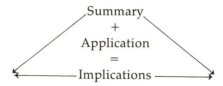

Example

Thesis: Since 1911 the definitions of poverty given by sociologists have not changed, and solutions proposed have been basically similar, but the methods of measuring poverty have become more and more complex. Concluding statement: Because the definitions of poverty and proposed solutions to the problem remained the same for sixty years, while only the techniques for measuring human suffering became more sophisticated, it is no surprise that poverty continues to be one of the most vexing problems of our society.

3. *Has the writer invited the reader's confidence and support by reminding him why these conclusions are important for him?*
Just as the writer originally appealed to the reader's interests and needs, now he must remind the reader of the relevance of these conclusions to the reader's own concerns.

4. *Has the writer maintained a tone consistent with the rest of the essay?*
The writer should refrain from exhortations and moralizing inconsistent with the rest of the essay. In a philosophical or religious essay we expect a more profound conclusion, a sense of intense vision and wisdom. But do not, for example, end a time–motion study on work procedures in the kitchen with a ridiculous attempt to impress the reader:

> The efficient kitchen worker completes his task with an air of confidence in the value of his work. His entire being seems to say, "By the manner in which I load this dishwasher I demonstrate my confidence in the benevolence of God and the dignity of labor. I am here to serve, and in my kitchen the will of God will not be thwarted." Let each of us, in our daily labors, strive to make our tasks worthy of those noble sentiments.

Exercise: Evaluating conclusions

Although you cannot fully evaluate the appropriateness of the following conclusions without the essays for which they were written, you can make tentative judgments about their value. Apply the questions listed above to these conclusions and criticize their effectiveness.

a. The next time you are walking down a street in New York or Philadelphia or San Francisco and a fellow walks by who is about seven feet tall, wearing a beret and sunglasses with a small beard, walking two dogs and looking like he doesn't want to be disturbed by questions about the weather, don't disturb him. If he's Wilt Chamberlain, he may put you under his arm like a suitcase. Then again, it may not be Wilt Chamberlain. You might just be embarrassing a tall mailman who is trying to look inconspicuous.

b. The only question left to be settled now is: are women persons? And I hardly believe any of our opponents will have the hardihood to say they are not. Being persons, then, women are citizens; and no state has a right to make any law, or to enforce any old law, that shall abridge their privileges or immunities. Hence, every discrimination against women in the constitutions and laws of the several states is today null and void, precisely as is every one against Negroes. (Susan B. Anthony, "Are Women People?" Written following her arrest and trial for casting a ballot, 1873)

c. For the future, therefore, the question is not what we can do, for we will increasingly be able to create miracles and marvels and to humanize man and his environment. The question has not to do with our capacity, but with our will; not with our imagination, but with our restraint; not with our acumen, but with our aspiration.

   The question is this: Will society slow its growth, revitalize itself in the process, and begin to talk with science? The question is this: Will we put an end to fragmentation and view the whole picture? The question is this: *Will-we-use-our-knowledge?* (Stewart L. Udall, "But Then Came Man")

d. The microelectronics laboratory at Rice University has had a very modest beginning, but there is more to come. It has already stirred the interest and imagination of students and faculty. The students, through their tireless efforts, deserve a major share of credit for developing and refining the laboratory. Their work, frequently late in the evenings and on Saturdays, has made them an integral part of the laboratory and very much a part of the ongoing microelectronics revolution.

e. Things would be even worse for the girls if the college government were fully elected the previous year, which would leave them totally unrepresented. Even if it weren't, the chance of minority members' being elected would be slim, since as newcomers they would not be well known. Clearly some sort of system would be needed to ensure proper representation; otherwise, women entering a formerly all-male college would be politically powerless.

f. History's jury is still out on our only true Texas President—it does not seem to matter much that Dwight Eisenhower happened to have been born in Denison and left while still in dresses—and, one supposes, the disputes will long rage over what Texas did to him or for him. One of the few eloquent passages in *The Vantage Point* is revealing, however, in expressing some sense of wonder that a boy from Johnson City could have scaled the heights. Of his first night back at The Ranch, after leaving the White House for good, LBJ wrote:

"I went outside and stood in the yard again, looking up at the moon in the broad, clear Texas sky. My thoughts went back to that October night in 1957 when we had walked along the banks of the Pedernales River and looked for the Soviet Sputnik orbiting in the sky overhead. I thought of all that had happened in the years between. I remembered once again a story I had heard about one of the astronauts from the crew of Apollo 8, which a month ago had circled the moon only a few miles above its surface. Soon after his return to earth the astronaut had stepped into his backyard at home and had looked up at the moon. He had wondered if it really could be true that he had been there. I had recounted this story a few days ago to a group of friends. Perhaps, I told them, the time would come when I would look back on the majesty and the power and the splendor of the Presidency and find it hard to believe that I had actually been there." (Larry L. King, "Bringing Up Lyndon," *Texas Monthly*)

Review

To evaluate an introduction, ask the following questions:

1. Does the introduction arouse the reader's interest in the thesis or central theme of the essay?
2. Does the introduction move from the inclusive to the particular, directing the reader's attention from a broad, general idea to a specific thesis?
3. Does the introduction act as a funnel to limit the topic and focus the controlling idea?
4. Does the introduction establish the desired relationship between writer and audience?

To evaluate a conclusion, ask the following questions:

1. Does the conclusion focus the reader's attention on his central concern? Does it summarize the main arguments? Does it offer an apt quotation that is easy to remember?
2. Does the conclusion invert the funnel structure of the introduction, moving from definite conclusions to their broader implications?
3. Does the conclusion invite the reader's confidence and support by reminding him why these conclusions are important for him?

4. Does the conclusion maintain a tone consistent with the rest of the essay?

Asking questions and making decisions

Exercise: Evaluating introductions

Review the questions above, and then evaluate each of the ten introductions that follow. Some of them are good; some are poor. Write a short paragraph about each one, explaining your judgment.

a. Introduction to a six-page article

Dear Friend:
   In the last six months of 1977, 894 children under the age of 14 were murdered by American parents who flogged, burned, starved and tortured their offspring to death. In the same period, the number of child prostitutes in "kiddie porn" films increased by fifty percent. Four small children were tied up in blankets in stifling airless rooms, causing three of them to die of heat prostration and the other to suffer brain damage.
   Every one of the statements in that paragraph is false. But were you quite sure, as you read them, that they weren't true? Didn't you, in fact, assume that they were accurate? And, if so, did you feel anything more than the customary twinge of weary nausea with which one reacts to the daily barrage of evil news about child abuse? The human capacity to be shocked is not unlimited, and the lies I have cooked up differ only in degree from the truths you already know about the strange and ferocious war that adults conduct. What if you believed my facts were accurate and were genuinely upset? How could you have protested and how could you have rescued those children who will die tomorrow? More particularly, what is it like to live in a nation where such statements are likely to be true? What has happened to the dreams of justice and harmony that once guided our future?

b. Introduction to a three-page student paper

The Parking Problem at Midwestern University
This topic is a big problem. Just last night I was forced to park my car a full half-mile from my 7:30 p.m. class. That was a long walk to class and a long walk back. The walkways are not very well lighted, either. A lot of girls don't like that. And when it rains it is really a problem. Maybe more students have cars now than when the parking lots were fixed. Some of the tree-filled areas could be turned into new parking lots, but that would make the ecology people mad. However, even they have to get to class on time.

c. Introduction to a five-page paper

The world today is asking a terrible question—a question which every citizen of this Republic should ask himself: what sort of people are we, we Americans? And the answer which much of the world is bound to return is that we are today the most frightening people on this planet.

d. Introduction to a ten-page essay

No aspect of human life seethes with so many unexorcised demons as does sex. No human activity is so hexed by superstition, so haunted by residual tribal lore, and so harassed by socially-induced fear. Within the breast of urban-secular man, a toe-to-toe struggle still rages between his savage and his bourgeois forebears. Like everything else, the images of sex which informed tribal and town society are expiring along with the eras in which they arose. The erosion of traditional values and the disappearance of accepted modes of behavior have left contemporary man free, but some-what rudderless. Abhoring a vacuum, the mass media have rushed in to supply a new code and a new set of behavioral prototypes. They appeal to the unexorcised demons. Nowhere is the persist-ence of mythical and metalogical denizens more obvious than in sex, and the shamans of sales do their best to nourish them. Nowhere is the humanization of life more frustrated. Nowhere is a clear word of exorcism more needed.

How is the humanization of sex impeded? First it is thwarted by the parading of cultural-identity images for the sexually dispos-sessed, to make money. These images become the tyrant gods of the secular society, undercutting its liberation from religion and transforming it into a kind of neotribal culture. Second, the authentic secularization of sex is checkmated by an anxious cling-ing to the sexual standards of the town, an era so recent and yet so different from ours that simply to transplant its sexual ethos into our situation is to invite hypocrisy of the worst degree.

Let us look first at the spurious sexual models conjured up for our anxious society by the sorcerers of the mass media and the advertising guild. Like all pagan deities, these come in pairs—the god and his consort. For our purposes they are best symbolized by The Playboy and Miss America, the Adonis and Aphrodite of a leisure consumer society which still seems unready to venture into full postreligious maturity and freedom. The Playboy and Miss America represent The Boy and The Girl. They incorporate a vision of life. They function as religious phenomena and should be exorcised and exposed. (Harvey Cox, "Sex and Secularization," *The Secular City*)

e. Introduction to a five-page student paper

Euthanasia has been a subject of growing controversy over the past decade. Euthanasia is the mercy killing of an incurably ill person through means by which the patient will generally not suffer any great deal of discomfort. Many people have not made up their minds. The church and the government are the only ones which seem to have a definite stand on this very important issue. The situation should be turned over to doctors and medical experts. Before allowing a person to die, the doctors must determine the extent of the illness, if there is a cure or hope for a recovery, and whether euthanasia would be better for the person involved. In most cases the doctors are in favor of the mercy killing. The person who is going to die might be consulted also.

f. Introduction to a five-page student paper

The power of bureaucracies is feared and denounced, but they continue to flourish. A bureaucracy as a system of administrative bodies is characterized by specialized functions, adherence to fixed rules, and a hierarchy of authority with a good deal of power. As "the working core of government," a bureaucracy's power is due to (1) the abdication of Congress to make policies in the face of demand, (2) public support of policies, (3) expertise of bureaucracies, (4) the organizational spirit of these agencies and, (5) the leadership of the bureaucracy.

g. Introduction to a chapter of a book

The fury of the Dorian Conquest is said to have reached its height about the year 1050. During the ensuing epoch, as we have already seen, the invaders settled down; political combination within certain limited areas produced a more or less clear-cut arrangement of independent states; and by the Eighth or Seventh Century the map of Greece had assumed in general outline the recognized divisions of historic times. But the process of expansion was not as yet complete and during these two centuries fresh settlements were made on the surrounding coasts. The age of haphazard wandering was over; but the age of colonization was yet to come. (Cyril E. Robinson, *A History of Greece*)

h. Introduction to a three-page student paper

The Problem of Narcotics
It means many kinds of problems, really. The problems are difficult to solve, just as the problems of life are difficult to solve. Life can be hard, as the experience of everyone shows. The problems we face and how we solve them are the way in which the world sees us.

i. Introduction to a seven-page student paper

> The Greek term *polis* connotes a community of people striving for a collective ideal. The social movements of our time have produced an upheaval that seems hardly consistent with the ancient ideal. Yet out of today's turmoil there seems to be emerging a new vision of community based upon some extraordinarily complex but profoundly human values. One example is Daniel Moynihan's analysis of lessons to be learned from the failure of the war on poverty. It is hoped that the social organization of the future will be characterized by the belief that, in Hannah Arendt's phrase, "truth can only exist where it is humanized by discourse." In other words, we must learn again what the Greeks knew: that the strength of the *polis* rests upon our ability to talk to one another.

j. Introduction to a fifteen-page essay

> Cervantes is known to the world as the author of *Don Quixote,* and although his other works are numerous and creditable, and his pathetic life is carefully recorded, yet it is as the author of *Don Quixote* alone that he deserves to be generally known or considered. Had his wit not come by chance on the idea of the Ingenious Hidalgo, Cervantes would never have attained his universal renown, even if his other works and the interest of his career should have sufficed to give him a place in the literary history of his country. Here, then, where our task is to present in miniature only what has the greatest and most universal value, we may treat our author as playwrights are advised to treat their heroes, saying of him only what is necessary to the understanding of the single action with which we are concerned. This single action is the writing of *Don Quixote;* and what we shall try to understand is what there was in the life and environment of Cervantes that enabled him to compose that great book, and that remained imbedded in its characters, its episodes, and its moral. (George Santayana, "Cervantes")

Exercise: Writing an introduction

> Return to the first exercise in this chapter (p. 149) and complete one of the introductions, applying what you have learned about introductions. Then write an evaluation of your introduction, using the questions applied in the preceding exercise.

Exercise: Writing conclusions

In this exercise you will read two essays and write a conclusion for each. The thesis sentence is indicated by italics.

a. This essay, called "Strategy in Football," could serve as part of a sports handout for physical education classes. The author's own conclusion has been deleted. Supply a conclusion that would fit Joseph Bevill's essay.

Football is a game of strategy, not just brute force. Sometimes if a weaker team has the right offensive scheme they can overcome a team of much greater talent. The two most widely used offensive schemes are the Wishbone and the Power-I attacks. Teams using the Wishbone include power-houses such as Oklahoma and Texas, while teams installing a Power-I include Penn State and L.S.U. *In choosing between these two offensive formations, coaches must evaluate offensive strategy as well as the skill of the players.*

First, the Wishbone is an offensive formation with three backs as well as a quarterback in the backfield. The whole system works on the idea that the quarterback is given three options. He can give the ball to the fullback, or the halfback, or run with it himself. In the Power-I formation there are only two backs in the backfield along with the quarterback. This system leans more toward the passing game. The backs can either pass, block, or run out for a short swing pass in case the quarterback gets in trouble. Of course, a team can also run a lot out of this formation but passing is more important in most cases.

In deciding whether to install the wishbone or the Power-I, coaches must first evaluate their players' skills. Generally, teams running a wishbone do so because they have players with both outstanding speed and strength. Power-I teams can compensate with smaller linemen because pass blocking is easier than run blocking. This makes the Wishbone basically a running formation— although, again, passing can be important. Also, an excellent all-around quarterback is necessary to make the Wishbone go. The quarterback running the Wishbone has to know his options, and when to pitch and when to keep the ball. He must also be an accurate passer because, although he does not have to pass often, when he does he must be right on target. The situation is usually critical when a Wishbone team has to pass. The Power-I quarterback's qualification is mainly his passing ability. He *has* to be a good passer. His running ability can be questionable, unlike that of a Wishbone leader. The running backs can be the same for both formations, although Wishbone backs must be more run-oriented. Both have to be strong and quick, and run without fumbling when hit hard by opposing players.

The Wishbone and the I also create different strategic playing advantages. The Wishbone is more of a controlled, conservative offensive designed to get small chunks of yardage with each play. The perfect Wishbone team marches up and down the field, using large time periods and long drives, topped with the fullback barreling in from one, two, or three yards out. This type of playing uses up precious time and gives the defensive players a much-needed rest on the sidelines. The I formation is usually a more radical wide-open type of football. The ideal I team would control the ball for a couple of minutes on the ground, then throw a long unsuspected pass for a touchdown. The run in the I sets up the pass.

b. In the following paper an anthropology student attempts to integrate information about the findings at various archae-ological sites, to answer the question "What happened in the Lowland Iron Age to the North European Lowland people, after disasters, invasions, inventions, and climate changes threatened to destroy them and their culture?" Complete the conclusion to the paper so that Delphia Clarke, the student author, can turn it in to her anthropology professor (footnotes and references have been omitted).

Around 700 B.C. the Early North European Lowland people were suffering a tri-faceted depression. During the previous Bronze Age they had had a very effective economy, importing foreign metals and exporting the finished bronze manufactures. But when iron replaced bronze in tools, trade collapsed. Further-more, the adoption of iron techniques among these people was so slow that the recovery of their trading economy took centuries. In addition to failing commercialism, increasing rainfall and colder weather complicated an agriculture and husbandry subsistence. Worst of all, Scythian-like bands began to burn and sack the villages. Grave goods, sacrificial finds, and village excavations document a later recovery. *During the Lowland Iron Age, the North European people overcame the collapse of their economy and developed one that could support an expanding population.*

Grave goods illustrate the history of these people well. During the Bronze Age, personal belongings had accompanied the body. We know of no religious changes in attitudes that might have affected this custom. But by the seventh century B.C., apparently as a result of the suffering economy, the amount of wealth in burials, religious offerings, and mercantile hoards decreased. Sixth-century burials were even poorer. Compared with other centuries, in fact, this period offers few archaeological finds. By the time of Christ, however, the quality and quantity of grave goods were increasing. A more materialistic concept of death at this stage resulted in the burial of peasants, as well as wealthy Jutland nobles, at tables set with feasts. In the richest graves were magnificent drinking vessels and large containers of bronze, glass, and silver. A Lowland chieftain was well outfitted with goods: a bronze dish; silver goblets made by Greek craftsmen; a series of Roman-made objects—a wine jug, wine bucket, saucepan, and dish; and lastly, more personal objects such as bow brooches, knives, bone pins, and gold rings. A woman at Jelling in the same district carried with her to the land of the dead hair pins, necklets, costume jewelry, gold and silver rings, a bronze knife, a pair of scissors, and cut and ground glass vessels of Roman origin. In short, grave goods imply an expanding economy both by sheer quantity and by the fact that so many are not local and probably come from trade or looting.

The gradual dominance of Nerthus, a fertility goddess, during the early Iron Age coupled in the late Iron Age with a shift to the glorification of war gods, suggests the transformation from a low subsistence level to a prosperous economy dependent on trading and war spoils. First, the nature of artifacts found and the presence of so many of them in bogs (sites often associated with Nerthus) hint at their connection with a fertility goddess. Nerthus was worshipped as far back as the Neolithic period, as seen in amulets, on necklets, and in decorations on pottery vessels. But by the early Iron Age, female figurines are more numerous than male. The female figures wear only the characteristic torcs and hold their hands under their breasts. Throughout the Iron Age, these twisted necklets or torcs symbolize the cult of Nerthus. Indeed, in the late Iron Age torcs found in bogs became so heavy that they could only have been special offerings for the goddess. This focus on the fertility goddess shifts, however, to worship of war gods. Offerings to the god of war increased toward the end of the Roman Iron Age, and a score of them have been found in peat-bogs. Many are large, containing hundreds of weapons and other war-booty. One contained three boats as well. These are evidence of troubled times and great tribal battles, and show the command of the war-god over men's minds.

Last, village excavations from the late Iron Age reveal fortifications and foreign influences. One village, Borre Fen, was built on an island in a fen and was surrounded by a deep defensive ditch. The dirt from this ditch was thrown on the inside to form a rampart, while the surface of the fen was dug away to make a swamp. The only entrance, over a paved road under water, was flanked by deep ditches so that only the experienced could reach the island. The dangers of looting must have been great to inspire such detailed planning of village building. Two settlements on the same spot in Grønloft have been excavated. Both show traces of an enclosing stockade with lockable gates.

Foreign influences are seen at two sites: Ginderup and Vendsyssel. Ginderup is an Iron Age village in Thy, Northwest Jutland. Under excavation it revealed Roman coins and mosaic hearths, similar to Roman mosaics. Vendsyssel cellars resembled deep storage pits in Gaul, in both structure and content. Tacitus suggests such cellars were also used for refuge from danger. In short, village excavations underline the war- and trade-based economy of the late Iron Age.

In summary, during the Lowland Iron Age, the North European peoples . . .

10 *The whole essay: decisions from start to finish*

Objectives

Before a play opens the actors rehearse for weeks, working first on one scene and then on another, perfecting each section, learning how to draw a certain response from the audience. A writer who wishes to improve his or her writing also rehearses various parts of the writing process, learning how to make judgments and elicit certain responses from an audience of readers. The improving writer, like the rehearsing actor, works on introductions, thesis sentences, patterns of organization, and use of evidence so that when he writes whole papers, essays, letters, or other documents, he will have the greatest freedom, the widest command of resources, the greatest capacity to express himself fully and exactly to his reader—and therefore to get what he wants: a job, a consensus, or an "A." Writing differs from the theater, however, because the writer is author, producer, and actor. Whereas the dramatic actor follows someone else's concept, organization, and choice of words, the writer must both plan and deliver the performance.

In the earlier chapters of this book you have learned to ask questions, mostly about other writers' works. Now it is time to employ questions that will guide your own writing, to do your own decision-making.

Preliminary decision-making

Preliminary writing decisions involve the audience, the subject, and the writer. Decisions in writing, as in driving or playing cards, can be deliberate and planned or semi-automatic and arbitrary. Bad writing and bad card-playing rely on luck without much thinking; the outcome is often disappointing.

Audience awareness

Careless thinking overlooks the audience, one of the most common failings among poor writers. Making conscious decisions about your audience is an important step in improving your writing. Here are some questions to guide many of your writing decisions:

1. How clearly can I identify my readers?
2. What are their assumptions about the topic?
3. What do they know about the topic?
4. How do they feel about the topic?
5. What power do they have to respond?
6. How will the context in which they read this writing affect their response?
7. What questions will the audience ask about this topic?

Skills practiced earlier can help you answer these questions. You will remember from Chapter 1 that audiences cannot always be identified precisely; but the more you can infer about them, the more accurately you can make decisions. Once you have identified the audience as fully as possible, you can plot a ladder of particular to inclusive terms (the kind discussed in Chapter 2) that will suggest what your readers are likely to know and feel about the topic. This ladder will help you check your perspective against theirs. You might start with a word-association test, the sort that many people play as a game. Beginning with a word or phrase for your topic, ask yourself what terms this might suggest to your readers.

Suppose you are a student who feels that women's volleyball games are not getting enough coverage in the campus newspaper. Before writing a letter, you could guess what words the phrase "women's volleyball" might suggest to the newspaper editor. You might imagine that in his perspective women's volleyball games are lumped together with other sports that the paper's sports writers handle. You might guess that he would answer "football," "basketball," "swimming," or "baseball" in a word-association game.

The terms the editor would associate with "women's volleyball" can become the starting point for a ladder of particular to inclusive terms representing part of a model in his professional perspective. Thinking about what these terms have in common can help you arrive at the next level of inclusiveness, such as "campus sports."

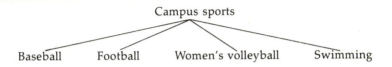

Similarly, you might guess that the editor would associate "campus sports" with "campus social events," "campus politics," and other campus activities covered by the newspaper. These activities are the topics on which his paper reports because of its responsibility to students. After thinking about your subject from the editor's perspective, you could draw a ladder to describe part of the model that guides his perceptions:

If you think the paper doesn't give women's volleyball enough coverage, you probably use a different model. To you, meager newspaper coverage may be just one more example of discrimination against women:

Comparing the two ladders will show how differences in perspective determine what the issues are likely to be and how you might manage the argument of your letter. Both of you see sports as part of a group of events, "campus activities," that the newspaper could cover, but the editor looks at these as "topics of interest to students," whereas you think of them as "unfair press coverage." The editor rates events by how many students are interested in them. If only a few want to read about women's volleyball, then he will consider his responsibility for covering women's volleyball to be reduced. In your view, as a student, women's volleyball deserves attention as an official campus activity, regardless of the number of students interested in it.

The issue between you and the editor is whether the newspaper's responsibility is to serve the students by reporting on activities of interest to the majority, or on all activities that happen on campus.

Examining the ladders can also disclose ways to persuade the reader. While both ladders have "campus activities," the inclusive terms at the level above differ: "unfair press coverage" and "topics of interest to students." In one persuasive approach, you might show the editor that his view of his purpose, reporting on "topics of interest to students," coincides with what you want, more coverage of "women's sports." You do this by defining "women's sports" as a topic increasingly interesting to students. You might describe the many readers who are eager to read about women's volleyball, a sport with a growing number of fans across the country, both male and female. The more difficult approach might be necessary at a school with many more male students than female students or where volleyball had few fans. You would have to convince the editor that his job was not to publish articles with majority appeal but to report all activities equally.

Another way to discover a persuasive strategy is to see what external models are suggested by the reader's perspective ladder. For example, the editor's ladder shows he would be thinking about this topic in terms of the newspaper's responsibility and operation. The model of how a newspaper operates might suggest how to persuade the editor to cover more volleyball games. Since the sports editor and his staff are actually doing the writing, you might spare the general editor a sense of being blamed, and appeal to his sense of being in control, by arguing that he could bring the paper closer to its ideals by instructing the sports editor to be more fair in his assignments given to reporters. Such a model of persons in the organization gives you insight into the appropriate procedure for the editor to accomplish your request. In turn, you can write more effectively by letting that awareness shape your argument.

Both you and your reader may be influenced by the situation, as well as by your perspectives. Supplement your decisions about the audience with these questions about the situation:

1. Will the situation make my audience stress certain values, beliefs, opinions, or actions?
2. Does the situation make any demands on me?
3. (If the situation is academic) What exactly is the assignment?

A person's values at a given period in his life may be fairly constant from day to day. Most people do not champion honesty, compassion, and justice on Wednesday, and prefer lying, brutality, and tyranny on Thursday. However, certain situations will bring into play selected aspects of a person's belief or value system. At a church meeting one expects emphasis on the moral issues of a community problem; but expects a political and legal discussion of that same problem at the city council meeting. Although boards of deacons may occasionally discuss politics, and city councils may discuss moral issues, these situations are less likely and less looked for.

Considering your audience's perspective will help you decide what to emphasize. If your topic is "controlling costs" and your audience is a construction engineering society meeting for an annual convention, you could ask what inclusive terms they might use to group ideas about "controlling costs." Because the context of your paper is an annual professional meeting, these construction engineers are not likely to think about controlling costs with reference to their family budgets, but as related to their work. How would the topic fit into their professional work? What questions would they ask? Perhaps they would ask, "Why should I control costs as part of my work?" The answer to this question suggests one level for your ladder:

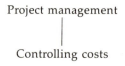

Project management

Controlling costs

What is the next level of the ladder from their point of view? How does a construction engineer view project management? Project management is one part of a construction engineer's professional activity, something he would like to do well. At a higher level of inclusiveness, he thinks of project management as efficient engineering:

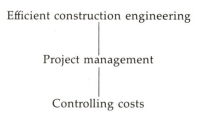

Efficient construction engineering

Project management

Controlling costs

Considering the context often helps determine whether your more inclusive terms embody concepts suitable to the audience.

The situation, whether academic or professional, may also affect the kind of writing. For the most part, student writers are asked to do academic writing, whose purposes are humanistic. This writing is designed to show the student's familiarity with important concepts, theories, and procedures; to improve his reasoning powers; and to expand his perceptions and experiences. The audience for most academic writing is a professor or his teaching assistant, a person who knows much more about the topic than the student writer. The only action the professor is likely to take after reading the essay is to confer a grade and make a few comments on the paper. Thus, academic writing is a special type of writing that is part of the educational process.

The purpose of professional writing (away from the campus) is almost always to change the audience: to alter their knowledge, or their actions, or their feelings. Thus, in professional writing the writer will choose evidence primarily to persuade, rather than to demonstrate his familiarity with concepts on which the audience is expert. Indeed, in professional situations the audience is usually *less* expert than the writer, who must supply information gleaned from his recent work with the topic, client, project or program. Thus the relationship between the writer, his audience, and his subject matter differs substantially in academic and professional writing.

Whether you are writing in a professional or an academic setting influences the intention you are likely to have toward your audience, and the *persona* you use. After you identify your audience and your situation, you should determine your intention and your role with your answers to these questions:

1. What is my intention toward these readers?
   a. Do I want them to take action?
   b. Do I want them to make a judgment?
   c. Do I want them to hold an opinion?
   d. Do I want them to understand something or remember certain facts?

2. What stance or *persona* will achieve my purpose?
   a. What degree of knowledge should I demonstrate?
   b. What attitude should I take toward my subject?
   c. How formal or informal should I be in my treatment?
   d. How directly should I express myself?
   e. What attitude should I take toward my audience?

If these questions are not clear to you, review Chapter 1.

The student writer who wanted the newspaper editor to give more coverage to women's volleyball might have answered the first set of questions in this way:

Intention
a. I want the editor to give more coverage to women's volley-ball.
b. I want him to judge the paper's past coverage to be inade-quate.
c. I want him to hold the opinion that many students are interested in women's volleyball.
d. I want him to understand that interest in women's volleyball is growing, both on campus and across the country.

The answers to the second set of questions are a bit harder to illustrate, because they involve the personality and ex-perience of the individual writer. The student's answers will govern many decisions as she writes her letter to the editor.

Stance or *persona*
a. I must show: (1) that I have an accurate and unbiased knowledge of what the paper has published on women's volleyball, and (2) that I have reliable information about the popularity of this sport on campus and across the country.
b. I should be formal enough to be taken seriously, as a student with a right to be heard; but informal enough to seem like a reasonable, human being.
c. I should be direct, using the second person "you."
d. I should express dissatisfaction with the coverage in the newspaper rather than with the editor himself, so that instead of reacting defensively he will be free to change his actions and hold the opinion I want him to adopt.

Notice that if the student's letter is likely to appear in the "Letters to the Editor" column, then the student will have *two* kinds of readers—the editor, and other students who read the newspaper. The writer then would also need to imagine the perspective of most students, and make additional decisions about this second audience: what in-tention (action, judgment, opinion and understanding) and *persona* might be appropriate for them. The ladder for the students' perspective might be:

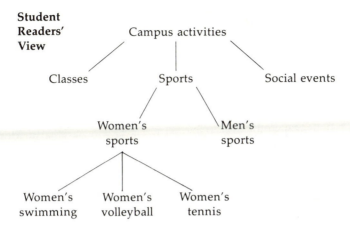

Student Readers' View

The writer might form this intention toward the student audience:

a. I want students to write similar letters.
b. I want students to agree that past coverage of women's volleyball has been too limited.
c. I want students to believe that women's volleyball is as important as other women's sports, and *ought* to rank equally with men's sports.
d. I want them to know that interest in volleyball is growing.

Next she would have to compare these two intentions and decide whether to modify the stance or *persona* chosen earlier. There are a few important differences in the intentions toward the two audiences. Whereas the writer wants the editor to think that many students are interested in women's volleyball, she wants the students to believe that women's volleyball is as important as other campus sports. Also, she wants the general editor to give more coverage to women's volleyball, whereas she wants the students to write similar letters to the editor. These intentions should work well together, because if the students are convinced that women's volleyball is important enough to write additional letters to the editor, the editor will be more likely to believe that student interest in women's volleyball is growing.

In adapting her stance or *persona* to suit both audiences, the writer may wish to demonstrate the same level of knowledge and the same degree of formality. She will probably decide to address the editor directly and other students indirectly. In order to motivate the student readers to write similar letters she will probably emphasize her identity as a student even more strongly than in the original plan.

Choosing a topic

Sometimes the writer's topic is not as clearly identified, in the beginning, as in the women's volleyball example. How to discover a topic and ideas about it can be another preliminary concern. The questions used in Chapters 5, 6, and 7 can be adapted as investigative techniques for early decision-making. An orderly procedure for investigating a topic is called a "heuristic" technique. Although some ideas may occur to you intuitively, in a flash of insight, others must be uncovered by a regular procedure for topic analysis. Often, people find both methods important. Frequently, they report going through these stages:

1. Reading about the topic to acquire a general but thorough understanding of it.
2. Asking deliberate and organized questions about the topic (heuristic procedure).
3. Considering the audience and the situation.
4. Allowing time to "mull it over."
5. Gaining insight, or choosing particular questions.
6. Additional reading to find out other information, if needed.
7. Working on the thesis, outline, and essay.

If a bright idea has not struck you after you complete stage one, and even if it has, you should run through the following questions, allowing at least thirty seconds for each one.

1. How can this topic be defined? What external model could I apply?
2. What internal model can be applied to this topic to analyze its parts?
3. How could this topic be compared to something else?
4. Is this topic the result of something, or the cause of something?
5. Is this topic an example of some general principle or theory or pattern? Can I make some generalization about it?

6. Does this topic occur in time or in space in an interesting way?

Add to these any questions you think the reader might ask about the topic, and any questions you could answer because of your special background of courses, travel, experience, training, hobbies, or beliefs. Among the answers to these questions you should find aspects of the topic and related ideas that will help you fashion your thesis.

Making decisions about the thesis

Deciding on a thesis requires answering more questions, but after that you are likely to find selecting a thesis much easier than it ever was in the past. Begin on the following questions, in order to narrow your topic:

1. In view of what I already know about this general subject, the amount of time available, and the proposed length of my paper, what are some more limited topics?

As you will recall from Chapter 3, you can restrict or limit a topic in two ways: by substituting an inclusive phrase that is a subsection of the topic, or by adding modifiers to make the topic more particular.

Topic: Cost control
Substitution: Inventory maximization
Modification: Highway project cost control

Topic: Movie heroes
Substitution: Gun fighters
Modification: French movie heroes of the 1950s

2. Based on my analysis of the audience's interests, my own interests, and my use of heuristic techniques, what controlling questions might I ask about this limited topic?

Join your limited topic and these controlling questions to produce several thesis sentences for evaluation. For example,

Topic: French movie heroes of the 1950s
Question: With what group could they be compared?
Thesis: French movie heroes of the 1950s showed a much narrower range of emotion and expression than German movie heroes of the same period.

Topic: Inventory maximization
Question: Does this topic cause something to happen?
Thesis: Inventory maximization improves cash flow for
a small grocery business.

Once you have fashioned several thesis sentences, you should select the best one for your essay by applying the questions used to evaluate thesis sentences in Chapter 3:

1. Is this thesis so commonplace that the audience will not pay attention to it? Will it interest my audience?
2. Can this thesis be adequately discussed in the time and length available?
3. Do I know, or can I find out, enough to develop this thesis?
4. Is the topic clear—does it appear as the subject of the independent clause?
5. Is the controlling idea properly emphasized—does it appear in the predicate of the independent clause?
6. Are the words precise and exact?
7. Are the grammatical constructions clear, correct, and easy to understand?

Suppose a student were asked to write a paper on "jobs" for an economics class, and jotted down several possible thesis sentences:

Jobs are important in our everyday lives.

Many new kinds of jobs have developed in the last two hundred years.

Blind people in rural communities need more job opportunities.

With strong public relations campaigns, it can be seen how programs are providing more job opportunities for the blind.

Using the questions above, he could eliminate several of these options. "Jobs are important in our everyday lives," a generalization about the topic, would be eliminated by the first question, because the thesis is so commonplace and general that no reader would find it interesting. The second possible thesis, "Many new kinds of jobs have developed in the last two hundred years," would be too broad a topic to discuss in a five-to-ten page paper. The third thesis, "Blind people in rural communities need more job opportunities," might be interesting, but the student might find it difficult to obtain information on jobs available to blind persons in *rural* communities. There might be more articles and books on urban opportunities because agencies collecting such information would be likely to locate in areas with larger numbers of blind people needing services. The fourth possible thesis, "With strong public relations campaigns, it can be seen how programs are providing more job opportunities for the blind," would also need to be revised. Because the point is that a certain action can produce a particular result, the main topic is "strong public relations campaigns" and this should be the subject of the thesis, not part of an ambiguous introductory phrase. The idea about this topic, "provide more job opportunities for the blind," should be the predicate of the independent clause: "Strong public relations campaigns can provide more job opportunities for the blind." This revised thesis, which has a cause-effect pattern, is much clearer, more forceful, and easier to understand. Testing the thesis can make organizing and drafting the essay much easier.

Implementing your decisions

Organizing the essay

First, decide what patterns of organization your thesis needs, by asking

What is the dominant pattern of the thesis?

What subordinate patterns are implied?

Chapter 8 lists seven basic patterns: definition, analysis, comparison, cause and/or effect, interpretive generalization, recommendation, and the subject in time or space. Analyze the structure of the thesis and identify any necessary subordinate patterns. For example, the thesis "Ben Jonson's later plays emphasized malice in human nature, and satiric themes, because he saw that humanistic ideals were being abandoned by society," has as its independent clause "Ben Jonson's later plays emphasized malice in human nature, and satiric themes," which is a two-part generalization about the restricted topic "Ben Jonson's later plays." The other part of the sentence, "because he saw humanistic ideals were being abandoned by society" suggests a cause-effect pattern showing that Jonson's view of events in society influenced the themes of his plays.

Next, decide how the dominant and subordinate patterns should be related in the outline. Will the reader need to understand one of them before he is ready or able to understand the others? Is there a pattern of relationship between the dominant and subordinate patterns? In the example above, one might say that the change in Jonson's plays was the result of current events; but one could also point to a comparison implied between events of the day and themes of the plays. Because it is very difficult to show the causal mechanism in the first case, a writer would probably not choose to claim that events of the time literally *caused* the plays. Instead, using either "A then B" or "point by point," he would make a comparison between the themes of Jonson's plays and his opinion of events. For example:

Thesis: Ben Jonson's later plays emphasized malice in human nature, and satiric themes, because he saw that humanistic ideals were being abandoned by society.

I. Jonson, whose love for the classics had led him to promote humanistic ideals such as justice, wisdom, moderation, loyalty to the state, and other virtues, deplored practices and policies that abandoned these ideals.
   A. He felt that Italianate intrigues such as the gunpowder plot would wreck the state, and replace the common good with the petty strivings of individuals, if such rebellions were not put down.
   B. He believed the fraudulent use of law, learning, and the arts posed a serious threat to the common good, especially during times of civil crisis such as plague and war.
II. Jonson's later plays show human nature to be full of malice that defeats humanistic ideals.
   A. In *Sejanus* and *Catiline: His Conspiracy,* Jonson gave society a tragedy of political adventure that mirrored the times, and specifically the conspiracy trial of Essex.
   B. *Volpone, The Alchemist,* and *Bartholomew Fair* are filled with characters guilty not only of follies (as in his earlier plays), but of crimes; and these people pervert learning, law, and religion for personal gain.

This abbreviated outline uses "A then B" parallel order for points of comparison. The writer first considers Jonson's reactions to current trends, then turns to how these attitudes were shown in the plays. Decide what topic sentence really expresses your controlling idea for each section, and list the major points of support to complete an outline with topic sentences. You can evaluate the outline as a whole by asking the following questions:

1. Are the divisions of the outline those suggested by the structure of the thesis?
2. Are the topic sentences of the outline complete and clear enough to control subordinate parts of the essay?
3. What does the thesis obligate me to prove?
4. Is this obligation fulfilled in the outline?
5. Are any topics in the outline unnecessary or irrelevant to the thesis?
6. Are sections of equal importance given equal rank and space?

A treatment of public relations campaigns for the blind would need a major section to analyze successful ones, and further sections to describe their results. If the student omitted major examples of such programs or their results, the fourth question would alert him to revise the outline. A section on the fun of participating in a public relations campaign would be eliminated if the student applied question five.

Depending on the patterns of organization you have chosen for your outline, apply the questions for those patterns to the sections of the outline:

Definition
Is the external model clearly explained?
Is the model justified, implicitly or explicitly?

Comparison
Are all topics measured by the same bases of comparison?
Are the bases clearly defined? (For example, if "effectiveness" is a point of comparison, have you established criteria for "effectiveness"?)
Are topics of equal weight given equal attention or space?
Will the pattern of organization (either "A then B" or "point by point") put the stress where you want it for your readers?

Generalization
Have you chosen enough examples to support your general statement?
Are the examples typical?
Are the examples given in enough detail to be convincing?

Analysis
Is the model for describing the parts or subsystems of the topic clearly explained?
Is the model justified, either explicitly or implicitly?

Cause and Effect
Is the evidence representative?
Is every generalization based on the right kind of evidence?
Is there any contrary evidence you have ignored?
Is the causal hypothesis too general or vague?
Is the causal hypothesis too simplistic? Does it fail to recognize multiple causes?
Does the hypothesis involve a *post hoc* error?
Does the hypothesis rely on a faulty analogy?
Are the links, between the inclusive premises and the evidence, clear and logical?
Are there any relevant principles you might have left out? (Check a logic textbook for deductive fallacies, if you have any doubts.)

Planning the introduction and conclusion

The introduction and conclusion are not usually considered part of the outline. In planning these extra parts of the essay it helps to consult those ladders of inclusive and particular terms sketched to represent the audience's perspective and your own. Looking at these ladders, can you find a common point between your two views of the topic? Do you share values or attitudes or interests? Is there a level of shared knowledge on which to build more detailed understanding? For example, the student in her letter to the editor, to be read by other students, might begin:

Like other students, I enjoy going to see a game and supporting our Cougar teams. No one can get to every game, however, so students sometimes have to rely on the newspaper to find out how the teams are doing. More and more students want to follow women's volleyball, both in person and by reading the *Daily Cougar*. Recently, the coverage of women's volleyball in the *Daily Cougar* has been so sparse that students can't easily find out whether our team has won or lost.

This writer refers to what she has in common with student readers: pleasure in going to exciting sports events, desire to read about sports in the student paper, and inability to attend all the games. Since student interests are the concern of the editor, this introductory paragraph would be relevant to the editor also.

Values, knowledge, or professional concerns are all useful points of common ground that you can use to begin a general introduction of your topic. From that point, plan the introduction like a funnel that narrows both the general topic and the controlling idea to a concise thesis statement. Define any terms the reader must know in order to grasp the thesis. Show him why he should be interested in the topic, and help him understand the scope of the essay.

Plan a conclusion that focuses the reader's attention on the central concern of the essay. If you have used a dialectical argument, your main points will have been interrupted several times by opposing views, so provide a review of your main points for your reader. Restate your thesis in a way the audience will remember. Draw out the implications of your conclusions, showing their broadest significance. Make clear to the reader any future action that should be taken.

Drafting the essay

Write a first draft of your essay. Many writers find it practical to write on every other line so that later revisions can be inserted easily. As you write, remember there is a reader out there who needs guidance in following your thoughts and feelings. Signal relationships with pointers that help your reader: "In contrast," "similarly," "because," "therefore," "afterwards," "nearby," "indeed," "nevertheless," and "finally."

Revising the essay

Immediate revision seldom improves an essay. Instead, go to a movie, play a game of tennis, work in the laboratory, or read a book. When you come back to your essay a day or two later, try to read it the way your audience would read it. Look especially for leaps from one subject to another where relationships are unexplained. Watch for terms that might be unfamiliar to the reader, even though *you* use them or hear them daily. If you have used the decision-making model of essay writing, you will probably have less revision to do than other writers, but you should *not* omit this step. Use the following questions to evaluate the essay:

Overall effects on the audience
1. Does the essay achieve the persuasive or informative intention chosen in your preliminary decision-making?
2. Would the essay be interesting to the reader?
3. Does the essay suit the situation in terms of length, language, and degree of knowledge displayed?
4. Is the essay unified? Do all the parts develop logically from the topic and idea announced in the thesis? Are there any digressions?

Organization, argument, and use of evidence
1. Is the essay organized in a way that is implied by the structure of the thesis sentence?
2. Is the essay complete in its use of evidence? Is every major point supported?
3. Are the transitions clear from one part of the essay to the next?
4. Is the argument complete? Are principles and premises explained and justified? Are any premises skipped?
5. Are the paragraphs unified, consisting of sentences that all relate to the topic sentence? Is each point of information clearly relevant?

Look at the two paragraphs below. The first has a topic sentence to which all the other information is related. In the second, information unrelated to an assertion is all jumbled together.

Since 1969, the U.S. Postal service has operated autonomously to achieve full cost recovery. Rational pricing policies for services were intended to eliminate the chronic deficits annually incurred by the old U.S. Post Office. The Reorganization Act required the Postal Service to set rates sufficient to cover the directly attributable costs of services, and to end deficits within a reasonable time.

First class mail is a form of communication that uses hard copy (paper) rather than electrical impulses or radio waves. If the quality of service provided is independent of the rate applied, then variations in volume associated with rate changes can be identified. Transactions between businesses and households create a large volume of communication demands. The average salary for mail carriers last year was $12,500.

Style
1. Are all the sentences grammatically correct?
2. Are the words and phrases precise?
3. Are relations between sentences emphasized by pointers?
4. Is the language suitable for the audience? Vivid? Interesting?
5. Are there any words of whose spellings you are unsure? Check these words in a dictionary.
6. Does the tone of the language create an appropriate *persona* for the writer, suggesting that he knows his subject, has an appropriate attitude toward the audience, and is interested in the subject?

After answering these questions, decide where the writing deserves reworking, and make the right adjustments. Few writers, if any, do everything perfectly the first time; but if you follow this guide and treat your writing as a decision-making process, it is likely to be organized, convincing, effective, and suited to your audience—in short, *decisive writing*.

Exercise: Writing the essay

Using all the skills you have reviewed in this chapter, write an expository essay of 700 words. This should be either a "comparison" essay or a "cause-effect" essay. Several general topics are suggested, which you can limit to form a viable thesis. If none of the suggested topics interests you, your instructor may permit you to choose your own. Keep your outlines and early drafts, as well as your final revised version of the essay, so that you can compare different versions of your paper.

Proposed Topics for Comparison:
Two kinds of student government
Two ways of increasing an employee's productivity
Two attitudes toward the supernatural
Two methods for dealing with another person's criticism
The poetry of two authors.

Proposed Topics for Cause-Effect:
Causes of racial attitudes in college students
Probable effects of changing to a coed dormitory system
Effects of being abandoned by a loved one
Causes of teenage divorce.

11 *Research*

Objectives

Student writers would not dread research assignments if they recognized that a research paper is essentially the same as other compositions. It needs very few new writing skills in addition to those already considered in this book. The research paper, like all other writing, is a response to a writing situation. The writer may simply want to collect information about a topic for his own needs—to satisfy his curiosity about killer bees, to determine the job potential in oceanography, or to discover what has already been done in solar refrigeration. More often, he will be responding to an outside demand—preparing an article on Norman Lear's impact on television for his church magazine or investigating market trends in bubble gum for his supervisor at Beechnut, Inc.

The college writer is nearly always responding to one situation—an assignment for a particular course. Such a research project challenges him to make discoveries about a topic. Usually the professor supplies the topic, but the student still has important decisions to make about his project. The professor may be specific, asking the student to prepare a ten-page paper on the presentation of human beings in the creation myths of five Indian tribes; or he may be quite general, suggesting a term paper on "something about tax reforms in the 1960s." In either case, the writer must ask questions and make decisions about his own interests, abilities, and time.

The writer must ask the following:

1. What does the situation require me to find out about the topic?
2. Where can I find such information?
3. How can this information best be collected?
4. What is the most suitable way of organizing collected information?
5. How should the information be presented and documented?

The professor will often set a length for the paper and a deadline. To fulfill the assignment the student must gather information, but he must do more than that. Beyond the research task, he has a rhetorical task as well. He must show that he can apply concepts from the course to his research information. Moreover, he must present his paper in a conventional form. The author of a successful research paper keeps all these requirements in mind.

The objective of this chapter is to add to your essential writing skills the capacity to conduct research and to organize, present, and document your research paper. You will learn to use a five-step process in its preparation.

Step 1: Limiting a topic

Although a research topic is usually specified in the assignment, it still must be limited to suit the writer's ability and intention, his audience's desires, the time available, and the length recommended. To limit a research topic the writer asks:

How much do I know about this, and how much can I find out in the time available?

What are the possible ways of looking at this topic, or what questions would a student in this field ask about it?

Your answers to these questions define the boundaries of your research.

Exercise: Limiting a topic

Choose one topic from the list below. After reading a general treatment of this topic—an encyclopedia entry, the introduction to a book on the subject, or a long magazine article—suggest a more limited version of the topic, appropriate to some class you might be taking. For example, if the class were a sociology or a linguistics class, the topic "dolphins" might be limited to "attempts to analyze the language of dolphins." If the class were concerned with genetics or ecology, the topic might be limited to "reproductive patterns of dolphins."

List for Selection of Topics:
Navajo Indians
Symbolism in Oriental Rugs
John Keats and Fanny Brawne
Stained Glass
Narcosynthesis
John Birch Society
Troubadours
The Cuban Missile Crisis of 1962
Zen Buddhism

Step 2: Finding possible sources of information

"But Dr. Kelly, there's nothing on my topic in that library!" Such laments usually fall on unsympathetic ears, for the Dr. Kellys who assign research topics are skilled researchers with keys to the storehouse of information in a college library. Without such keys, a student researcher will have a hard time finding what he needs. The student who knows how to use the library is at a great advantage. You can use your college library easily once you know about its basic research tools.

The *card catalog*, the first important tool, is usually the best place to start. The card catalog lists each book in the library's collection alphabetically in three ways: (1) by author, (2) by title, and (3) by subject. For research purposes the subject listings are the most helpful. However, even here a little shrewd detective thinking helps. Subject headings are often subdivided. For example, "history of France" would not be a separate heading under "H" but a subdivision under "France." The writer whose imagination fails him in his search for the right card catalog heading can find help in a large book, usually kept in the reference room of the library, called *Library of Congress Subject Headings* (pre-1975 editions of this book have the title *Subject Headings*

Used in the Dictionary Catalogs of the Library of Congress). This book lists subject headings and their subdivisions. Reference librarians working in the reference area will usually help students find the correct headings.

Exercise: Using the card catalog

Using the topic you chose above, go to the library and make a list of all relevant card-catalog headings you find. Be sure to notice cross-references given on the cards and, if necessary, consult the *Library of Congress Subject Headings*.

A library contains far more than books. It offers a collection of bound periodicals, often dating far into the past. To use these effectively, the writer must consult the various indices to periodical publications in the reference area of the library. The basic index to periodicals is *The Reader's Guide to Periodical Literature*, which lists articles from 125 magazines published in the United States. Most of these magazines are popular (attracting a general audience) rather than scholarly. A similar index to more scholarly articles is the *Social Sciences and Humanities Index*. In both indices, articles are listed alphabetically, both under the author's name and under Library of Congress subject headings. (This means the list prepared in the previous exercise will also serve you here. The list will guide you to the right places in each index to find the articles you need.)

In addition, much periodical material is covered in specialized indices (*Education Index, Art Index, Psychological Index, PMLA*) and in abstracts, which offer brief summaries of all articles listed, such as *Chemical Abstracts, Dissertation Abstracts, Pollution Abstracts*. These tools of research are also located in the reference area.

There are a few other guides to shorter materials. Articles about living people may be located in the *Biography Index*. Newspaper events may be traced in *The New York Times Index*. Book reviews are indexed in *Book Review Digest*, and essays that are part of larger collections may be located by consulting the *Essay and General Literature Index*.

Exercise: Locating articles through the index

Locate the above indices available in your library, and write down the library call number for each. Use the appropriate index to find the following articles. Indicate which index supplied each answer, and the volume and page number of the index.

a. An essay on *violence* collected in a volume about Alfred Adler published in 1974.
b. An article in 1971 explaining John Lindsay's views on the church and politics.
c. A more scholarly article in the *Sociological Quarterly* (1973) on religion and politics.
d. A review of Wilfred Mellers' book *Twilight of the Gods: The Music of the Beatles* (1974), which finds Mellers' style "too technical" but recommends the book for students of modern music.
e. A biographical monograph on N. Scott Momaday, Indian author and teacher, published in 1974.

Exercise: Making a working bibliography

Now that you know how to unlock the storehouse of library materials, make a tentative (or working) bibliography, a list of possible sources of information on the topic you chose, using the card catalog and the indices. Include both books and periodical material. Record each source on a 3" x 5" card, using this form.

Author's name	Library call number
Title of book or title of magazine article and name of magazine	
Publication data: City, State, Company, Year *or* Volume, Date, Pages	

Any other information you may want to remember

Jones, Ernst L.	PB847. 13Y
Nomenclature in Critics	
Newark, N.J.: River Press, 1970	

List at least 15 sources on separate cards, because there is almost always loss due to missing volumes, misleading titles, and repetition within sources. This list is your tentative bibliography.

Step 3: Collecting information

Once sources are located, the collection of data begins. This reading and note-taking is by far the most time-consuming part of research, and using an efficient method at this point often ensures the success of the paper.

Often it is impossible to read completely and record data from all the sources listed in the tentative bibliography. Selective reading is made easier by a tentative outline, or at least a list of questions to which the writing situation demands answers. For instance, a paper on "The Effect of the American Party on Presidential Politics" would require answers to these questions:

1. What is the nature of the party?
2. When did it begin?
3. What were the circumstances of its origin?
4. What were its immediate effects?
5. What seem to be its long-term effects?
6. What are its future prospects?

Such a list or tentative outline will guide the writer as he skims books and articles, in his decisions about what really needs to be taken down in his notes. Of course, questions or sections may be added, deleted, or combined as the researcher learns more about his topic.

Significant data or quotations, relating to a section in the tentative outline, should be recorded, usually on note cards. These notes should be brief and specific. Rather than a summary of an entire article, notes should record only details relevant to the limited topic.

Key to source listed in bibliography   Section of tentative outline to which note relates

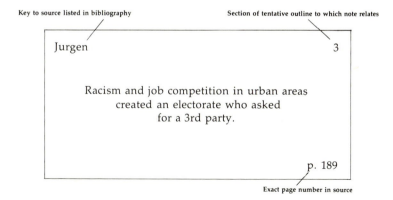

Jurgen   3

Racism and job competition in urban areas
created an electorate who asked
for a 3rd party.

p. 189

Exact page number in source

Verbatim excerpts (word-for-word quotations) from sources are rarely desirable. Direct quotation is necessary only if the style as well as the content of a passage is important. In most instances, it is best to paraphrase—to record what is relevant in your own words. Only data relevant to *one* section of your outline should be put on a single note card; if an article contains information for different sections of the research paper, notes should be put on separate cards. One article might supply as many as twenty notes. The advantage of this procedure is that the note cards can then be arranged according to their content and the section to which they belong, allowing the researcher to keep track of how much data he has gathered for each section of the topic.

Exercise: Taking notes

Prepare a tentative outline or list of questions for the topic you have chosen. Read at least three of the sources you have located. Take careful notes, and assign each card to the appropriate section of the outline or list of questions.

Step 4: Organizing the final paper

After most of your note-taking is done, a more formal outline should be prepared. The first step here is formulating the thesis. A research paper, like any other essay, must have a central, controlling idea about the topic. From this thesis will come the major divisions of the paper (see Chapter 8 to review your analysis of the thesis to determine the structure of the essay).

Topic: Political emergence of Howard Cosell
Thesis: Howard Cosell's political emergence was the result of a series of influences, each of which took him closer to becoming a public figure.
Analysis of the thesis: Cause-and-effect, multiple causes analyzed into a series, perhaps ordered by time.
Categories based on questions:

1. Family influences
2. Educational influences
3. Professional influences
4. Social influences

Notice that each division relates directly to a key word in the thesis, and that the headings are parallel in structure. Such divisions very often coincide with the sections of your tentative outline so that a body of notes about each is already assembled.

Your information on why Howard Cosell came to be involved in politics will contain several notes about family influences. You can group these notes to form the following sections of the outline:

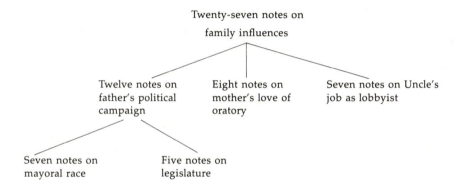

Twenty-seven notes on
family influences

Twelve notes on
father's political
campaign

Eight notes on
mother's love of
oratory

Seven notes on Uncle's
job as lobbyist

Seven notes on
mayoral race

Five notes on
legislature

I. Family influences
  A. Father's political campaigns
    1. For mayor
    2. For legislature
  B. Mother's love of oratory
  C. Uncle's job as lobbyist

This method of drawing up the outline has two advantages: it is based on the data you know you have on your note cards, and it assembles your notes into very workable writing units. For instance, the seven cards assigned to IA1 above could easily be turned into a single paragraph by writing a good opening sentence and tying the notes together with coherence devices.

Some points of outline structure need to be observed:

1. The introduction is not a major division of the thesis, and should not appear thus in the final outline. This also applies to the conclusion.
2. Headings of equal importance should be parallel in struc-

ture. All roman numeral sections are equivalent; the capitalized headings under a single roman numeral are equivalent; arabic numeral headings under a single capitalized heading are equivalent.

3. Headings should specifically define the boundaries of a given section.

Exercise: Organizing your information

1. After accumulating your information, formulate a thesis appropriate to your writing situation. Guided by that thesis, determine the major structural divisions of your paper.

2. When the major divisions have been determined, reclassify all your notes and assign each one to a major section of the paper. (Notes which do not seem to fit may be considered for the introduction or conclusion, or simply discarded.)

Step 5: Writing and documenting the paper

When you have taken careful notes and prepared an outline, writing the paper becomes simply a matter of incorporating the organized notes into a series of paragraphs. For instance, the outline on the political emergence of Howard Cosell (see Step 4) contained a section on family influences on Cosell's political life. Collected notes relating to Section IB, Mother's love of oratory, are as follows:

Note 1   Mother had majored in speech in college.

Note 2   Mother gave young Howard candy when he memorized and recited famous passages.

Note 3   Mother entered Howard in local speaking contests when he was ten years old.

Note 4   His mother insisted that he try out for his high-school debate team.

Note 5   Cosell has said, "She never let me forget that the golden tongue had more power than the bloody sword."

Note 6   For seven years she was president of the Women's Forum on Public Issues—a group which met monthly to hear speeches on a variety of local public problems.

The paragraph generated by reordering these notes would look something like this:

<table>
<tr><td>

Topic
sentence
provided by
writer

First note

Sixth note

Second note

Third and
fourth note

Fifth note, use
of direct
quotation

Summary
supplied by
writer

</td><td>

Although his father's campaigns gave young Cosell a taste for politics, it was his mother's love of oratory that lay behind the mastery of language he later found so effective in his own political life. Eva Cosell had graduated from college with a degree in classical oratory.[7] Her interest in public speaking continued after her marriage, and for seven years she was president of her city's Women's Public Forum, a group which held public debates on local urban problems.[8] This interest was also imposed on her son. As a child he was rewarded with candy when he memorized and recited famous literary passages.[9] When he was ten, his mother entered him in several local speaking contests, and she insisted that he try out for his high-school debate team.[10] Cosell has said, "She never let me forget that the golden tongue had more power than the bloody sword."[11] *This early and continued training in public speaking certainly helps to account for Cosell's poise and facility in his political speeches.*

</td></tr>
</table>

The writer has supplied only a topic sentence, a pattern of organization (time pattern in this case), a few transitions for coherence, and a summary sentence. To write this paragraph's topic sentence and concluding sentence, he chose inclusive words and phrases that were appropriate to the particular facts in his notes. For example:

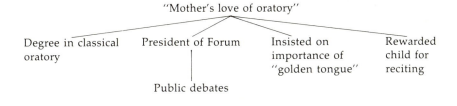

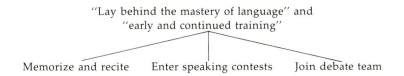

(You may review Chapter 2 for additional treatment of complete expression.)

Thus, the actual writing of careful research is little more than turning logically-arranged blocks of noted data into coherent and unified paragraphs. However, the information collected and presented in the paper must be documented; that is, its sources must be identified and credited. This documentation takes two forms: a listing of all works consulted or cited in the research (a final bibliography); and a specific identification of any statistics, direct quotations, or statements of opinion borrowed from other sources (footnotes).

Such documentation normally follows carefully prescribed patterns. You must always determine which of these patterns your writing situation demands. Following is a list of documentation manuals which are widely used in college-level research:

General:

> Kate Turabian, *A Manual for Writers of Term Papers, Theses, and Dissertations* (Chicago: University of Chicago Press, revised frequently).
>
> Wm. G. Campbell and S. V. Ballou, *Form & Style* (Boston: Houghton Mifflin Co., 1974).

Literature, Modern Language and Humanities:

> William Riley Parker, *The MLA Style Sheet* (New York: The Modern Language Association, revised frequently).

Science:

> American Institute of Biological Sciences, *Style Manual for Biological Journals* (Washington, D.C., 1960).

Social Sciences and Education:

> *A Manual of Style* (Chicago: University of Chicago Press, 1969).
>
> *The College of Education Style Manual* (Columbus, Ohio: Ohio State University Press, 1960).

Government:

> *U.S. Government Printing Office Style Manual* (Washington, D.C.: G.P.O., revised frequently).

Use the form recommended by the professor under whose direction you are writing the paper.

The bibliography appears at the end of the research paper and is always presented in a specified form. Special attention is given to indentation, spacing, and punctuation. Works are listed alphabetically by author (or by title if author is unknown).

Exercise: Making a final bibliography

> Choose a reputable style manual from the list above, and construct a bibliography from the list of sources you prepared in the fourth exercise.

Footnotes are more troublesome, for you must decide where they are needed, in what form to present them, and where to present them. Information in the form of statistics or tables or any direct quotations must be footnoted. But it is equally important to credit any borrowed judgment or opinion, even when the material has been skillfully paraphrased. In other words, the only material you may take full credit for is the framework, coherence devices, transitional passages, and statements of reasoning based on presented material. Your role in such writing is like that of the jewelry designer who creates a setting which shows off the diamonds to their best advantage.

Footnotes may be placed at the foot of each page or at the end of the paper. Again, the writing situation should determine this. There is a specified form for footnotes, and whichever style manual you are using should be closely followed.

Exercise: Writing a documented paragraph

> Using the notes you assembled and related to your outline, write a unified paragraph citing at least four sources and supplying the necessary footnotes.

There follows a sample research paper written by a student according to the system described here. She used the skills and the five research steps discussed in this chapter, to create the finished product.

In following these steps, she asked the general questions:

1. What does the situation require me to find out about the topic? (Step 1)
2. Where can I find such information? (Step 2)
3. How can this information best be collected? (Step 3)
4. What is the most suitable way of organizing the collected information? (Step 4)
5. How should the information be presented and documented? (Step 5)

The Individual's Right to Die
Research Paper

Gayle Michalk
English 131
April 24, 1975

Thesis: The problems involved in an individual's right to die relate to his actual facing of death, his right to make decisions about his treatment, and the moral and legal aspects of his situation. [Analysis into parts]

 I. The individual facing death has certain rights
    A. Fears but is entitled to truth
       1. Denial response
       2. Right to truth
    B. Entitled to dignity in his death
       1. Right to choose where
       2. Right to choose when
       3. Right to choose how
 II. The terminally ill person should be allowed to make decisions about his treatment
    A. Decisions regarding medication
       1. How often
       2. How much
       3. None at all
    B. Decisions regarding surgery
III. Moral aspects of the right to die involve the public, the medical profession, and the churches
    A. General public's attitude
       1. Humane view
       2. Practical view
    B. Conflicting views of physicians
       1. Their teachings
       2. Their emotions
       3. Their right to protection
    C. Consistent position of the church
       1. American Medical Association (A.M.A) survey
       2. Catholic moral teaching
IV. The legal aspects of the right to die are difficult to define
    A. Legal death
       1. Past definitions
       2. Current problems of defining death
    B. Current bills proposed to define death
       1. State legislatures
       2. A.M.A. proposals

C. The "Living Will" as means of clarifying legal confusion
   1. Contents
   2. Legal value

The Individual's Right to Die

Introduction

"A dying man needs to die, as a sleepy man needs to sleep, and there comes a time when it is wrong, as well as useless, to resist."[1] At a time in history when modern medicine has the ability not only to control birth but also to prolong life, it has become increasingly important for a person to seek out his right to die. The ability to prolong life brings with it the ability to prolong dying.[2] The Constitution of the United States has given the people many rights, but not the right to choose, when the time comes, to die as they wish. Although many people confuse the word euthanasia with mercy-killing, it is actually derived from the Greek word *eu,* meaning good, and *thanatos,* meaning death.

Thesis

Thus, the meaning is good death.[3] The problems involved in an individual's right to die relates to his actual facing of death, his right to make decisions concerning his treatment, and the moral and legal aspects of his situation.

Transition to I

In times past society viewed death as a natural event, even as a time of peace and dignity. Now people must wonder if modern medicine has not taken Mother Nature's work a little too far.

IA Topic sentence

People often express their fear of death by denying it; but they have a right to know, and should be told, the truth. Denial is expressed in many ways. Because man is frightened of death, he pretends it does not exist, telling himself it is other people who die.[4] Thus he will find excuses or reasons for his illness that are minor compared with the actual causes, making himself believe he is not really that sick. For instance, a sick person who is worried about his loss of weight, and fears death, may go on a diet to provide a reason for the weight loss.[5] However, this is not always the case. While there are some who persistently refuse to discuss their impending death, most will eventually find the inner strength to do so, accepting it as a part of life.[6] Though he denies it, a dying person almost always knows when death is near. Trying to suppress it only compounds his fears.[7] Because death is an unpleasant topic, it seems to have replaced sex as a taboo subject of conversation.[8]

It is an individual's right to know the truth about his illness, so that the last days of his life can be truly his own. A patient told he is about to die, and allowed to speak of it, can better overcome his fears.[9] A common fallacy about the dying is for others to say as little as possible, refuse to answer their questions, and simply deny their impending death.[10] A dying person is often surrounded by well-meaning loved ones who refuse to acknowledge the impending death, thus making it difficult for the patient himself to accept it.[11] The patient has a right to the truth so that he may settle his affairs and plan for the future of his family.[12] To know the truth, to accept it, and to set his mind in order, can bring the peace he so desperately needs. When he is not told his illness is fatal, his last days are wasted, as he clings to an illusion.[13] " . . . No one has the right or authority to deprive another person of the opportunity to deepen that understanding of life which comes particularly when one has to face death."[14]

IB Topic sentence

Marked progress in medical science means that terminal illnesses now linger on and on, and the individual can no longer choose where, when, and how he spends his last days; he is thus denied death with dignity. At one time people died at home, with people they loved and in a familiar environment. Now they are dying alone in hospitals and nursing homes and, more often than not, drugged beyond control of their emotions.[15] Families are often forced to stand by helplessly, watching their loved one suffer, while doctors prolong a life that should already have been ended. Margaret Mead, the famed anthropologist, states: "I believe it is the right of an individual to choose not to endure destructive suffering that can only end in death."[16] Arthur E. Morgan, former president of Antioch College, cried as he told the Senate Special Committee on Aging how nurses forced his dying wife to eat by prying her jaws apart, depriving her of the right to die with dignity.[17] In such cases, death can be a welcome exit from an unbearable situation. People today die feeling weak and defeated instead of at peace with themselves.[18] If a terminally ill patient wants the relief of death, he should be allowed it; or at least the promise that his life will not be prolonged needlessly.[19]

Transition from I to II

Once a patient has come to terms with death and has been given the right to choose where, when, and how he will die, he must also have the right to make decisions about his treatment such as regulating his medication and, if he wishes, refusing surgery.

IIA Topic sentence

The terminally ill individual should decide how much medication he wants; or whether he wants it abandoned, and if so, when. In trying to prolong a life for a few days, a physician may be subjecting the patient to needless and unbearable pain.[20] Drugs are administered at sufficient intervals to avoid addiction. It would make no difference to a dying man if he did become addicted. He should be allowed to choose his own dosage intervals so that he suffers as little as possible. Doctors who plead addiction when refusing drugs to a terminally ill patient use this to cover their embarrassment that they cannot work miracles.[21] Stewart Alsop, a famous author who died recently of a rare form of leukemia, said the most painful experiences of his illness (much of which was spent in cancer wards with other terminally ill patients) were those in which he had to watch patients suffer needlessly because they were not allowed to have enough pain-killing drugs.[22] Some patients prefer to be alert and spend precious time talking with loved ones and getting their affairs in order, while others would rather not face the intense pain and their fear of death.[23] Whichever the case, if the patient is indeed dying, the decision should be his. He need not be drugged to the point of insensibility, but he should be asked how much pain-killer he would prefer.[24] A physician who sees the death of a patient as a personal failure may over-compensate, by prolonging a life now useless. An individual has the right to refuse further medical intervention. In some cases, however, a person who is critically ill is incapable of rationally deciding whether or not he wants his life prolonged.[25] In these cases, his family must be called upon for rational decisions at a time of extreme emotion.[26]

IIB   A dying person must also have the right to refuse surgery. Surgery, more often than not, is a necessary measure to save life; but in some cases it only serves to prolong a life that is useless, because death is a certainty. When a patient refuses surgery, doctors will often go to court for a decision for or against the surgery. In one such case, circuit court Judge David Popper said: " . . . A person has the right not to suffer pain. A person has the right to live or die in dignity."[27] Over the objections of his wife, 79 year old Clarence A. Bettman was given a pacemaker, whereby he lived a few months longer, although still a vegetable.[28] In this case the patient had to suffer not only the surgery, but also the knowledge that death still awaited. Moreover his wife suffered emotional agonies, watching and waiting for the end to come. In Milwaukee in 1972, Mrs. Gertrude Raasch refused to sign papers for further surgery because after sixteen previous operations she neither wanted, nor could stand, any more. She wanted to be permitted to die in peace. The court upheld her decision in spite of a request from her physician that he be allowed to operate anyway.[29]

Transition from II to III   The individual's right to face death in his own way, and to make decisions concerning his treatment, is clearly important. However, it is an issue only recently coming into focus. The moral aspects are being considered by the general public, physicians, and churches.

IIIA Topic sentence   The public's approach to the morality of a right to death is both humane and practical. Pressures for a moral position on death by choice are growing with the advancement of medicine.[30] The morality of medicine is geared to promoting life under all circumstances. Therefore, death is the enemy of medicine.[31] The questions the public has to face in judging the morality of a person's right to die place a tremendous sense of responsibility on its conscience. When a person is reduced to little more than a vegetable, does he not have a clear right to die? Stewart Alsop stated the need for public compassion:

> . . . It is not normal to feel so weak you can't play tennis or go trout fishing. And it is not normal either to feel a sort of creeping weariness and a sense of being terribly dependent, like a vampire, on the blood of others . . . after weeks of this kind of 'normal life,' the thought of death loses some of its terrors.[32]

In Margaret Mead's view, people should be able to decide in advance how they wish to die if they become terminally ill, to draw up a legal document stating under which circumstances they want medical help and when they want it abandoned.[33] Compassion is not the only matter to be considered. The living, as well as the dying, must be considered. David Hendrin writes: " . . . But if humanity and compassion for the dying are not enough, there is the matter of economics, the shameful waste of hospital space, manpowers, and money involved in special care when, by disease, age, or accident, the body's usefulness has been ended."[34] It is time for physicians to distinguish between their own instinct to save life, and what is best for the dying patient and the public interest.

IIIB Topic sentence

It is easy enough for the public to blame the physicians; but they too are constrained by their principles, their humane feelings, and their wariness of malpractice suits. Physicians today have been taught to save lives regardless of how little time is gained, and no matter how much the patient will suffer.[35] Now they are faced with the question of when and for how long they should use heroic measures to prolong life.[36] They are caught in the web of their profession and their own emotions. Dr. W. N. Hubbard, Dean of the University of Michigan Medical School, in a graduation address at Albany Medical College, stated: "To sacrifice human dignity at the time of death or to make the process of dying a burden upon the living, is not in the highest tradition of medicine, nor is it justified in the humanist traditions."[37] Partly because of their confusion between their teachings and their emotions, physicians are trying to gain some sort of protection for themselves and their patients. A committee of 1,776 physicians proposed a bill in New York state to legalize euthanasia and protect their patients and themselves from prosecution for a practice that is well known to be common.[38]

IIIC Topic sentence

Less confused than the general public and the physicians, the church seems to feel that death should come naturally when God calls and should not be prolonged by unnatural means. The American Medical Association took a survey of churches' views about letting a patient choose his own time of death, once his illness has been explained to him carefully by his doctor. The survey showed the churches strongly supported the patient's right of choice.[39] Traditional Catholic moral teaching is that life should be prolonged by normal means but not by extra-ordinary means.[40] In 1957 Pope Pius XII said: "The removal of pain and consciousness by means of drugs, is permitted by religion and morality to both the doctor and patient, even if the use of drugs will shorten life."[41]

Transition from III to IV   The moral attitudes in this issue are more easily defined than the legal. There is difficulty in determining what a legal death really is. Bills have been proposed, by both the legislatures and the American Medical Association, to clarify the individual's right to die.

IVA Topic sentence   Probably the most difficult legal problem is the traditional definition of death, and what the current definition should be. Twenty-five years ago death was not hard to determine. If a heart stopped beating and a person stopped breathing, he was automatically pronounced dead.[42] Today heartbeat and breathing can be revived by artificial means even though the brain may be dead; and a person can be kept "alive," if only as a living vegetable.[43] In December of 1973, the A.M.A. refused to settle on a legal definition of death, since machines are able to keep the vital signs going long after the "death" of the brain.[44] In the context of modern medicine, should we define legal death as brain death rather than heart death?[45] The inability to define death, and the ability to create situations where death would appear to be preferable, are the most perplexing things about scientific progress.[46]

IVB Topic Sentence   Bills have been proposed by state legislatures and by the A.M.A., in an effort to determine a person's rights. As of now, no action has been taken regarding death by choice. A bill for euthanasia is pending in the Hawaii Legislature, and the Montana Constitutional Convention has been urged to let citizens choose their manner of death.[47] In December of 1973 the A.M.A. passed a resolution making it possible for terminally ill patients or their families, if the patient is unconscious, to sign a statement indicating their wish for large doses of drugs to kill pain and hasten death. They may also request that lifesaving machines and devices be removed. This resolution was the first time in history that the A.M.A. has faced the moral and legal problems of prolongation of life, or has tried to establish a policy concerning death.[48]

IVC Topic sentence   Despite all the current legal confusion, there is hope in the future for the individual's right to die in the form of the "Living Will." In 1973, over fifty thousand people requested copies of a "Living Will" from the Euthanasia Educational Fund in New York. The "Living Will" is a short testament which is given to a person's family, physician, clergyman, and lawyer.[49] Part of the "Living Will" states:

> If there is no reasonable expectation of my recovery from physical or mental disability, I request that I be allowed to die and not be kept alive by artificial means or heroic measures. I do not fear death as much as I fear the indignity of deterioration, dependence, and hopeless pain. I ask that drugs be mercifully administered to me for terminal suffering, even if they hasten the moment of death. . . .[50]

Conclusion The "Living Will" is not yet legally binding, but there have been proposals to the legislatures of thirteen states to make it so.[51]

The individual's right to die is a problem that must be handled by all the people of this country, not just those directly involved. If moral pressure is applied, perhaps the legal problems can be resolved. In the meantime, although the "Living Will" carries no legal weight, physicians and families cannot in good conscience ignore it.[52] "There is a time to live but there is also a time to die."[53]

author   title of article   periodical

Periodical citation 1. Stewart Alsop, "Stay of Execution: Excerpts, S. Alsop," *Saturday Review World*, 18 Dec. 1972, p. 22.

date   page on which material appeared

2. "Death with Dignity . . . the Debate Goes On," *Science News*, 19 Aug. 1972, p. 118.

3. Christopher P. Anderson, "A Joint Suicide . . . and the Right to Choose a 'Good Death,' " *People*, 17 Mar. 1975, p. 40.

4. Avery Weisman, "Toward a Better Death: Views of A. Weisman," *Time*, 5 June 1972, p. 60.

Second citation of a source 5. Weisman, "Toward . . .," p. 60.

6. W. Kitay, "Let's Retain the Dignity of Dying," *Today's Health*, 44 (May 1966), p. 64.   volume number

7. Weisman, "Toward . . .," p. 61.

8. Dael Wolfe, "Dying with Dignity," *Science News*, 168 (June 1970), p. 1403.

9. Weisman, "Toward . . .," p. 61.

author   title   place of publication

Book citation 10. Avery D. Weisman, *On Dying and Denying* (New York: Behavioral Publications, 1972), p. 29.

publisher   year   page

11. Weisman, "Toward . . .," p. 60.

12. Barney G. Glaser and Anselum L. Strauss, *Awareness of Dying* (Chicago: Aldine Pub. Co., 1965), p. 128.

13. Kitay, p.63.

14. Kitay, p. 63.

15. Kitay, p. 62.

16. Margaret Mead, "What Are Your Views on Euthansia?" *Redbook*, 141 (July 1973), p. 34.

17. "Death with Dignity . . .," p. 118.

18. Kitay, p. 62.
19. David Hendrin, *Death as a Fact of Life* (New York: Norton, 1973), pp. 78, 79.
20. "Death with Dignity . . .," p. 118.
21. Weisman, "Toward . . .," p. 60.
22. Alsop, p. 21.
23. Weisman, "Toward . . .," p. 60.
24. Weisman, "Toward . . .," p. 60.
25. "Right to Die," *America*, 3 Aug. 1968, p. 64.
26. "Right . . .," p. 64.
27. Hendrin, p. 83.
28. Hendrin, p. 66.
29. Hendrin, p. 67.
30. Daniel C. Maguire, "Death by Chance, Death by Choice," *Atlantic*, 233 (Jan. 1974), p. 59.
31. Maguire, "Death by Chance . . .," p. 59.
32. Alsop, p. 22.
33. Mead, p. 34.
34. Hendrin, p. 79.
35. Kitay, p. 62.
36. R. S. Morison, "Dying," *Scientific American*, 229 (Sept. 1973), p. 55.
37. "Right to Die," p. 64.
38. Maguire, "Death by Chance . . .," p. 62.
39. "A.M.A. Passes Death with Dignity Resolution," *Science News*, 15 Dec. 1972, p. 375.
40. "Right to Die," p. 65.
41. Anderson, p. 41.
42. Maguire, "Death by Chance . . .," p. 62.
43. Maguire, "Death by Chance . . .," p. 63.
44. "A.M.A. Passes . . .," p. 375.
45. Maguire, "Death by Chance . . .," p. 63.
46. Maguire, "Death by Chance . . .," p. 58.
47. Maguire, "Death by Chance . . .," p. 62.
48. "A.M.A. Passes . . .," p. 375.
49. Maguire, "Death by Chance . . .," p. 62.
50. Maguire, "Death by Chance . . .," p. 62.
51. Anderson, p. 43.
52. Maguire, "Death by Chance . . .," p. 62.
53. Alsop, p. 23.

Bibliography

Alsop, Stewart. "Stay of Execution: Excerpts, S. Alsop," *Saturday Review World*, December 18, 1972, pp. 20–3.
"A.M.A. Passes Death with Dignity Resolution," *Science News*, December 15, 1972, p. 375.
Anderson, Christopher P. "A Joint Suicide . . . and the Right to Choose a 'Good Death,' " *People*, March 17, 1975, pp. 40–3.
"Death with Dignity . . . the Debate Goes on," *Science News*, August 19, 1972, p. 118.

Glaser, Barney G. and Anselum L. Strauss. *Awareness of Dying*. Chicago: Aldine Pub. Co., 1965.

Hendrin, David. *Death as a Fact of Life*. New York: Norton, 1973.

Kitay, W. "Let's Retain the Dignity of Dying," *Today's Health*, May 1966, pp. 62–4.

Maguire, D.C. "Death by Chance, Death by Choice," *Atlantic*, January 1974, pp. 56–65.

Mead, Margaret. "What Are Your Views on Euthanasia?", *Redbook*, July 1973, pp. 33–4.

Morison, R. S. "Dying," *Scientific American*, September 1973, pp. 54–60.

"Right to Die," *America*, August 3, 1968, pp. 64–5.

Weisman, Avery D. *On Dying and Denying*. New York: Behavioral Publications, 1972.

————. "Toward a Better Death: Views of A. Weisman," *Time*, June 5, 1972, pp. 60–1.

Wolfe, Dael. "Dying with Dignity," *Science News*, June 19, 1970, p. 1403.

12 *Critical essays*

Objectives

Critical writing is distinguished by its humanistic purpose. The writer intends to clarify the meaning of the novel, poem, drama, film, painting, or sculpture he has experienced; to sort out the relationships of its parts; to judge its worth; or to relate it to other parts of a cultural heritage. He does this primarily for his own benefit—to enhance his perception, his reasoning power, and his comprehension of the values and aesthetic heritage of a civilization. Those who read such essays, such as professors and friends and subscribers to journals, are interested in the writer's humanistic skills and in comparing their own critical perceptions with the writer's. Unlike the audience for a technical report, the audience for a critical essay will not march to the laboratory, sign a purchase order, or take any other obvious action after reading the essay, but this does not mean that writing critical essays is less important than writing a technical report. Indeed, writing critical essays may benefit the individual even more than other kinds of writing, because of its humanistic effect: it is the *writer* whose perceptions, reasoning, and comprehension of human culture improve. It is the objective of this chapter to teach you how to adapt the skills you have already practiced to achieve this humanistic purpose.

Critical intentions

Critical essays usually answer one of three different questions. The first kind of critical essay offers an interpretive analysis of the literary or artistic work, answering the question "What does the work (or a part of it) mean?" Because

203

different patterns of perceived details can support different interpretations, interpretive analysis involves a subsidiary question: "How do the parts of this work create a significant whole?" or "How does a particular part or set of parts contribute to the meaning of the whole?" Such essays have characteristic thesis sentences, usually naming an element of the work as the "topic" of the thesis and using a generalization about its significance as the "idea" of the thesis. For example:

> The various houses in *Portrait of a Lady* represent different stages
>   topic   +   idea
> in the heroine's moral growth.   (or generalization about meaning)

A second kind of critical essay makes a judgment about the work. The writer considers how well the parts form a whole, how important the work is when judged by some standard, how well it has been received, how valuable or influential it has been, or what personal significance it has for the writer of the essay. In general, the judgmental essay replies to the question "How important is this work?" For example, the thesis *"Gravity's Rainbow* is the most important American novel of the late twentieth century" introduces a judgmental essay.

The third kind of critical essay relates a literary work, a part of a work, or several works, to a larger literary concept or to something outside the work itself. This kind of essay, a correlational essay, usually answers the question "How does this work relate to something else?" Essays of this kind can treat a broad range of subjects, as the following titles suggest: "The Influence of Shakespeare on Melville's *Billy Budd,*" "Nineteenth Century Political Theory in Zola's *Germinal,*" "The Effects of Swift's 'Drapier's Letters' on English Mercantilist Policy in Ireland, 1724–26," "Vaughan's Lyrics and English Baroque Style," "Surrealistic Painting and Guillaume d'Apollinaire's Poetry." The correlational essay is usually organized as a comparison or a cause and effect essay.

In summary, critical essays are usually concerned with answering one of three questions:

1. What does this work mean? How do the parts of the work create or contribute to the meaning of the whole? (Interpretive essay)

2. How important is this work, according to some standard? (Judgmental essay)
3. How does this work, or something in it, relate to something outside the work? (Correlational essay)

The three critical emphases may be conveyed by the same types of thesis sentences you analyzed in Chapter 8.

Interpretive essays

The following two essays on Robert Frost's poem "Design" demonstrate how interpretation relies on analysis of the work's parts. The first essay follows the organization of the poem, tracing a movement from description to doubt. The writer offers an interpretive generalization about each section, and then supports his statement with a description of details from the poem. The second essay examines references to black and white in the poem, and interprets their role in the speaker's reasoning about "design" in events.

Design
I found a dimpled spider, fat and white
On a white heal-all,* holding up a moth
Like a white piece of rigid satin cloth—
Assorted characters of death and blight
Mixed ready to begin the morning right,
Like the ingredients of a witches' broth—
A snow-drop spider, a flower like froth,
And dead wings carried like a paper kite.

What had that flower to do with being white,
The wayside blue and innocent heal-all?
What brought the kindred spider to that height,
Then steered the white moth thither in the night?
What but design of darkness to appall?—
If design govern in a thing so small.

(Robert Frost)

Interpretive Analysis 1

A lyric poem might be described as a mind's encounter with an event and what that mind makes of the encounter. Robert Frost's sonnet "Design" describes one such encounter, but the

* A heal-all is a flower, usually blue, used for medicinal purposes.

Thesis nature of the event is such that the mind comes to no firm decision about its meaning. The speaker in the poem speculates whether there is a power that designs events in the universe.

The octet* of the sonnet describes the troubling perception of an event—a spider holding a dead moth on top of a heal-all. This cluster of objects is striking because all three are a ghostly and unnatural white. These "assorted characters of death and blight" strike the speaker as supernatural, "the ingredients of a witches' broth."

This supernatural quality leads the speaker to ask a series of questions in the sestet † about what force could be responsible for bringing the moth and the spider to their fatal meeting atop the flower: in short, what is the design? He first concludes that the event can only result from an evil force, "the design of darkness." The speaker momentarily thinks that the universe is ruled by an evil force that brings creatures together in curious patterns of destruction.

However, the final lines question the already pessimistic conclusion that the universe is ordered by evil. The speaker wonders if the universal design extends to such insignificant creatures as spiders and moths. Perhaps the event that teased his mind with its apparent significance is totally without design and meaning. And, if this is the case, might not man's faith in his own place and significance in the universal design be equally misplaced? The question is implied, "Does design govern in a thing so small as man, or is there any design in the universe at all?" Frost provides no final answers to these last and most troubling questions.

The writer of Interpretive Analysis 1 asks: "What does this poem mean? How do the parts of the poem contribute to the meaning of the whole?" He begins by defining the whole of the poem as a mind's encounter with an event and what the mind makes of the encounter. He then offers a thesis about the response the mind makes to the event in "Design." The second paragraph describes the speaker's perceptions and his initial reaction to the sight of the three white objects. The third paragraph begins with a topic sentence describing the mental actions of the speaker in response to the event—a series of questions and a temporary conclusion. The fourth paragraph probes the meaning of the last two lines by an examination of the speaker's speculations. In each paragraph the topic sentence, containing

*First eight lines
†Last six lines

an interpretive statement about the poem, is supported by a description of elements in the poem. In this way, key ideas are substantiated by brief phrases and quotations showing how elements in the poem, in this case the mental operations of the speaker, justify a particular interpretation.

Interpretive Analysis 2

In his sonnet "Design" Robert Frost suggests that when man is faced with something out of the ordinary he demands an explanation; but often no explanation is forthcoming. This failure to get an explanation could result from man's dependence on certain methods of perception and evaluation that are too crude. The arbitrary linking of color and ethical interpretation is one method of understanding that will not answer man's deepest questions. Thesis The speaker's reliance on a pattern of black and white to guide his judgments is too simple, and leads him only to troubled confusion.

The speaker's first attempt to analyze his perceptions through a pattern of opposites proves more confusing than enlightening. Man's basic tendency to categorize his experience places perceptions into mutually exclusive ethical groups designated good and evil, symbolized almost universally by the colors black and white. In the octet, the speaker is confronted with a strange grouping of plant and animal specimens—a spider, far from his web, holding a dead moth atop a heal-all bloom. What bothers him is not so much the chance capture of the moth, as the fact that all three objects are white. He dwells on this compulsively, using the adjective "white" three times in the first three lines. According to his method of interpreting perceptions through the simple opposition of black and white, this scene should be firmly on the good side of the ledger.

Instead of being comforted, the speaker is perplexed, because in this case white is an unnatural color: the creatures are albinos, freaks of nature. They are instances of nature's failure to conform to our notions of her design. The heal-all, which is usually blue, in this case has healed nothing and has become part of a pattern of death. The speaker is made even more uneasy by the white but sinister scene because he instinctively associates whiteness with the harmless "snow-drop," "froth," and a "paper kite"; now, however, he is faced with something that strikes him more like a "witches' broth." He wants to know what this contradiction means; nervously, he leaps to his other column of categories for understanding, and concludes that hidden in all the whiteness is a "design of darkness." Instead of being mutually exclusive, white and black become one; in an evil universe, even white has its place in the overall pattern of blackness.

Finally, in the last line, the speaker takes a further step and radically questions his "black and white" approach to understanding the world. Shaken by nature's failure to conform to his preconceived ideas of the meanings of black and white, the speaker comes to an even more terrifying doubt: it may not be so much that our understanding is faulty, as that there is no design in nature to perceive, after all. Black and white have proved inadequate as a means of organizing experience for him. In showing that nature does not conform to simple moral categories of "good" and "bad," traditionally depicted by "white" and "black," Frost hints that human notions of morality are inadequate for understanding nature, which may be morally neutral or "colorless."

In answering the question "How do the parts of the poem contribute to the meaning of the whole?" the writer of this essay has paid close attention to the way the speaker uses images of white and black. This writer sees the poem as a statement about the failure of a simple way of interpreting experience, and describes why the speaker's way of thinking leaves him disturbed and confused. Instead of interpreting the poem section by section, as the writer of the first essay did, the second writer uses his first paragraph to present the speaker's images of white and black and his initial expectations. In the second paragraph, he explains why these expectations are defeated rather than supported. In the last paragraph, he interprets the speaker's doubts about his original approach. In the middle paragraphs of the essay, the writer details the development of the poem to support what he has said about the speaker's use of black and white as a moral model. Both essays interpret the meaning of the poem and do so by analyzing its parts.

Judgmental essays

A judgmental essay compares a work with some standard or measure to determine its worth or significance. Many book reviews are judgmental essays. In the following review, Monroe K. Spears, a scholar and authority on modern poetry, evaluates a recently published volume of Robert Lowell's poems. The standards by which he tests the book are usefulness to readers and students and balance in presentation of the best poems from each phase of the poet's work. In the first part of the essay, he justifies these criteria by showing the problems readers have had in obtaining an overall view of Lowell's work from the various collections published over the years. In the rest of the essay he explains how the new volume meets these standards, describing the contents of each section to support his judgment.

The best of a major poet: Robert Lowell, Selected Poems
This handsome and substantial volume is a great success, presenting Lowell's own choice, as he nears the age of 60, of his best work so far. For three decades, Lowell has been widely regarded as the leading American poet of the postwar era.

Lord Weary's Castle in 1946 established him as master of a formal, elaborately allusive "metaphysical" style. But by 1959 he responded to the trend toward openness in form and personal directness in content with *Life Studies*, which rode this new wave farther up the beach than anyone else. A third stage began with *Notebook 1967-8*, recording with a new closeness the public and private involvements of a year. The first version was rapidly succeeded by two others, each larger and more incoherent. Finally in 1973, Lowell published another revised and expanded version as *History*, with the poems about his former wife and daughter in a separate volume, *For Lizzie and Harriet*; and a new volume, *The Dolphin*, about his new wife and son. All these books from 1967 to 1973 were in the same form, the "sonnet" of 14 unrhymed lines; Lowell's obsession with this form, and his incessant revision of his earlier work (which he appeared willing to destroy through forcing it into this later mold) left his readers confronted with an impossibly overgrown and confused body of work.

The appearance of this eminently sane and responsible *Selected Poems*, is therefore especially welcome. There is no longer any effort to make the later work swallow up the earlier; past work and past selves are treated with proper respect. To leave no doubt on the point, Lowell says he has made no changes in poems of the first 20 years except to cut parts of some of the longer ones. In recovering from the excess of the 1960's, Lowell has once more followed an intensely private path that mysteriously coincides with the broad highway of public attitudes; he has changed with the nation. (He has also recovered from his "sonnet" obsession; none of the poems he has published in magazines since 1973 are in this form.)

Lowell has admirably restrained the partiality which any poet must feel for his most recent work, giving roughly ninety pages to the last decade, one hundred and fifty to the first two. Especially in view of the enormous bulk of the later work, this is a reasonable proportion. In dealing with the later work, he follows the sensible procedure of choosing "possible sequences, rather than atomizing favorite poems out of context," and confines himself to "a few slight changes" which often simply go back to discarded versions.

From *History* he selects (or composes) two sequences. The first examines the whole panorama of history, from Cain and Abel to the assassinations and upheavals of 1968, in search of ultimate significance and of relation to the self. God appears in history as cruel and senseless; the self is seen as flawed, guilty, corrupting public motives by private. There are brilliant and witty perceptions, like the portrait of Cicero as Ezra Pound ("the old sheep sent out to bite the frosty stubble") and the parallel of Henry VIII and Mohammed, who "got religion in the dangerous years, and smashed the celibates," and wonderfully condensed portraits, like those of Rembrandt or Charles V. But probably the best of all are those explicitly personal ones treating the ideals of revolutionary politics and open or naked poetry with the same candor and irony.

The second sequence uses the opposite method, beginning with an explicit autobiographical narrative and generalizing its significance. The subject is Lowell's relation to his parents, and specifically the incident in which he knocked his father down in 1936; this becomes the archetype of rebellion in both the psychological and the political realm. Both parents are finally accepted at last (now long after their deaths), and "To Daddy" makes amends for many previous revealing portraits.

"Mexico," the third sequence, is printed as from *History*, though in fact it comes from *For Lizzie and Harriet*; dealing with the themes of love and cruelty in marriage, it forms an introduction to that sequence which describes the long and agonizing process of Lowell's leaving his wife and daughter for another woman.

Finally, "The Dolphin" relates the story of his relation to the new wife, but also dwells on his own sickness, the continuing agony of the separation from Lizzie and Harriet, and the relation of art to life. (Monroe K. Spears, author of *Dionysus and the City: Modernism in 20th Century Poetry*)

Correlational essays

The third type of critical essay, the correlational essay, points to relationships between something inside the work and something outside—for example, between the plot of a play and a famous incident in history, or between the theme of a poem and a popular philosophical concept. Often the purpose is to show where literary themes begin; the writer of a correlational essay may explain how ideas or events in an earlier work have been borrowed and transformed by a later author. For example, he might discuss how in *Paradise Lost* Milton relied on Spenser's notions of true and counterfeit earthly paradises in *The Faerie Queene*. Or he could analyze how American frontier tales borrowed plots from medieval legends of knights and villains. Sometimes the main concern is to draw parallels between literature and other cultural events. In such essays, the writers choose bases of comparison and then compare a literary work or trend with a painting or a style of painting—such as the *Leatherstocking Tales* of Cooper and the landscape style used by the painters known as the "Hudson River school." Again, the writer might compare the behavior of a dramatic character with a kind of behavior defined by a current psychological theory.

Occasionally the three central questions about literature, "What does this work mean?", "How important is this work?", and "How does this work or part of it relate to something else?" may be combined. A writer might investigate the relationship between parts of a play by first explaining the notions about the structure of tragedy that probably influenced the dramatist as he wrote. After the comparison between the contemporary theory of drama and the structure of the particular play, he might interpret the play in the light of structural references developed in the comparison. Usually one of our three questions is dominant, and other questions are subordinated to it, just as certain expository patterns of organization can be subordinated when developing an argument (see Chapter 8).

Exercise: Analyzing critical intentions

The direction a critical essay will take is determined by what question is asked about the work. In this exercise, the many thesis sentences about Shakespeare's play *Hamlet* will give you an idea of the range of essays that can be written on a single work.

A. Which of the three critical questions does each seem to answer?
1. What does this work mean? How do the parts of the work create or contribute to the meaning of the whole? (interpretive analysis)

2. How important is this work? (judgment)

3. How does this work or something in it, relate to something outside the work? (correlation)

B. Which of the regular thesis sentence patterns does it fit? (See Chapter 8 if necessary.)

Examples

King Lear shows more significant depth and complexity of characterization than *Hamlet* or *Othello*.

A = judgment, of importance or value, indicated by the phrase "more significant"

B = comparison

Although he is mentioned but a few times and speaks only in the last scene, Fortinbras contributes to the concept of "honor" in *Hamlet*.

A = interpretive analysis (The independent clause promises to show that Fortinbras contributes to the meaning of a key concept in the play.)

B = interpretive generalization

a. The costuming of Ophelia can reinforce the audience's grasp of her mental deterioration in *Hamlet*.

b. The motivation of several characters in *Hamlet* can be explained in terms of the psychological theory of Shakespeare's time.

c. Far from being the villain in *Hamlet*, Claudius is an admirable character who stands in contrast to Hamlet, the living principle of death and evil.

d. The changes in Hamlet's understanding of the concept of honor mark the important changes in his mental state as the play progresses.

e. The differences between the principal characters in *Hamlet* can be seen in the different ways they define "honesty."

f. Several lines in *Hamlet* seem to refer to events in the later years of Elizabeth's reign.

g. Hamlet's condition fits the Renaissance definition of "melancholy."

h. Shakespeare's play *Hamlet* violates the Renaissance theory of classic tragedy accepted in the universities of that time.

i. The ritualistic scenes in *Hamlet* emphasize the discordant purposes of the major characters.

j. Although *Hamlet* has enjoyed continuous popularity since the seventeenth century, not every age has been fascinated by the same aspect of Hamlet's character.

k. Analysis of two soliloquies shows how Hamlet's moods of grief and determination are reflected in the verbal rhythms of his speeches.

l. *Hamlet* is the tragedy of a man who could not make up his mind.

Supporting critical arguments

One of the greatest difficulties students have in writing essays for literature classes is understanding the differences between a "critical" essay and a "descriptive" essay. In the early grades of school, students are often asked to write short descriptive essays, called book reports, about stories and books they read. Seven-year-olds are not taught to ask the three critical questions we have been discussing. Instead they are told to write answers to the questions "What happened in this book?" and "What was this book about?" This last question is *not* quite the same as "What does this work mean?" As the student advances in school, differences between the writing demands of his early years and the demands of advanced study are not always made clear to him. A plot summary is a description, not an interpretation of a work. Unless the student understands the distinction, he may have trouble in writing critical essays.

The thesis (topic + idea) of a critical essay usually has an interpretive, judgmental, or correlational phrase as its controlling idea. Note the following examples mentioned earlier:

Topic	Idea
The various houses in *Portrait of a Lady*	represent different stages in the heroine's moral growth.
Gravity's Rainbow	is the most important American novel of the late twentieth century.
The political theories advocated by characters in Zola's *Germinal*	reflect the major conflicts in political ideology of the nineteenth century.
The meaning of Billy Budd's fate	is ambiguous because all the characters in the novel express conflicting opinions of him.

The phrases in the Idea column are the critical assertions related to the three critical questions. They are also inclusive phrases, in the sense in which we used the term in Chapter 2.

The critical essay supports the inclusive critical assertion of its thesis with descriptive elements from the work itself. If these descriptions of characters, events, and themes are not *subordinated* to or *supportive* of the inclusive critical assertions, the essay cannot be called a critical essay. The argument of a critical essay is developed by the pattern of inclusive terms that justify the critical idea of the thesis. For example:

. . . represent different stages in the heroine's moral growth.

early naïve beliefs in simplistic system of moral opposites

gradual understanding of moral complexity and difficult choices

perception of the possible discrepancies between appearance and moral character

self sacrifice and commitment to moral integrity in order to rehabilitate a corrupt moral order

Support for this argument comes from describing specific events and characters in the work that justify the critical assertion. For example, the last assertion above might follow this development:

. . . represent different stages in the heroine's moral growth.

↑
More
inclusive

"Self sacrifice and commitment to moral integrity in order to rehabilitate a corrupt moral order"

More
particular
↓

heroine rejects simplistic solution of being rescued by Caspar Goodwood, who offers her a new marriage and a return to America

she returns to dissolute husband's villa in order to help his child, who needs her

returns determined to advocate moral integrity of the self caught in a web of deceit

Similarly, the particular terms support the critical assertion in this paragraph:

The meaning of Billy Budd's fate is ambiguous because all the characters in Melville's short novel express conflicting opinions of Billy, the hero. For the ordinary sailors, Billy is "the fresh young image of the Handsome Sailor." To the author of the naval record, Billy is simply "the criminal" whose punishment was salutary. To Captain Vere, Billy sometimes seems the trigger for mutiny, a guilty murderer; sometimes his innocent son, whom he must condemn. And Claggart, "apprehending the good, but powerless to be it," perceives in Billy utter innocence and comes to hate him. The variety of possible responses to the hero of the novel has made *Billy Budd* controversial ever since its publication.

In this description of the characters and their beliefs about Billy Budd, we can find a pattern of related inclusive and particular terms, just as we found in other essays:

More inclusive

More particular

The meaning of Billy Budd's fate

is ambiguous because all the characters in the novel express conflicting opinions of him.

the Handsome Sailor   the criminal   son who must die   utter innocence

The evidence in a critical essay is provided by the writer's description of what happens in the work, of the words used by the author, of the dialogue, plot structure, and theme. This description must be subordinated to or supportive of critical assertions—assertions that may be interpretive, judgmental, or correlational. When the description is not subordinated, a plot summary or a character sketch results. Therefore it is vital to remember to subordinate description of the work to critical assertion. Introduce any description of the content of the work with inclusive assertions that develop the thesis.

Exercise: Evaluating critical assertion and supportive description

In this exercise, you will read two commentaries based on each of three topics. For each topic, decide which author creates a better pattern of inclusive-particular phrases and related description of elements from the work. Explain your opinion. (Can you draw a ladder of inclusiveness for each case?)

"Jade Flower Palace"

a. "Jade Flower Palace" is a lovely poem containing much reality. Everything the poet describes is real and would exist.

This is a free verse poem without the characteristics of rhythm and rhyme that most poems possess and therefore seems more like prose. However, because of its language it is poetry.

Everything we do now will eventually fall into ruin and be forgotten, the poem says. The author also seems to be saying that everything will go back to nature. He talks about the stream, wind, pines, ghost fires, storm, leaves, dust, grass and water which are all parts of nature, and relates the ruins to these objects and forces as if saying: "here is where it all ends up." The primary purpose of this poem is to say that nothing man-made can last forever.

b. "Jade Flower Palace" reminds the reader of the futility of man's attempts to create anything of permanence. The ancient Chinese poet observes and records for us the decomposing remains of a once-impressive palace. All the man-made objects are disintegrating. The cheeks of the dancing girls painted on the walls, like the cheeks of the girls who once danced there, have crumbled to dust. The fine tiles have cracked and washed away. The statue of the horse, a symbol of authority, remains; but the name of the prince or noble it represented is unknown. Beside the frail remnants of human glory, the relentless and indomitable forces of nature seem omnipotent. Phosphorescent moss has replaced the household fire in the hearth. Wind and water wear away the materials of the palace. The power of nature is expressed in the verbs "swirls," "moans," "slips," "scurry," and "shattered." The verbs depict a world in a state of change and decay. The run-on lines also imitate a world in constant flux, a world carried away without pause. Man's arrogance seems trivial before such forces. Twentieth-century readers join in the last line of "Jade Flower Palace": "Who can say what the years will bring?"

Mr. Sammler's Planet

a. Mr. Sammler's ideas and beliefs do not agree with those of Angela, his best friend's daughter. Angela likes all sorts of unusual sex acts. Mr. Sammler thinks she is gross and vulgar. Mr. Sammler thinks she should be more respectful toward her father, Dr. Gruner, who is dying. Shula, Sammler's daughter, doesn't always obey her father. She does things like stealing Dr. Lal's manuscript, something Mr. Sammler doesn't like. Wallace, Angela's brother, only cares about thrills and money. All their indifference to the usual human obligations offends Mr. Sammler, who affirms the responsibility of people for each other, even at the end of the book.

b. Throughout *Mr. Sammler's Planet*, Mr. Sammler's belief in our personal responsibility for one another is contrasted with the selfish and meaningless behavior of several of the minor characters. Mr. Sammler believes that each individual has an assignment that requires him to be responsible for other people. Mr. Sammler argues with Angela over what he believes is her obligation to her dying father. Angela, who spends much of her time satisfying her yen for new sexual experiences, resists Sammler's admonition that she should ask her father's forgiveness before he dies. Wallace, Dr. Gruner's son, also neglects his father, giving all his attention to flying planes and searching for hidden money during his father's last illness. This contrast between indifference and commitment, which has been a central theme throughout the book, culminates in the novel's final scene when Angela's and Wallace's indifference to their dying father is set against Sammler's struggle to reach the bedside of his friend. In the last lines of the book, Sammler continues to assert that affirmation of personal relationships is "part of our contract," one of the terms under which we claim the right to human dignity and life.

"Loveliest of Trees"

a. In his short poem, "Loveliest of Trees," A. E. Housman carefully discusses the miracle and essence of God's universe, death and rebirth, and expresses the amazement he feels toward this miracle.

  The first stanza of the poem contains a great deal of hidden action although on the surface it merely describes a cherry tree. The cherry tree, which may be interpreted as a symbol of the cross, is "hung with bloom along the bough," while snow still clings to its branches. The key to the meaning of this statement is found in the term "Eastertide." The cherry tree's blooms are appearing through snow, the symbol of winter or death. The flowers are being reborn after a period of ritual death, just as Christ was reborn after his death on the cross. The ultimate product of this rebirth of the blooms is a fruit, a cherry, which symbolizes the promise of rebirth to mortals that was made possible by that first "Easter." The poet has realized that the promise of God appears in nature, and that the meaning of his own life can be discerned in the world around him.

b. "Loveliest of Trees" is written with rhythm and rhyme scheme *aabb, ccdd, eeff*. It is written in a standard, old-fashioned form. The theme, too, is age-old. The poet uses poetic language and alliteration in "wearing white" and "seventy springs a score," among others.

  The poet writes of the cherry tree, a religious symbol, "wearing white for Eastertide." He realizes that twenty years of his life are over, and he can never live them again. Assuming that he will live to be 70, that leaves him only 50 more years to enjoy spring, he says.

  Spring is obviously the poet's favorite time of year, and the cherry tree the "lovliest of trees." Religion and nature go hand-in-hand. The cherry tree is personified by "wearing white for

Eastertide." To the poet, being close to nature is being close to God.

Death awaits the poet so he makes the best use of time and dwells in nature, since fifty years are not enough to enjoy nature. The poet does not appear to be afraid of death.

Exercise: Understanding a critical argument

In the following student essay, note how each of the three unsuccessful narrators mentioned in the thesis is discussed in different sections. Identify and underline the topic sentences, and draw lines for the patterns of inclusive terms that trace the interpretive analysis of a writer's task.

Faulkner wrote in his Nobel Prize acceptance speech that he believed man would not merely survive but prevail, because "he has a soul, a spirit capable of compassion and sacrifice and endurance." To help man prevail, Faulkner said, the writer must transcend time to remind man of the old verities of the heart, share the mystery of existence, and encourage his spirit. In Faulkner's novel *Absalom, Absalom!* several narrators fail to fulfill Faulkner's definition of the writer's task: Rosa is too religious; Mr. Compson too rational; and Quentin and Shreve are too academic, but Faulkner himself succeeds.

In telling her version of the story, Miss Rosa relies on religious oversimplification. Her description of Sutpen patterns itself after the story of God's creation of the world in Genesis. She describes Sutpen as a "warhorse-demon" "who came out of nowhere and without warning upon the land" to "drag house and formal gardens violently out of the soundless Nothing and clap them down like cards upon a table beneath the up-palm immobile and pontific creating the Sutpen's Hundred, the 'Be Sutpen's Hundred' like the oldentime 'Be Light'." Furthermore, she sees Sutpen as "the evil's source and head," who forbade his daughter's marriage "without rhyme or reason or shadow of excuse." Like the wrathful God of the Old Testament, Sutpen does evil for no adequate reason. In short, Miss Rosa uses Old Testament religion and a pessimistic romanticism to create her interpretation.

Miss Rosa succeeds in suspending time in her narration, although she is unable to make her reader "become at one with" her characters. Two reasons for this are obvious: first, she is too involved, too much a part of the lives of the characters whose story she is telling. She cannot disengage herself from her emotions long enough to "step back" and gain some perspective. Anyone who would wear black for forty-three years is tied too closely to the characters to see them from a universal angle.

Second, Miss Rosa lacks imagination. Instead of trying to understand why Sutpen didn't want Judith to marry Charles, she chose to believe he had no reason, which fitted her preconceived notion of Sutpen as Old Testament God. Finally, although she is romantic, she fails to express the "truths of the heart" that Faulkner insists are essential. Miss Rosa is so entangled in her religious views that she can only see Sutpen as evil incarnate, and therefore cannot convey the emotional complexity of her characters. Her involvement in the story, her lack of imagination, and her rigid moral view prevent her from fulfilling her duty as poet.

Mr. Compson's interpretation of the past is likewise inadequate, focusing too heavily on rational explanations. He turns to logic and scientific examination, but these tools do not solve the mysteries. He tells Quentin, "Yes, Judith, Ben, Henry, Sutpen: all of them. They are there, yet something is missing; they are like a chemical formula exhumed along with the letters from that forgotten chest, carefully, the paper old and faded and falling to pieces, the writing faded, almost indecipherable, yet meaningful, familiar in shape and sense, the name and presence of volatile and sentient forces; you bring them together in the proportions called for, but nothing happens; you re-read, tedious and intent poring, making sure that you have forgotten nothing, made no miscalculation; you bring them together again and again nothing happens: just the words, the symbols, the shapes themselves, shadowy inscrutable and serene, against the turgid background of a horrible and bloody mischancing of human affairs." Mr. Compson asks the same question as Sutpen does about the failure of his design: I had all the right ingredients, so what went wrong? Both he and Sutpen believe in the superiority of reason. But their method is too simple. Mr. Compson admits this when he explicitly describes the actions of his characters as "simple passion and simple violence." Mr. Compson reasons that Henry, acting independently of Sutpen's desires, killed Charles to prevent his sister from marrying a bigamist. Mr. Compson approaches his story in a calm, deliberate, almost legalistic manner and achieves just that: a precise, logical series of events that nonetheless fails to satisfy.

The strength of Mr. Compson's interpretation is twofold. Because his approach is retrospective, he achieves some "distance" from the characters. Most of the book is Mr. Compson's interpretation, the clearest presentation of the events that the reader encounters. Second, Mr. Compson makes some important conjectures—conjectures that Quentin and Shreve find essential in the development of their own interpretation. But Mr. Compson fails in the most basic ways: he cannot capture the complexity of human emotions in his characters, nor is he able to reach universality, to display the immortality and the endurance of man.

Quentin and Shreve, who give the third narration, come closest to meeting Faulkner's ideal; but, like Mr. Compson, they simplify the mysteries they encounter. Quentin and Shreve gain the distance needed to express the universality of the characters, and to offer a broader perspective than either Miss Rosa or Mr. Compson. For example, Quentin realizes while creating the story that "if I had been there I could not have seen it this plain." On the other hand, they become so close to Henry and Charles, empathize so completely with them, that they become them: "So that now it was not two but four of them riding the two horses through the dark . . . : four of them and then just two—Charles-Shreve and Quentin-Henry." Finally, in their version of the story, Quentin and Shreve pinpoint the old verities of the heart. In *Absolom, Absolom!* Faulkner confirms: "That was why it did not matter to either of them which one did the talking, since it was not the talking alone which did it, performed and accomplished the overpassing, but some happy marriage of speaking and hearing wherein each before the demand, the requirement, forgave condoned and forgot the faulting of the other . . . in order to overpass to love, where might be paradox and inconsistency but nothing fault nor false." Thus Quentin and Shreve are able to remove themselves far enough from the story to gain a broad perspective, to dig out and express the "truths of the heart" that they recreate in their characters, and to become so close, so much a part of their characters that they transcend time itself. Their belief in rationality, in logic, is their only drawback. They simplify their characters to the point that no mystery is left; eventually, they seem like God—looking down and understanding all. If life were so simple and so logical man would not have to endure, or listen to his soul. As Mr. Compson believed, living would be just like the baking of a cake: put certain ingredients in, and out would come the desired result.

Each narrator attempts to fulfill the task of the writer. Miss Rosa expresses some truths, but they are clouded by a strong moral sense, close involvement, and a lack of imagination. Moreover, although she is the only one to recognize the complexity of life, she attributes it to an arbitrary and wrathful God. Mr. Compson contributes perspective and imagination in clarifying certain events, but his dedication to logic prevents any transcendence of time, any communication of emotions or any appreciation of the mysteries of life. Quentin and Shreve also suffer from a heavy reliance on logic. It is this fault that keeps them from seeing that their interpretation is inadequate, precisely because it over-simplifies. Thus, through the failure of each narrator, the mysterious gossamer quality of life flouts our reason, our logic, and our religion.

Faulkner, however, succeeds. By accepting and affirming the inconsistencies of life, he reassures us. He writes of the complexity of life, of the misunderstandings and mysteries that can never be resolved, of its lack of logic and reason, and of the brief meeting of souls that makes life bearable. Finally, Faulkner in *Absolom, Absolom* expresses his belief in man's immortality: "at least it would be something just because it would have happened, to be remembered even if only from passing from one hand to another, one mind to another, and it would be at least a scratch, something, something that might make a mark on something that *was* once for the reason that it can die someday, while the block of stone can't be *is* because it never can become *was*." The block of stone can never be alive, as man is, because it cannot die. Man's immortality springs from awareness of his own mortality, his truth from the recognition of complexity and contradiction. (Delphia Clarke, student)

Asking questions and making decisions

Exercise: Writing critical essays

Now you are ready to plan and write some critical essays. For each of the following literary selections, follow the instructions that accompany each selection. You will be asked to create a thesis for a three- to five-page essay (750 to 1,000 words), to prepare an outline, and to write the essay.

Selection 1: "My Old Man"

Read the story at least twice. Create a thesis that would offer an interpretive analysis of the story. The following questions suggest some considerations in choosing a thesis:

a. The title of the story is "My Old Man." Is this story primarily about the father, or the son, or about the relationship between them? Is the story about the failure of a plucky hustler or about the boy's change from innocence to experience?

b. Will the boy get over his feelings of distress, or will this discovery change his attitude toward his father forever?

c. Notice where the boy makes emotional comments about his father or the situation, using terms like "swell." How do these comments influence the reader's view of the father?

d. When Kzar loses the race, the boy calls George Gardner "a son of a bitch." This echoes someone else's statement earlier in the story. Is the boy's comment evidence of moral growth or change?

e. Look at the passage where the narrator describes the race in which his father is killed. How does the sentence structure create suspense?

f. What kind of *persona* does Hemingway create for the narrator? Is he omniscient or limited? How does that affect your response to the narrator?

g. How does Hemingway give clues to the father's behavior so that the reader realizes what he has been doing before the boy does?

My Old Man
ERNEST HEMINGWAY

I guess looking at it, now, my old man was cut out for a fat guy, one of those regular little roly fat guys you see around, but he sure never got that way, except a little toward the last, and then it wasn't his fault, he was riding over the jumps only and he could afford to carry plenty of weight then. I remember the way he'd pull on a rubber shirt over a couple of jerseys and a big sweat shirt over that, and get me to run with him in the forenoon in the hot sun. He'd have, maybe, taken a trial trip with one of Razzo's skins early in the morning after just getting in from Torino at four o'clock in the morning and beating it out to the stables in a cab and then with the dew all over everything and the sun just starting to get going. I'd help him pull off his boots and he'd get into a pair of sneakers and all these sweaters and we'd start out.

"Come on, kid," he'd say, stepping up and down on his toes in front of the jocks' dressing room, "let's get moving."

Then we'd start off jogging around the infield once, maybe, with him ahead, running nice, and then turn out the gate and along one of those roads with all the trees along both sides of them that run out from San Siro. I'd go ahead of him when we hit the road and I could run pretty stout and I'd look around and he'd be jogging easy just behind me and after a little while I'd look around again and he'd begun to sweat. Sweating heavy and he'd just be dogging it along with his eyes on my back, but when he'd catch me looking at him he'd grin and say, "Sweating plenty?" When my old man grinned, nobody could help but grin too. We'd keep right on running out toward the mountains and then my old man would yell, "Hey, Joe!" and I'd look back and he'd be sitting under a tree with a towel he'd had around his waist wrapped around his neck.

I'd come back and sit down beside him and he'd pull a rope out of his pocket and start skipping rope out in the sun with the sweat pouring off his face and him skipping rope out in the white dust with the rope going cloppetty, cloppetty, clop, clop, clop, and the sun hotter, and him working harder up and down a patch of the road. Say, it was a treat to see my old man skip rope, too. He could whirr it fast or lop it slow and fancy. Say, you ought to have seen wops look at us sometimes, when they'd come up, going into town walking along with big white steers hauling the cart. They sure looked as though they thought the old man was nuts. He'd start the rope whirring till they'd stop dead still and watch him, then give the steers a cluck and a poke with the goad and get going again.

When I'd sit watching him working out in the hot sun I sure felt fond of him. He sure was fun and he done his work so hard and he'd finish up with a regular whirring that'd drive the sweat out on his face like water and then sling the rope at the tree and come over and sit down with me and lean back against the tree with the towel and a sweater wrapped around his neck.

"Sure is hell keeping it down, Joe," he'd say and lean back and shut his eyes and breathe long and deep, "it ain't like when you're a kid." Then he'd get up before he started to cool and we'd jog along back to the stables. That's the way it was keeping down to weight. He was worried all the time. Most jocks can just about ride off all they want to. A jock loses about a kilo every time he rides, but my old man was sort of dried out and he couldn't keep down his kilos without all that running.

I remember once at San Siro, Regoli, a little wop, that was riding for Buzoni, came out across the paddock going to the bar for something cool; and flicking his boots with his whip, after he'd just weighed in and my old man had just weighed in too, and came out with the saddle under his arm looking red-faced and tired and too big for his silks and he stood there looking at young Regoli standing up to the outdoors bar, cool and kid-looking, and I says, "What's the matter, Dad?" 'cause I thought maybe Regoli had bumped him or something and he just looked at Regoli and said, "Oh, to hell with it," and went on to the dressing room.

Well, it would have been all right, maybe, if we'd stayed in Milan and ridden at Milan and Torino. 'cause if there ever were any easy courses, it's those two. "Pianola, Joe," my old man said when he dismounted in the winning stall after what the wops thought was a hell of a steeplechase. I asked him once. "This course rides itself. It's the pace you're going at, that makes riding the jumps dangerous, Joe. We ain't going any pace here, and they ain't any really bad jumps either. But it's the pace always—not the jumps that makes the trouble."

San Siro was the swellest course I'd ever seen but the old man said it was a dog's life. Going back and forth between Mirafiore and San Siro and riding just about every day in the week with a train ride every other night.

I was nuts about the horses, too. There's something about it, when they come out and go up the track to the post. Sort of dancy and tight looking with the jock keeping a tight hold on them and maybe easing off a little and letting them run a little going up. Then once they were at the barrier it got me worse than anything. Especially at San Siro with that big green infield and the mountains way off and the fat wop starter with his big whip and the jocks fiddling them around and then the barrier snapping up and that bell going off and them all getting off in a bunch and then commencing to string out. You know the way a bunch of skins gets off. If you're up in the stand with a pair of glasses all you see is them plunging off and then that bell goes off and it seems like it rings for a thousand years and then they come sweeping round the turn. There wasn't ever anything like it for me.

But my old man said one day, in the dressing room, when he was getting into his street clothes. "None of these things are horses, Joe. They'd kill that bunch of skates for their hides and hoofs up at Paris." That was the day he'd won the Premio Commercio with Lantorna shooting her out of the field the last hundred meters like pulling a cork out of a bottle.

It was right after the Premio Commercio that we pulled out and left Italy. My old man and Holbrook and a fat wop in a straw hat that kept wiping his face with a handkerchief were having an argument at a table in the Galleria. They were all talking French and the two of them were after my old man about something. Finally he didn't say anything any more but just sat there and looked at Holbrook, and the two of them kept after him, first one talking and then the other, and the fat wop always butting in on Holbrook.

"You go out and buy me a *Sportsman*, will you, Joe?" my old man said, and handed me a couple of soldi without looking away from Holbrook.

So I went out of the Galleria and walked over to in front of the Scala and bought a paper, and came back and stood a little way away because I didn't want to butt in and my old man was sitting back in his chair looking down at his coffee and fooling with a spoon and Holbrook and the big wop were standing and the big wop was wiping his face and shaking his head. And I came up and my old man acted just as though the two of them weren't standing there and said, "Want an ice, Joe?" Holbrook looked down at my old man and said slow and careful. "You son of a bitch," and he and the fat wop went out through the tables.

My old man sat there and sort of smiled at me, but his face was white and he looked sick as hell and I was scared and felt sick inside because I knew something had happened and I didn't see how anybody could call my old man a son of a bitch and get away with it. My old man opened up the *Sportsman* and studied the handicaps for a while and then he said, "You got to take a lot of things in this world, Joe." And three days later we left Milan for good on the Turin train for Paris, after an auction sale out in front of Turner's stables of everything we couldn't get into a trunk and a suit case.

We got into Paris early in the morning in a long, dirty station the old man told me was the Gare de Lyon. Paris was an awful big town after Milan. Seems like in Milan everybody is going somewhere and all the trams run somewhere and there ain't any sort of a mix-up, but Paris is all balled up and they never do straighten it out. I got to like it, though, part of it, anyway, and say it's got the best race courses in the world. Seems as though that were the thing that keeps it all going and about the only thing you can figure on is that every day the buses will be going out to whatever track they're running at, going right out through everything to the track. I never really got to know Paris well, because I just came in about once or twice a week with the old man from Maisons and he always sat at the Café de la Paix on the Opera side with the rest of the gang from Maisons and I guess that's one of the busiest parts of the town. But, say, it is funny that a big town like Paris wouldn't have a Galleria, isn't it?

Well, we went out to live at Maisons-Lafitte, where just about everybody lives except the gang at Chantilly, with a Mrs. Meyers that runs a boarding house. Maisons is about the swellest place to live I've ever seen in all my life. The town ain't so much, but there's a lake and a swell forest that we used to go off bumming in all day, a couple of us kids, and my old man made me a sling shot and we got a lot of things with it but the best one was a magpie. Young Dick Atkinson shot a rabbit with it one day and we put it under a tree and were sitting around and Dick had some cigarettes and all of a sudden the rabbit jumped up and beat it into the brush and we chased it but we couldn't find it. Gee, we had fun at Maisons. Mrs. Meyers used to give me lunch in the morning and I'd be gone all day. I learned to talk French quick. It's an easy language.

As soon as we got to Maisons, my old man wrote to Milan for his license and he was pretty worried till it came. He used to sit around the Café de Paris in Maisons with the gang, there were lots of guys he'd known when he rode up at Paris, before the war, lived at Maisons, and there's a lot of time to sit around because the work around a racing stable, for the jocks, that is, is all cleaned up by nine o'clock in the morning. They take the first batch of skins out to gallop them at 5:30 in the morning and they work the second lot at 8 o'clock. That means getting up early all right and going to bed early, too. If a jock's riding for somebody too, he can't go boozing around because the trainer always has an eye on him if he's a kid and if he ain't a kid he's always got an eye on himself. So mostly if a jock ain't working he sits around the Café de Paris with the gang and they can all sit around about two or three hours in front of some drink like a vermouth and seltz and they talk and tell stories and shoot pool and it's sort of like a club or the Galleria in Milan. Only it ain't really like the Galleria because there everybody is going by all the time and there's everybody around at the tables.

Well, my old man got his license all right. They sent it through to him without a word and he rode a couple of times. Amiens, up country and that sort of thing, but he didn't seem to get any engagement. Everybody liked him and whenever I'd come in to the Café in the forenoon I'd find somebody drinking with him because my old man wasn't tight like most of these jockeys that have got the first dollar they made riding at the World's Fair in St. Louis in nineteen ought four. That's what my old man would say when he'd kid George Burns. But it seemed like everybody steered clear of giving my old man any mounts.

We went out to wherever they were running every day with the car from Maisons and that was the most fun of all. I was glad when the horses came back from Deauville and the summer. Even though it meant no more bumming in the woods, 'cause then we'd ride to Enghien or Tremblay or St. Cloud and watch them from the trainers' and jockeys' stand. I sure learned about racing from going out with that gang and the fun of it was going every day.

I remember once out at St. Cloud. It was a big two hundred thousand franc race with seven entries and Kzar a big favorite. I went around to the paddock to see the horses with my old man and you never saw such horses. This Kzar is a great big yellow horse that looks like just nothing but run. I never saw such a horse. He was being led around the paddocks with his head down and when he went by me I felt all hollow inside he was so beautiful. There never was such a wonderful, lean, running built horse. And he went around the paddock putting his feet just so and quiet and careful and moving easy like he knew just what he had to do and not jerking and standing up on his legs and getting wild eyed like you see these selling platers with a shot of dope in them. The crowd was so thick I couldn't see him again except just his legs going by and some yellow and my old man started out through the crowd and I followed him over to the jocks' dressing room back in the trees and there was a big crowd around there, too, but the man at the door in a derby nodded to my old man and we got in and everybody was sitting around and getting dressed and pulling shirts over their heads and pulling boots on and it all smelled hot and sweaty and linimenty and outside was the crowd looking in.

The old man went over and sat down beside George Gardner that was getting into his pants and said, "What's the dope, George?" just in an ordinary tone of voice 'cause there ain't any use him feeling around because George either can tell him or he can't tell him.

"He won't win," George says very low, leaning over and buttoning the bottoms of his pants.

"Who will?" my old man says, leaning over close so nobody can hear.

"Kircubbin," George says, "and if he does, save me a couple of tickets."

My old man says something in a regular voice to George and George says, "Don't ever bet on anything, I tell you," kidding like, and we beat it out and through all the crowd that was looking in over to the 100 franc mutuel machine. But I knew something big was up because George is Kzar's jockey. On the way he gets one of the yellow odds-sheets with the starting prices on and Kzar is only paying 5 for 10. Cefisidote is next at 3 to 1 and fifth down the list this Kircubbin at 8 to 1. My old man bets five thousand on Kircubbin to win and puts on a thousand to place and we went around back of the grandstand to go up the stairs and get a place to watch the race.

We were jammed in tight and first a man in a long coat with a gray tall hat and a whip folded up in his hand came out and then one after another the horses, with the jocks up and a stable boy holding the bridle on each side and walking along, followed the old guy. That big yellow horse Kzar came first. He didn't look so big when you first looked at him until you saw the length of his legs and the whole way he's built and the way he moves. Gosh, I never saw such a horse. George Gardner was riding him and they moved along slow, back of the old guy in the gray tall hat that walked along like he was the ring master in a circus. Back of Kzar, moving along smooth and yellow in the sun, was a good looking black with a nice head with Tommy Archibald riding him; and after the black was a string of five more horses all moving along slow in a procession past the grandstand and the pesage. My old man said the black was Kircubbin and I took a good look at him and he was a nice looking horse, all right, but nothing like Kzar.

Everybody cheered Kzar when he went by and he sure was one swell-looking horse. The procession of them went around on the other side past the pelouse and then back up to the near end of the course and the circus master had the stable boys turn them loose one after another so they could gallop by the stands on their way up to the post and let everybody have a good look at them. They weren't at the post hardly any time at all when the gong started and you could see them way off across the infield all in a bunch starting on the first swing like a lot of little toy horses. I was watching them through the glasses and Kzar was running well back, with one of the bays making the pace. They swept down and around and came pounding past and Kzar was way back when they passed us and this Kircubbin horse in front and going smooth. Gee, it's awful when they go by you and then you have to watch them go farther away and get smaller and smaller and then all bunched up on the turns and then come around towards into the stretch and you feel like swearing and goddamming worse and worse. Finally they made the last turn and came into the straightaway with this Kircubbin horse way out in front. Everybody was looking funny and saying "Kzar" in sort of a sick way and them pounding nearer down the stretch, and then something came out of the pack right into my glasses like a horse-headed yellow streak and everybody began to yell "Kzar" as though they were crazy. Kzar came on faster than I'd ever seen anything in my life and pulled up on Kircubbin that was going fast as any black horse could go with the jock flogging hell out of him with the gad and they were right dead neck and neck for a second but Kzar seemed going about twice as fast with those great jumps and that head out—but it was while they were neck and neck that they passed the winning post and when the numbers went up in the slots the first one was 2 and that meant Kircubbin had won.

I felt all trembly and funny inside, and then we were all jammed in with the people going downstairs to stand in front of the board where they'd post what Kircubbin paid. Honest, watching the race I'd forgot how much my old man had bet on Kircubbin. I'd wanted Kzar to win so damned bad. But now it was all over it was swell to know we had the winner.

"Wasn't it a swell race, Dad?" I said to him.

He looked at me sort of funny with his derby on the back of his head. "George Gardner's a swell jockey, all right," he said. "It sure took a great jock to keep that Kzar horse from winning."

Of course I knew it was funny all the time. But my old man saying that right out like that sure took the kick all out of it for me and I didn't get the real kick back again ever, even when they posted the numbers up on the board and the bell rang to pay off and we saw that Kircubbin paid 67.50 for 10. All round people were saying, "Poor Kzar! Poor Kzar!" And I thought, I wish I were a jockey and could have rode him instead of that son of a bitch. And that was funny, thinking of George Gardner as a son of a bitch because I'd always liked him and besides he'd given us the winner, but I guess that's what he is, all right.

My old man had a big lot of money after that race and he took to coming into Paris oftener. If they raced at Tremblay he'd have them drop him in town on their way back to Maisons, and he and I'd sit out in front of the Café de la Paix and watch the people go by. It's funny sitting there. There's streams of people going by and all sorts of guys come up and want to sell you things, and I loved to sit there with my old man. That was when we'd have the most fun. Guys would come by selling funny rabbits that jumped if you squeezed a bulb and they'd come up to us and my old man would kid with them. He could talk French just like English and all those kind of guys knew him 'cause you can always tell a jockey—and then we always sat at the same table and they got used to seeing us there. There were guys selling matrimonial papers and girls selling rubber eggs that when you squeezed them a rooster came out of them and one old wormy-looking guy that went by with post-cards of Paris, showing them to everybody, and, of course, nobody ever bought any, and then he would come back and show the under side of the pack and they would all be smutty post-cards and lots of people would dig down and buy them.

Gee, I remember the funny people that used to go by. Girls around supper time looking for somebody to take them out to eat and they'd speak to my old man and he'd make some joke at them in French and they'd pat me on the head and go on. Once there was an American woman sitting with her kid daughter at the next table to us and they were both eating ices and I kept looking at the girl and she was awfully good looking and I smiled at her and she smiled at me but that was all that ever came of it because I looked for her mother and her every day and I made up ways that I was going to speak to her and I wondered if I got to know her if her mother would let me take her out to Auteuil or Tremblay but I never saw either of them again. Anyway, I guess it wouldn't have been any good, anyway, because looking back on it I remember the way I thought out would be best to speak to her was to say, "Pardon me, but perhaps I can give you a winner at Enghien today?" and, after all, maybe she would have thought I was a tout instead of really trying to give her a winner.

We'd sit at the Café de la Paix, my old man and me, and we had a big drag with the waiter because my old man drank whisky and it cost five francs, and that meant a good tip when the saucers were counted up. My old man was drinking more than I'd ever seen him, but he wasn't riding at all now and besides he said that whisky kept his weight down. But I noticed he was putting it on, all right, just the same. He'd busted away from his old gang out at Maisons and seemed to like just sitting around on the boulevard with me. But he was dropping money every day at the track. He'd feel sort of doleful after the last race, if he'd lost on the day, until we'd get to our table and he'd have his first whisky and then he'd be fine.

He'd be reading the Paris-Sport and he'd look over at me and say, "Where's your girl, Joe?" to kid me on account I had told him about the girl that day at the next table. And I'd get red, but I liked being kidded about her. It gave me a good feeling. "Keep your eye peeled for her, Joe," he'd say, "she'll be back."

He'd ask me questions about things and some of the things I'd say he'd laugh. And then he'd get started talking about things. About riding down in Egypt, or at St. Moritz on the ice before my mother died, and about during the war when they had regular races down in the south of France without any purses or betting or crowd or anything just to keep the breed up. Regular races with the jocks riding hell out of the horses. Gee, I could listen to my old man talk by the hour, especially when he'd had a couple or so of drinks. He'd tell me about when he was a boy in Kentucky and going coon hunting, and the old days in the States before everything went on the bum there. And he'd say, "Joe, when we've got a decent stake, you're going back there to the States and go to school."

"What've I got to go back there to go to school for when everything's on the bum there?" I'd ask him.

"That's different," he'd say and get the waiter over and pay the pile of saucers and we'd get a taxi to the Gare St. Lazare and get on the train out to Maisons.

One day at Auteuil, after a selling steeplechase, my old man bought in the winner for 30,000 francs. He had to bid a little to get him but the stable let the horse go finally and my old man had his permit and his colors in a week. Gee, I felt proud when my old man was an owner. He fixed it up for stable space with Charles Drake and cut out coming in to Paris, and started his running and sweating out again, and him and I were the whole stable gang. Our horse's name was Gilford, he was Irish bred and a nice, sweet jumper. My old man figured that training him and riding him, himself, he was a good investment. I was proud of everything and I thought Gilford was as good a horse as Kzar. He was a good, solid jumper, a bay, with plenty of speed on the flat, if you asked him for it, and he was a nice-looking horse, too.

Gee, I was fond of him. The first time he started with my old man up, he finished third in a 2,500 meter hurdle race and when my old man got off him, all sweating and happy in the place stall, and went in to weigh, I felt so proud of him as though it was the first race he'd ever placed in. You see, when a guy ain't been riding for a long time, you can't make yourself really believe that he has ever rode. The whole thing was different now, 'cause down in Milan, even big races never seemed to make any difference to my old man, if he won he wasn't ever excited or anything, and now it was so I couldn't hardly sleep the night before a race and I knew my old man was excited, too, even if he didn't show it. Riding for yourself makes an awful difference.

Second time Gilford and my old man started, was a rainy Sunday at Auteuil, in the Prix du Marat, a 4,500 meter steeplechase. As soon as he'd gone out I beat it up in the stand with the new glasses my old man had bought for me to watch them. They started way over at the far end of the course and there was some trouble at the barrier. Something with goggle blinders on was making a great fuss and rearing around and busted the barrier once, but I could see my old man in our black jacket, with a white cross and a black cap, sitting up on Gilford, and patting him with his hand. Then they were off in a jump and out of sight behind the trees and the gong going for dear life and the pari-mutuel wickets rattling down. Gosh, I was so excited, I was afraid to look at them, but I fixed the glasses on the place where they would come out back of the trees and then out they came with the old black jacket going third and they all sailing over the jump like birds. Then they went out of sight again and then they came pounding out and down the hill and all going nice and sweet and easy and taking the fence smooth in a bunch, and moving away from us all solid. Looked as though you could walk across on their backs they were all so bunched and going so smooth. Then they bellied over the big double Bullfinch and something came down. I couldn't see who it was, but in a minute the horse was up and galloping free and the field, all bunched still, sweeping around the long left turn into the straightaway. They jumped the stone wall and came jammed down the stretch toward the big water-jump right in front of the stands. I saw them coming and hollered at my old man as he went by, and he was leading by about a length and riding way out, and light as a monkey, and they were racing for the water-jump. They took off over the big hedge of the water-jump in a pack and then there was a crash, and two horses pulled sideways out off it, and kept on going, and three others were piled up. I couldn't see my old man anywhere. One horse kneed himself up and the jock had hold of the bridle and mounted and went slamming on after the place money. The other horse was up and away by himself, jerking his head and galloping with the bridle rein hanging and the jock staggered over to one side of the track against the fence. Then Gilford rolled over to one side off my old man and got up and started to run on three legs with his off hoof dangling and there was my old man laying there on the grass flat out with his face up and blood all over the side of his head. I ran down the stand and bumped into a jam of people and got to the rail and a cop grabbed me and held me and two big stretcher-bearers were going out after my old man and around on the other side of the course I saw three horses, strung way out, coming out of the trees and taking the jump.

My old man was dead when they brought him in and while a

doctor was listening to his heart with a thing plugged in his ears, I heard a shot up the track that meant they'd killed Gilford. I lay down beside my old man, when they carried the stretcher into the hospital room, and hung onto the stretcher and cried and cried, and he looked so white and gone and so awfully dead, and I couldn't help feeling that if my old man was dead maybe they didn't need to have shot Gilford. His hoof might have got well. I don't know. I loved my old man so much.

Then a couple of guys came in and one of them patted me on the back and then went over and looked at my old man and then pulled a sheet off the cot and spread it over him; and the other was telephoning in French for them to send the ambulance to take him out to Maisons. And I couldn't stop crying, crying and choking, sort of, and George Gardner came in and sat down beside me on the floor and put his arm around me and says, "Come on, Joe, old boy. Get up and we'll go out and wait for the ambulance."

George and I went out to the gate and I was trying to stop bawling and George wiped off my face with his handkerchief and we were standing back a little ways while the crowd was going out of the gate and a couple of guys stopped near us while we were waiting for the crowd to get through the gate and one of them was counting a bunch of mutuel tickets and he said. "Well, Butler got his, all right."

The other guy said, "I didn't give a good goddam if he did, the crook. He had it coming to him on the stuff he's pulled."

I'll say he had," said the other guy, and tore the bunch of tickets in two.

And George Gardner looked at me to see if I'd heard and I had all right and he said, "Don't you listen to what those bums said, Joe. Your old man was one swell guy."

But I don't know. Seems like when they get started they don't leave a guy nothing.

Selection 2: "The Shield of Achilles"

Read the poem several times. Read it aloud at least once. Write a thesis sentence for either a correlational essay or an interpretive analysis. You may want to consider the following points before forming your thesis:

a. How many different things are being contrasted in this poem, in addition to Thetis' expectations and Hephaestos' metalworking?

b. How does the line length of the different stanzas reinforce the contrast?

c. Study the words that rhyme. How do these reinforce key ideas in the poem?
d. Look at the words themselves and the way they define the difference between what Thetis expects ("vines," "olive trees," etc.) and what she sees ("no blade of grass," "nothing to eat," etc.).
e. Consider the rhythm of the short lines. How do rhythms like "Quick, quick, to music" contrast with rhythms like "Proved by statistics that some cause was just?"
f. What significance does this poem have in a post-Watergate era? What marks it as a World War II poem or a twentieth century poem?
g. Look up the passage in the *Iliad*, if you have read the *Iliad* before, and try to state the relationship between the epic, with its definitions of heroism and grandeur, and the "civilization" Auden describes.

Background
The *Iliad* is a famous long poem or epic about the siege of Troy, an ancient city, and the battles between the Trojans and the Greeks (Achaeans). Achilles is one of the greatest warriors of the Greek army. He is referred to as "the great runner" and the ideal of chivalry. But Achilles is also capable of selfish, irrational anger and terrible cruelty. After he kills Hector, the finest prince of the Trojans, he slits Hector's tendons at the heels, inserts leather straps, and drags the mutilated dead body behind his chariot around the walls of the city.

Thetis (pronounced tā'tis), a goddess who is Achilles' mother, has helped her son by obtaining a special set of armor for him from Hephaestos (pronounced hĕ fī'stos), the metal-working god. In the *Iliad*, Achilles' great shield shows the universe in miniature, including the solar system, the arts of agriculture, music, dancing, warfare, and justice before a lawful court. Thetis believes that the outcome of a military victory will be an ideal civilization.

W.H. Auden, writing during World War II, presents a different version of this well-known scene from the *Iliad*.

The Shield of Achilles
W.H. AUDEN
She looked over his shoulder
For vines and olive trees,

Marble, well-governed cities
    And ships upon wine-dark seas;
But there on the shining metal
    His hands had put instead
An artificial wilderness
    And a sky like lead.

A plain without a feature, bare and brown,
    No blade of grass, no sign of neighborhood,
Nothing to eat and nowhere to sit down;
    Yet, congregated on the blankness, stood
    An unintelligible multitude,
A million eyes, a million boots, in line,
Without expression, waiting for a sign.

Out of the air a voice without a face
    Proved by statistics that some cause was just
In tones as dry and level as the place;
    No one was cheered and nothing was discussed,
    Column by column, in a cloud of dust,
They marched away, enduring a belief
Whose logic brought them, somewhere else to grief.

She looked over his shoulder
    For ritual pieties,
White flower-garlanded heifers,
    Libation and sacrifice:
But there on the shining metal
    Where the altar should have been
She saw by his flickering forge-light
    Quite another scene.

Barbed wire enclosed an arbitrary spot
    Where bored officials lounged (one cracked a joke)
And sentries sweated for the day was hot;
    A crowd of ordinary decent folk
    Watched from outside and neither moved nor spoke
As three pale figures were led forth and bound
To three posts driven upright in the ground.

The mass and majesty of this world, all
    That carries weight and always weighs the same,
Lay in the hands of others; they were small
    And could not hope for help, and no help came;
    What their foes liked to do was done; their shame

Was all the worst could wish: they lost their pride
And died as men before their bodies died.

> She looked over his shoulder
>   For athletes at their games,
> Men and women in a dance
>   Moving their sweet limbs,
> Quick, quick, to music;
>   But there on the shining shield
> His hands had set no dancing-floor
>   But a weed-choked field.

A ragged urchin, aimless and alone,
    Loitered about that vacancy; a bird
Flew up to safety from his well-aimed stone:
    That girls are raped, that two boys knife a third,
    Were axioms to him, who'd never heard
Of any world where promises were kept
Or one could weep because another wept.

> The thin-lipped armorer
>   Hephaestos hobbled away;
> Thetis of the shining breasts
>   Cried out in dismay
> At what the God had wrought
>   To please her son, the strong
> Iron-hearted man-slaying Achilles
>   Who would not live long.

Selection 3: *Antigone,* Scene One

Read the scene at least twice. Write a critical essay. Consider some of the following points before you formulate your thesis:

a. What does each character consider to be the supreme source of moral authority?
b. How does each character describe the motives of others?
c. Is there a contrast between each character's concept of the supreme moral authority in human affairs, and the motives he or she attributes to others? Notice that Kreon relies on "the good of the state" as the basis of moral judgments, but accuses most people of acting because they have been bribed.
d. How many times does Kreon mention money?
e. What does each of the characters want most?

f. What are the sources of conflict between characters in the first scene?

g. Are the moral arguments employed by these characters still used today?

h. *Antigone* has nearly replaced Sophocles' most famous work, *Oedipus Rex*, in popularity. Why would *Antigone* be popular today?

A square in front of the Theban palace. The palace faces south. In the foreground is an altar. This is the hour of dawn. As the action proceeds, the area gradually brightens. ANTIGONE *waits on the audience's side of the altar.* ISMENE *comes forward from the palace and approaches hesitantly.*

ANTIGONE Ismene?
Let me see your face:
my own, only sister,
can you see
because we are the survivors
today Zeus is completing in us the ceremony
of pain and dishonor and disaster and shame
that began with Oedipus?
And today, again:
the proclamation, under the rule of war
but binding, they say, on every citizen. . . .
Haven't you heard? Don't you see
hatred marches on love
when friends, our own people, our family
are treated as enemies?

ISMENE No, Antigone,
since the day we lost our brothers,
both in one day, both to each other,
I haven't thought of love—happy or painful, either.
Last night the enemy army left.
I know nothing further.
Nothing makes me happy, nothing hurts me any more.

ANTIGONE I know. But I called you here for a reason:
to talk alone.

ISMENE I can see there's something important. Tell me.

ANTIGONE It's the burial. It's our brothers:
Kreon, honoring one and casting the other out.
They say he has buried Eteokles

with full and just and lawful honors due the dead;
but Polyneices, who died as pitiably—
Kreon has proclaimed that body will stay unburied;
no mourners, no tomb, no tears,
a tasty meal for vultures.
That's what they say this man of good will
Kreon has proclaimed, for you, yes and for me;
and he is coming here to announce it
clearly, so that everyone will know.
And they say he intends to enforce it:
"Whoever shall perform any prohibited act
shall be liable to the penalty of death by stoning
in the presence of the assembled citizens."
You can see that you'll have to act quickly
to prove you are as brave today
as you were born to be.

ISMENE What can I accomplish? There's nothing left.
What can I do or undo?

ANTIGONE Will you join with me? Will you help?
Ask yourself that.

ISMENE Help with what?

ANTIGONE The body. Give me your hand. Help me.

ISMENE You mean to bury him? In spite of the edict?

ANTIGONE He's my brother and yours too;
and whether you will or not, I'll stand by him.

ISMENE Do you dare, despite Kreon?

ANTIGONE He cannot keep me from my own.

ISMENE Your own?
Think of Oedipus, our own father,
hated, infamous, destroyed;
found his crimes, broke his eyes,
that hand that murdered,
two in one—
and Mother, remember,
his mother and wife,
two in one,
her braids of rope that twisted life away—
then our brothers,
two in one day,
the hands that murdered
shared twin doom—

now us, sisters, two alone,
and all the easier destroyed
if we spite the law and the power of the king.

No, we should be sensible:
we are women, born unfit to battle men:
and we are subjects, while Kreon is king.
No, we must obey, even in this,
even if something could hurt more.
But because I will obey,
I beg forgiveness of the dead;
my plea is that I am forced;
to intervene would be senseless.

ANTIGONE Then I won't urge you. No.
Even if you were willing to "be senseless"
I wouldn't want the help you could give.
It's too late.
You must be as you believe.
I will bury him myself.
If I die for doing that, good:
I will stay with him, my brother;
and my crime will be devotion.
The living are here,
but I must please those longer
who are below; for with the dead
I will stay forever.
If you believe you must,
cast out these principles which the gods themselves
honor.

ISMENE I won't dishonor anything; but I cannot help,
not when the whole country refuses to help.

ANTIGONE Then weakness will be your plea.
I am different. I love my brother
and I'm going to bury him, now.

ISMENE Antigone, I'm so afraid for you.

ANTIGONE Don't be afraid yet, not for me.
Steer your own fate. It's a long way.

ISMENE Promise not to say anything.
Keep this secret. I'll join you in secrecy.

ANTIGONE No, shout it, proclaim it.
I'll hate you the more for keeping silence.

ISMENE Hate me?
This ardor of yours is spent on ashes.

Will is not enough.
There is no way, without power.

ANTIGONE When my strength is spent, I will be done.
I know I am pleasing those whom I must.

ISMENE With no hope, even to start is wrong.

ANTIGONE Talk like that, and you'll make me hate you;
and he, dead, will hate you,
and rightly, as an enemy.
Leave me alone, with my hopeless scheme;
I'm ready to suffer for it and to die.
Let me. No suffering could be so terrible
as to die for nothing.

ISMENE Since you believe you must, go on.
You are wrong. But we who love you
are right in loving you.

ANTIGONE *and* ISMENE *part,* ANTIGONE *to the left, the
west,* ISMENE *to the right. Bright daylight now pours
from the right where the* CHORUS *enters, fifteen white-
bearded gentlemen, whose courtiers' garb, spangled
with golden dragons and sunbursts, reflects the color
of new day. They about-face toward the sun. They pray:*

CHORUS Sun-blaze, shining at last,
you are the most beautiful light
ever shown Thebes
over her seven gates;

and now, higher,
widening gaze of gold day,
you come,
over the course of our west river.

In whole armor,
come out of Argos
(his shield shone white)
you have expelled the man,
exiled in unbridled and blinding flight.

Out of the crisis of a dubious quarrel
Polyneices had roused him against our country.
As shrill as an eagle on wings white as snow
he flew onto the country,
feathered in armor,
many men full-armed
and plumes on their helmets.

Stood there, over our roofs;
circled our gates, Thebes' seven faces;
spears, set for the kill,
snarling about the wall;

a gullet gaping,
dry for a fill of our blood;
fires
ready to catch our wreath of towers;

but then nothing.
Now he was gone,
fled the war god's crash,
snared in flight by the war god.
Futile to have struggled with dragon Thebes.

Zeus hates the noise of a bragging tongue.
When he saw them come against us
in a great gush, grandiose with splashing gold,
he whirled fire;
and the man who was rushing like a racer to the goal
on the heights of our battlements
and was signaling victory,
Zeus hurled him down with that fire.

Swung and then fell,
with the torch in his hand still,
on our land;
struck, and the land returned the shock.

He who had raved drunk, raged to attack,
who had howled with sweeps of the wind of hatred,
fell baffled;
and the grand war god allotted the rest their own
dooms,
pressed as they failed,
gained us the contest.

Our seven gates were their seven stations,
and standing against our own, their seven captains,
who were turned by Zeus and ran
and to Zeus abandoned their bronze squadrons.
But on either side, one man remained, out of hatred,
seed of one father, birth from one mother,
planted spears against each other,
and both of them conquered,
sharing a twin death.

Victory comes
bringing glory to Thebes,
answers a smile
to our many chariots that cheer her.
Now that the war is over, forget war.
We'll visit every god's temples,
for a whole night, dancing and chanting praise.
Dionysos leads us,
rules Thebes,
makes the land tremble.

KORYPHAIOS But look, the new king of the country,
Kreon, is coming:
a new kind of man for new conditions.
I wonder what program he intends to launch,
that he should call the elders into special conference.

From the palace KREON *enters, in armor, with a military*
retinue

KREON Gentlemen, the state!
The gods have quaked her in heavy weather.
Now they have righted her.
The state rides steady once again.

Out of all the citizens, I have summoned you,
remembering that you blessed King Laios' reign
when Oedipus ruled, you stood by him;
and after his destruction stood by his sons,
always with firm counsel.
Both sons died in one day, struck and stricken,
paired in doom and a twin pollution.
Now I rule, as next of kin.
They are dead; I am king.

It is impossible to know a man's soul,
both the wit and will,
before he writes laws and enforces them.
I believe that he who rules in a state
and fails to embrace the best men's counsels,
but stays locked in silence and vague fear,
is the worst man there.
I have long believed so.
And he who cherishes an individual beyond his home-
land,
he, I say, is nothing.
Zeus who sees all will see I shall not stay silent
if I see disaster marching against our citizens,
and I shall not befriend the enemy of this land.

For the state is safety.
When she is steady, then we can steer.
Then we can love.

Those are my principles. The state will thrive through them.
Today I have proclaimed more laws akin to those.
These concern the sons of Oedipus:
Eteokles, who fought in defense of the nation
and fell in action,
will be given holy burial,
a funeral suited to greatness and nobility.
But his brother, Polyneices, the exile,
who descended with fire to destroy his fatherland and family gods,
to drink our blood and drive us off slaves,
will have no ritual, no mourners,
will be left unburied so men may see him
ripped for food by dogs and vultures.

This is an example of my thinking.
I shall never let criminals excel good men in honor.
I shall honor the friends of the state
while they live, and when they die.

KORYPHAIOS These opinions, sir,
concerning enemies and friends of the state,
are as you please.
Law and usage, as I see it,
are totally at your disposal
to apply both to the dead and to us survivors.

KREON Think of yourselves, therefore,
as the guardians of my pronouncements.

KORYPHAIOS You have young men you can put on duty.

KREON No, No! Not the corpse. I have guards posted.

KORYPHAIOS Then what are your orders?

KREON Not to side with rebels.

KORYPHAIOS No one is such a fool. No one loves death.

KREON That's right, death is the price.

All the same, time after time,
greed has destroyed good men.

A SENTRY *runs in from the left.*

SENTRY King Kreon,
I'm going to
explain about
why I made it
down here all out of wind,
which for one thing
is not on account of going
fast,
because even when I started out
it wasn't light-footed.
No, and I kept stopping to think,
and all the way I was going in circles
about turning right back.
Yes, and my soul keeps telling me things.
Says: What are you going to go there for,
when as soon as you get there you're sure to pay for it?
And then: What are you standing here for?
If Kreon finds out about this from somebody else first
you'll be the one that suffers.
I kept rolling that over in my mind,
and moved along slow,
like on my own time:
you can go a long way, walking a short distance.
In the end the thought
that acutally did win out
was to go right ahead to you, sir.
And even if what I'm about to explain
really isn't anything,
I'm going to say it anyhow,
because here I am,
yes, and with a handful of hope
that nothing more will happen to me
but what the future has in store already.

KREON What's the matter with you? What are you afraid of?

SENTRY Well, first I want to tell you about me,
because I didn't do it, and don't know who did,
so it wouldn't be right either way
if I fell into some kind of trouble.

KREON You aim well before you shoot.

You virtually encircle the business, you build a block-
ade.
Clearly your news is extraordinary.

SENTRY Sir, it's awful; it was so strange
I can hardly bring myself to say it.

KREON Tell me now,
then I'll dismiss you,
and you'll go.

SENTRY Well, I am telling you:
somebody up and buried the corpse and went off:
sprinkled dust over it
and did the ceremonies you're supposed to.

KREON Who? Who dared?

SENTRY I don't know.
There wasn't any cut from a pickax or scoop of a hoe.
The soil is hard and dry,
no breaks in it from wagon wheels.
No, whoever the one who did it was,
there's no sign of him now. Nothing at all.
When the first daytime sentry showed us
we all thought it was a miracle.
We couldn't see the body; and he wasn't really buried;
it was like someone tried to drive the curse out:
a fine dust on it.
No game tracks or dog tracks,
no sign of being tugged at.

Next thing there's a flurry of harsh words,
with one sentry cross-examining the other;
and we'd have wound up fighting,
with nobody there to stop us, either,
because everybody did it, and no one saw him do it,
and everyone testified he knew nothing about it.
We were ready to hold hot iron, walk through fire,
swearing by the gods we didn't do it
and never knew who did or planned it, either one.

But in the end, when we'd tried everything,
one man speaks up
and sets us all hanging our heads
looking at the ground afraid,
because we couldn't say a thing against it
and couldn't expect good to come of doing it.
He said we couldn't hide what happened,

we had to tell you.
And that idea won out.
With my bad luck, the lot fell on me,
and I'm the winner, and here I am,
and I don't want to be
and I know you don't want me here
because no one who hates what you say loves you.

KORYPHAIOS My lord, we have been considering
whether a god might not have done this. . . .

KREON Stop, before you say too much.
You're an old man. Are you senile?
Intolerable talk,
as if gods had any concern for that corpse,
covering him up,
honoring him presumably as a public benefactor,
when he was the one who came to burn their temples,
the circles of pillars and the holy treasures
and the country that is theirs,
smashing the laws.
Is that your idea?
Can you see gods honoring criminals?
Impossible.

No. For a long while now
certain men in this city, as they would have it,
have scarcely been able to stand up under my commands.
They mutter about me, they hide, shake their heads
instead of properly shouldering the yoke and working with the team
which is the one way of showing love to me.
Those are the men that did this, I'm positive.
They were seduced with money.

Money: nothing worse for people
ever has sprouted up and grown current.
That's what ravages nations and drives men from their homes,
perverts the best human principles,
teaches men to turn to crime,
makes everything they do and think unholy.

Everyone they hired to do this will pay for it.
As Zeus accepts my prayers,
understand this well, I'm talking on oath,
to you (*to* SENTRY)

unless you find me the perpetrator of this burial
death won't be enough,
you'll hang alive till you tell me who did it,
just so you'll, all of you, know from then on
not to take bribes, and learn that your love
of getting what you can where you can is wrong.
You'll see: When you have it, shame makes you hide
it;
that kind of money wrecks men,
and few escape alive.

SENTRY Will you give me a chance to answer,
                  or should I just go?

KREON Don't you know yet your talk irritates me?

SENTRY Does it hurt in your ears, sir, or in your soul?

KREON What is this? Anatomy?

SENTRY The man who did it irritates your mind.
I just bother your ears.

KREON You can't stop talking, can you?
You must have been born this way.

SENTRY Anyway, I never did what you said I did.

KREON Yes you did! For money! You sold your soul.

SENTRY Sir, it's terrible; you make your mind up
when even what's wrong looks right.

KREON I'll leave the subtleties to you. I make decisions.
But unless you show me the responsible parties in this case
you will learn that easy money buys suffering.

13 Technical writing

Objectives

Technical writing is a necessity of our time, because scientific knowledge is valuable only when it is applied and shared. Unless discoveries in the research laboratory can be conveyed to others, they will benefit no one. Therefore, both as a student and later as an engineer, technical management person, or scientist, your writing ability will enhance your effectiveness.

In technical writing situations, the basic principles you learned in the first ten chapters of this book still apply. What you will need to know is how to use those basic concepts. In this chapter you will become familiar with the techniques of reader-oriented technical writing, and will learn the usual structure of four major technical reports: the physical research report, the laboratory report, the progress report, and the feasibility report.

Reader-oriented technical writing

Good technical writing is reader-oriented. If technical writers wrote only for themselves, nearly any kind of prose would be acceptable. There could scarcely be any doubt that the writers would understand their own sentences. But technical writing is valuable chiefly as a means of communication, not self-expression. Therefore, you should aim to put down on paper what someone else needs to know about your work. Ask yourself what there is about it that matters to your readers. What do they already know, and how much more do they need to know? Some readers' interests will differ from others. You will often need to make your writing useful to a diverse audience.

Keeping the readers' needs in mind will help you plan your report. Many choices, including material selection, discussion length, and terminology, can depend on the kind of audience that will receive your report. If you are writing for colleagues who are expert in your general field, you will want your report to provide the extensive technical details that concern them. If you are writing for less expert readers you will omit or summarize certain information, and provide explanations that would be unnecessary for those who know the field. Focusing on what your reader needs to know will improve your technical writing.

Techniques for reader-oriented writing

In addition to selecting the right kind and amount of information for the reader, the expert technical writer makes the physical form of letters, memoranda, and reports as useful to the reader as possible. Often he can rely on conventions familiar to his readers. Among these conventions are specific patterns of organization for certain types of reports, techniques for arranging materials on the page, methods of constructing graphs and tables, and technical writing style.

Technical writing style

Good technical writing is clear, vigorous, and specific. Apply the principles of objectivity, honesty, and precision to your writing just as you apply them to your research. Technical writers want to be understood, and therefore they assume the obligation of being clear, concise, and complete. You should tell the reader precisely and concisely what you want him to understand or do. Indeed, you should strive to write so precisely that your meaning cannot be misunderstood.

Writing to avoid reader error and to foster exact interpretation implies careful word choice and unambiguous syntax. Checking to make sure that relationships between ideas are clearly stated will improve your style. Some adverbs should be used very carefully to prevent temporary misunderstandings. Use "since" and "while" to mean "after" and "during," because these are the primary and most common uses of the words. Using "since" to mean "because" may oblige the reader to correct his interpretation after four or five words of your clause; that brief break in his attention is a waste of time and an opportunity for misunderstanding. Also, avoiding jargon nearly always makes your meaning more exact and earns your reader's approval.

Visual emphasis through listing

The listing technique emphasizes related ideas of about the same importance. Lists are useful for pointing out elements in instructions, procedures, and summaries. The writer may list, (1) by starting each separate point on a new line, or (2) by using numbers within a line, as in this sentence. Placing a key term as close as possible to the beginning of each item will help your reader remember the division. Read the following examples and note how the use of key terms improves the effectiveness of the listing technique. Note also how the first and third examples use the "point by point" comparison form you learned in Chapter 5.

Example 1: Good use of listing technique

January 28, 1975

Dear Mr. Brown:

The recently enacted Employee Retirement Income Security Act of 1974 has greatly modified the Federal Tax Code of 1954. The salient features prior to 1975 were as follows:

a. *Fiduciaries were liable only* in the event of fraud or other crimes.
b. *Rights of employees* were neither guaranteed nor assured.
c. *Funding of deferred compensation plans* was arbitrary and at the discretion of management.
d. *Employees had no right of recourse* against their employer, because employers were insulated from amounts held in trust funds.

However, the recently enacted legislation has had the following effects:

a. *Fiduciaries are not only liable* for their own judgment, *but also* for the judgment of other fiduciaries.
b. *Rights of employees* are now financially guaranteed by a newly chartered agency administered by the Department of Labor.
c. *Funding of deferred compensation plans* is now required to be systematic, and subject to fines if funding standards are not maintained.

d. *Employees* and/or the Labor Department *may seek relief* in the federal courts for violations of employee rights. Also, employee deferred compensation plans may attach a portion of the employee's net worth—up to 30% of such worth.

I trust that this summary will enable you to view the new law with greater insight. If you have any questions, however, please call.

Sincerely,
William P. Burke

Parallel
topics   William Burke's letter helps his client understand the changes in the law by listing the corresponding features of the old law and the new law in parallel order. By using the "A then B" form, he visually separates the provisions of the old law from the provisions of the new one. By using parallel order and key terms near the beginning of each item, he makes it easy for the reader to recognize the parallel items in the first and second parts.

Example 2: Poor use of listing technique

Requirements of Applicants for Grant Assistance under Public Law 92–500

In order to aid in elimination of pollution in our rivers and streams, the Federal Government has initiated a grants assistance program providing funds for seventy-five percent of the cost (excluding land) of designing and constructing publicly-owned treatment works facilities or any improvements thereto.

Public Law 92–500 is an act of the 92nd Congress passed on October 18, 1972.

The objectives of this act are as follows:

"1. it is the national goal that the discharge of pollutants into the navigable waters be eliminated by 1985;

"2. it is the national goal that wherever attainable, an interim goal of water quality which provides for the protection and propagation of fish, shellfish, and wildlife, and provides for recreation in and on the water, be achieved by July 1, 1983;

"3. it is the national policy that the discharge of toxic pollutants in toxic amounts be prohibited;

"4. it is the national policy that Federal financial assistance be provided to construct publicly-owned waste treatment works;

"5. it is the national policy that area-wide/regional waste treatment management planning processes be developed and implemented to assure adequate control of sources of pollutants in each State; and

"6. it is the national policy that a major research and demonstra-

tion effort be made to develop technology necessary to eliminate the discharge of pollutants into the navigable waters,
waters of the contiguous zone, and the oceans."

The administration of the grant is separated into four phases:
(1) application, (2) facilities planning, (3) plans and specifications,
and (4) construction. To apply for a grant, an official of the
governmental entity desiring assistance requests a pre-application
conference with the Water Quality Board. The results of this
conference are used to determine a priority rating. The priority
rating reflects each applicant's total pollution impact on water-
courses in the state. Priority ratings are established at six-month
intervals and funds are allocated accordingly.

The writer achieves nothing by separating the objectives
of Public Law 92–500 into six vertically listed items. The
listing is not related to the reader's needs or to the function
of this information in the whole composition. If the reader
works hard to figure out connections between the vertical
list and the next section of the notice, he will probably
infer (eventually) that the grants assistance program is supposed to further the objectives of Public Law 92–500—but
the writer has not specifically said so. Furthermore, when
the list is concluded, the writer jumps to new topics: administration of the grant and review of applications. Thus, the
vertical listing of the law's objectives does not relate to any
need to refer back arising from the content of the following
paragraph. The list within the line explaining the four
phases of grant administration is somewhat more useful,
because it groups together the actions of the applicant in
the sequence in which they will occur. One irregularity,
however: application for the grant occurs *before* the person
knows whether he has received it; "application," therefore,
is hardly part of the "administration of the grant," which
suggests procedures necessary *after* the grant is received.

In the following example, two forms of an alcohol are
compared. In the introduction, the writer explains that the
two compounds are structurally identical except for the
placement of the hydroxyl group. The important bases of
comparison—their occurrence in nature, their odors, and
their commercial uses—are associated with this difference
in structure, which the listing technique emphasizes. Key
words are used at the beginning of each numbered point
of comparison.

A numbered list is useful either when the list is very long and the number helps the reader find his way among the many items to be discussed, or when the writer would like to refer to each item simply by number rather than a descriptive phrase. Using a phrase like "option three" can be much easier than a long phrase, such as "the option to resynthesize the compound with an aldol reaction."

The questions used to evaluate a listing technique include:

1. Does the list emphasize important relationships between parts of the whole or series?
2. Does the list relate parts of that particular section more clearly to parts of another section, or to other parts of the whole composition?
3. Are key words placed near the first of each item to signal its basic idea?
4. Are numbers required to make reference to parts of the list easier, or to facilitate reference when the wording of the items is cumbersome in discussion?

Example 3: Good use of listing technique

A Comparison of cis-3-hexen-1ol and cis-3-hexen-2ol

$$\overset{\text{OH}}{\underset{|}{C}}-C-C=C-C-C \qquad C-\overset{\text{OH}}{\underset{|}{C}}-C=C-C-C$$

Introduction
Cis-3-hexen-1ol and cis-3-hexen-2ol are naturally occurring unsaturated alcohols. The former is often referred to as "leaf alcohol"; the latter, by its chemical name. These alcohols are straight chain, unsaturated compounds. In the six-carbon chain, the location of the unsaturated bond is in both cases the third carbon atom. The hydroxyl group (OH) in the first alcohol is located on the end carbon of the chain and in the second alcohol on the second carbon atom. The carbon atom attached to the hydroxyl group is numbered *one*. Cis indicates that both the hydrogen atoms of the unsaturated bond are on the same side of the bond. It is the position of the hydroxyl group in these two alcohols that determines their organoleptic or odor qualities.

Points of comparison
1. Occurrence: Both cis-3-hexen-1ol and cis-3-hexen-2ol are found in nearly all fresh fruits and berries. The original work leading to the isolation and identification of these alcohols was done in Japan on tea leaves, hence the name leaf alcohol.

2. Odor: It is the cis-3-hexen-1ol that conveys the chemical message to your nose that the fruit is fresh. This note, as perfumers call it, is soft, floral, and sweet, the odor noticed when a lawn is mowed. The second compound, cis-3-hexen-2ol, is described as being intense or sharp green. Some species of weeds will be found to contain more of this alcohol than of cis-3-hexen-1ol.
3. Commercial uses: Both alcohols appear in the GRAS list of compounds. This acronym is derived from Generally Regarded As Safe. The addition of a very small amount of cis-3-hexen-1ol to frozen fruits lends appeal because smell and taste associate freshness with this odor. Cis-3-hexen-2ol is used in perfumes, bath oils, and similar preparations to sustain a strong natural note.

Conclusions
These two similar compounds illustrate the difference in odor obtained when a functional group such as hydroxyl is shifted by one position. The fact that these are natural alcohols, and as such find use in foods and perfumery, makes them valuable commercial chemicals.

Technical correspondence

Technical correspondence facilitates cooperation between professionals. Correspondence will be more effective if you follow these guides:

1. Show the reader why the subject is of interest to him in the opening paragraph, by identifying yourself, your purpose in writing, and the problem or situation.
2. Prepare your reader for whatever data you intend to offer by using inclusive terms to introduce information.
3. Always make clear what you want the reader to do. Don't hide instructions or requests in the middle of a paragraph; place them at the beginning or end. In this respect, paragraphs are like freight trains: you notice the locomotive and the caboose more than individual cars in between.
4. Both the writer and the reader have professional identities indicated by the language of the letter. The writer should sound confident, competent, professional, and energetic. "I would be happy to review your plans and specifications" conveys a more positive identity for the writer than "I am anxious to see your drawings." The reader also can infer the writer's attitude toward him from the tone of the letter. Always emphasize the reader's ability to contribute to the

solution of a problem or the achievement of a goal. "This is to inform you that the final decision of the committee is to reject your proposal to . . ." tells the reader that the writer considers him an outsider. "The committee received with interest your proposal to offer a tour of the analytical services laboratory to new personnel. Because the schedule for orientation week is already crowded, we will have to delay this tour until other parts of training have been completed" treats the reader with more courtesy and dignity, as someone who is part of the group that has to tolerate the delay rather than as an outsider of no consequence.

Compare the effectiveness of the following two letters, on the basis of these guides.

Version 1

> Longbridge Engineering Co.
> 2414 Weinberg Road
> Jackson, Texas 77578

January 24, 1977

Mr. Milton Hernandez
Texas Water Quality Board
P.O. Box 13246, Capitol Station
Austin, Texas 78711

> Subject: WPC-Tex-1048
> City of Jackson

Dear Mr. Hernandez:

Who is writing? Project designated WPC-Tex-1048 was reviewed and approved for advertisement for bids by the City Council of the City of Jackson on January 23, 1977, subject to the review and approval of governmental agencies having jurisdiction. *Why?* Plans and specifications and *Why "note" this?* a brief job description are attached. It is noted that the West Main Street Sanitary Trunk Sewer was initially proposed as a new *Who investigated?* twenty-one-inch trunk sewer. Subsequent field investigations revealed the existence of a fifteen-inch and a ten-inch line not indicated by City records. As discussed with Mr. Charles Wilson *Who decided?* of your office earlier this month, it was decided to rehabilitate the existing lines to accomplish the project objective in the most *What action shall the* cost-effective manner.

reader take? The treatment plant plans and specifications conform with the approved plan of action dated November 12, 1976.

Yours truly,
Elmer Wharton

Version 2

Longbridge Engineering Co.
2414 Weinberg Road
Jackson, Texas 77578

January 24, 1977

Mr. Milton Hernandez
Texas Water Quality Board
P.O. Box 13246, Capitol Station
Austin, Texas 78711

Subject WPC-Tex-1048

Dear Mr. Hernandez:

Who is writing and why? The Jackson City Council approved project WPC-Tex-1048 for bids on January 23, 1977, subject to review and approval by your agency. *What is included?* I have attached plans, specifications, and a brief job description of this project for your review and action.

Information introduced? We have recommended one modification in the project. Instead of installing the new 21-inch trunk sewer originally proposed as the West Main Street Sanitary Trunk Sewer, we suggest that the *Who investigated?* fifteen- and ten-inch lines discovered by our field investigators be rehabilitated. We discussed this change with Mr. Charles Wilson *Who decided?* from your office earlier this month, and everyone agreed that this modification will accomplish the project objective more economically.

The treatment plant plans and specifications fully conform to the plan of action approved by your office on November 12, 1976. *Instructions and requests?* Please review the project documents. The Jackson City Council would like to announce this project for bids by March 15, so they will need your approval within the next month. If you have any questions, please call me.

Yours truly,
Elmer Wharton

Process descriptions

Even when your purpose is to describe rather than to persuade, you must still concern yourself with the reader's needs and interests. You might think that in describing a process, something "out there," the writer could be less concerned about the reader, but that is not the case. Readers of process descriptions are not all alike. Generally, they can be grouped into two classes with very different needs.

Some readers can be called participants, because after they read the description they are going to perform actions that require the most complete understanding of every detail in the process. Participants include laboratory technicians who will use the process, or plant design engineers, who will plan or construct equipment to carry out the process.

Other readers are observers or non-participants. They will not go to the laboratory to carry out the process, but they will need to understand basic reactions or events or principles involved. They often need to know why such processes are important, or how they can be applied. Observers include investors, managers, and persons who must advertise and hire people to carry out the process, or perform some other ancillary function.

The basic pattern for process descriptions is the same for participants or observers. For both types you should include:

1. Significance of the process
2. Underlying principles
3. List of major steps
4. Analysis of each step
5. Conclusion

The emphasis, however, differs, depending on your reader. Participants need more detailed information in steps 3 and 4; observers need fuller treatment of steps 1 and 2.

Written for a participant:

Use a small glass bulb having a capacity of about two cubic centimeters and a capillary stem about three centimeters long. This glass bulb should have very thin walls. After weighing the bulb, gradually heat the bulb to expel a large part of the air. While the bulb is still warm, dip the capillary tip down into the sample to be tested for heating value. . . .

Written for an observer:

Liquid fuels with a high volatility can be tested for heating value by weighing a sample in a capillary tube and bulb device.

Exercise: Process description

Look up the word *sulfur* in at least two encyclopedias or technical books, and learn about the Frasch process of sulfur mining. Write a description of the Frasch process suitable for an observer.

Technical reports

In his book, *Composition for Technical Students*, J. D. Thomas offers this definition of the technical report:

A report is a communication concerning work done, with or without recommendations concerning work yet to be done. It is prepared by an expert or specialist, or a group of experts and specialists, and addressed to a superior, official, employer, or client; to other experts and specialists; to a particular group of laymen, such as the shareholders in an enterprise; or rarely, to the general public. Although most reports are in some sense technical, the term technical report has limited reference to those specifically concerned with science and technology.

Four kinds of reports are particularly important to the student: the laboratory report, the physical research report, the feasibility study, and the progress report. Professor Thomas points out that all reports, regardless of length or type, invariably answer the same three questions: (1) What was the objective of the project, study, or experiment? (2) What was done? (3) What was the outcome? Some reports also answer another question, What is recommended for the future? Different types of reports emphasize the answers to different questions.

The physical research report answers questions (1)–(3) by recording the equipment, procedures, and results of physical experiments and observations. The laboratory report is a version of the physical research report.

The feasibility study answers all four of the above questions and is organized to stress the recommendations based on research. For example, a feasibility study might make recommendations about which artificial sweetener a company should use in diet soft drinks; or about the suitability of a particular material for lining containers used for shipping ammonium hydroxide.

The progress report explains how the work completed on a particular project during a certain period of time relates to the overall project. Often it summarizes work done in preceding periods, explains in greater detail the work done in the period that has just ended, and describes the work planned for the next period.

Physical research report

The physical research report usually follows a standard plan of organization:
Abstract
Introduction
Background of theory

or review of literature
Equipment
Procedures
Results
Discussion
Conclusions
References
Appendices

An *abstract* is a summary of a report, set out on a separate page of the report. There are two types of abstract: the descriptive or topical abstract and the informative abstract. The descriptive abstract tells about the report's purpose and organization without revealing any of the findings of the investigation. The informative abstract contains all the vital general statements in the report. An informative abstract is often made up of the topic sentences of the major divisions of the report. Reading the informative abstract, one knows the most important content of the report.

Descriptive abstract

This report presents the results of a study on preventing movements of the Alaskan pipeline downslope through liquefiable soil. Two types of slopes were analyzed. Recommendations are made to prevent movement.

Informative abstract

Areas of transition from above-ground construction to below-ground construction for the Alaskan pipeline are vulnerable to rupture, as a result of the pipeline's moving downslope due to the liquefaction of surrounding soils. Protective measures are required to prevent downslope movement. The slopes and soil conditions at all transition sections were reviewed, and the worst soil and slope conditions were selected for study. Two types of slope were analyzed: longitudinal slopes with a cross slope less than 2.5%, and longitudinal slopes with a cross/skew slope such that the true slope is greater than 2.5%. In both types, significant displacements of the pipeline can be prevented by replacing liquefiable soils of the transition section with non-liquefiable granular fill, and founding the pipe in it.

Abstracts are written in the third person, not the first person. Say "This report contains . . ." or "Areas of transition are vulnerable . . ." instead of "I have told in the report how . . ." or "I studied areas of transition that were vulnerable. . . ."

A good report *introduction*, like a good essay introduction, (1) announces the general topic or question under investigation, (2) offers historical background if necessary, (3) states the purpose and objectives of the investigation, (4) narrows the topic by explaining the scope and limitation of the work, (5) states or implies a plan of development, and (6) concludes with a thesis sentence.

The *background of theory*, or *review of literature*, section summarizes the relevant knowledge about the problem in texts and journals. The objective is to provide the reader with whatever information and concepts he needs to understand the approach used in the investigation.

The *equipment* section lists what equipment was used, and why. The writer should make this section more detailed for a participant reader.

The *procedures* section contains a description of (1) the conditions in which the experiment was performed, (2) the precautions taken, (3) the manner in which the experiment was assembled and operated, and (4) the way the results were recorded.

The *results* section presents the data, often in tabular and graphic form, along with necessary explanations. This section does not contain conclusions, only the data obtained by following the procedures of the experiment or investigation.

The *discussion* section is the most important part of the report. In it the writer discusses, reviews, and interprets the data presented in the results section. He relates the data to the issues or principles presented in the review of literature (or background of theory) section, and to the technical questions involved in the particular problem or situation described in the introduction. Patterns of organization may be suggested by the results: contrast or comparison, cause/effect, analysis into parts, or interpretive generalization about the topic. More than one pattern may be needed in the discussion. The original research question will probably become the thesis for this section, and its implied pattern of organization will usually be the dominant one.

The *conclusions* section, similar to the essay conclusion, works like an inverted funnel, moving from the major points supported by the discussion to the broad implications of the researcher's findings. The conclusion presents the major outcome of the investigation. Comments on the validity and reliability of the experiment are also appropriate here.

The *references* section presents a list of the works cited in the background of theory or review of literature section, and is analogous to the bibliography attached to other papers.

The *appendices* section consists of maps, diagrams, tables, price lists, and other supplementary materials that might be consulted by various readers.

Laboratory report

The laboratory report is a short form of the physical research report. Often a department or company will have its own style sheet for writing laboratory reports, or will provide forms to fill out. Check to see if there is a style sheet or standard form whenever you begin a laboratory course, in order to make your writing conform to the standard format.

The laboratory report contains the same sections as the physical research report. Because it is usually quite short, the abstract is often omitted and the introduction states the purpose of the experiment. In some schools the laboratory workbook or manual substitutes for the background of theory section; but in others, students are expected to write a review of the reactions and principles involved in the laboratory work.

Sample laboratory report (abstract omitted)

Separation of Two Liquids by Fractional Distillation
Introduction: The purpose of the experiment was to demonstrate that a mixture of toluene and chloroform can be separated by fractional distillation.

Background of theory:
Mixtures of two liquids with different boiling points may be mechanically separated by distillation. When the mixture is heated to its boiling point, the vapor rises in the distillation column. As it comes in contact with the core of packing material, the vapors condense. As the vapor continues to be produced, heat rises in the column, and the liquid with the lower boiling point will revaporize and recondense in the column before the one with the higher boiling point. The liquid with the lower boiling point will thus reach the top of the distillation column first, and run down the glass tubing to the collection flask. As the mixture

continues to be heated its temperature will rise, and the condensed vapor of the second liquid will also revaporize, move up the column, condense, and run down the tubing into the collection flask.

Equipment: Prepare the fractionating column and assemble the distillation apparatus as shown in the diagram and described under "assembly."

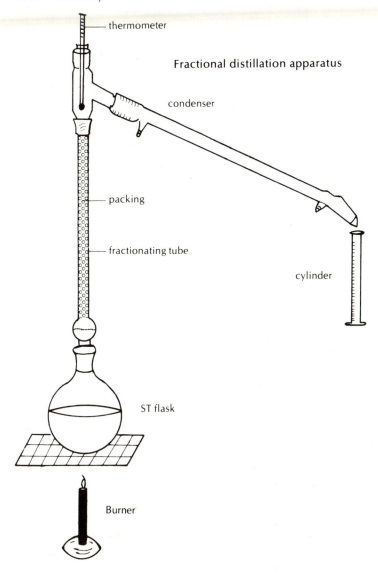

thermometer

Fractional distillation apparatus

condenser

packing

fractionating tube

cylinder

ST flask

Burner

Special Handling: The following rubrics should be observed. (1) Pack the steel wool neither too densely (causes "flooding") nor too sparsely (gives poor fractionalization). (2) Protect the flask with a wire gauze. (3) The slower the distillation, the better the separation will be.

Assembly: Fractionating column. The packing is to be accomplished by threading a three-foot copper wire through the empty fractionating tube, attaching it to a long, narrow piece of steel wool, and pulling it back through the tube with the assistance of spatula thrusts.

Distillation apparatus assembly. Place the sample mixture and a few boiling chips in a 100-ml. round-bottom ST flask. Use two ring stands and several universal clamps to secure the apparatus, consisting of: the loaded flask, the prepared fractionating column, a thermometer adapter, a 250° thermometer, a condenser, and a 50-ml. graduated cylinder. Place the thermometer bulb slightly below the level of the side arm of take-off distillation adapter (see diagram).

Procedure: Start circulating water through the condenser (at bottom), and begin heating the flask 10–15 minutes before the vapors rise to the top of the fractionating column. Maintain a distillation rate of 1–2 drops every 3–4 seconds by holding the base of the burner in the palm of the hand and rocking the burner. The consequent regular heating can be varied for precise control of the distillation rate.

When the first drop of distillate reaches the graduated cylinder, begin the temperature and volume recordings. Record the temperature at each additional 5-ml. of distillate until the temperature begins to rise. Thereafter, record the temperature at every 2-ml. rise.

Results

Temperature °C	Volume ml.
56	1
58	3
60	5
60	7
60.5	10
61	12
61.5	15
62	17
65	20
70	23
75	25

80	27
85	30
90	31
95	32
100	35
105	37
108	40
108.5	45
109	48

The distillation apparatus functioned as expected.
Yield: See graph of Fractional Distillation of 50 ml of 1:1 chloroform and toluene.

Fractional distillation curve for 50 ml. of 1:1 chloroform and toluene

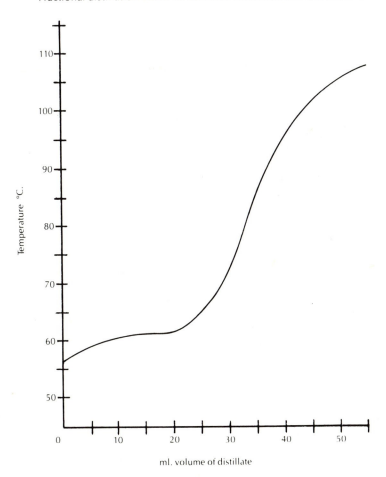

ml. volume of distillate

Discussion: The total volume of distillate was less than the original mixture because some of the vapor condensed on the surfaces of the metal sponge in the fractionating column. Some loss might also have occurred in spite of greasing all joints. The major loss, 3 ml., was probably due to the fractionating column. A change in pressure, such as the use of a partial vacuum, might have improved the fractionalization.

Conclusion: The difference in the boiling points of chloroform (60°C) and toluene (100°C) allows for effective mechanical separation of the two from a mixture by use of fractional distillation.

Progress report

The progress report is a convenient means of periodic communication between those who are doing work and those for whom work is being done. It gives the investor or client a chance to evaluate the rate of progress, the direction, and the emphasis of the project, and allows him to modify the project before more money and effort have been spent. The progress report is also valuable to the researcher or project director, because the process of writing may help him to see his work in a new perspective. Writing a series of progress reports helps the writer plan and execute a final report.

The first two sections of a progress report are the introduction and the project description. These may remain identical, or nearly identical, in a series of reports on the same project. The project description (also called the work statement or the contractual requirement) tells what the researcher must do or investigate in the entire project. The third section, the work done section, makes up the body of the report. This section may be organized according to topics investigated, tasks performed, or order of occurrence. In all but the final report, another section describes work to be done in the next period. The progress report ends with a conclusion and overall appraisal of the project to date.

Feasibility report

A feasibility report describes work done on a particular question in order to make recommendations for action. Should the company acquire a particular site for storing ammonia? Should the company replace locomotives of a certain design? The recommendations section is the key part of a feasibility report.

There are two different plans for organizing feasibility reports. The traditional plan arranges its units in the following order: Abstract, Introduction, Body, Conclusions, Recommendations, and References and Appendices. A second method is called the administrative plan. This plan focuses on the problem and the recommendations, placing the data collected, and other materials, in the appendices. The administrative plan arranges its units in the following order: Abstract, Introduction, Discussion (brief), Conclusions, Recommendations, Appendices (data, lengthy discussion, tables, other materials). Not every reader is expected to read the appendices. The possible disadvantage of this plan is that judgments may be made by people with an incomplete grasp of the complexities, based on the conclusions without details from the appendices.

In the following example of a student feasibility study, Warren White has used the traditional plan of organization. In the actual paper, however, the title, abstract, and contents would each appear on separate pages.

Feasibility Study

Lighting the Tennis Courts
at Rice University

Prepared for:
Mr. Russell Pitman
Assistant to the President

Prepared by:
Warren C. White
Civil Engineering Student
Rice University

24 March 1976

Abstract

Rice University has no lighted tennis courts. Installing a lighting system would be a service to the students and allow greater use of the courts, and would also provide the University with a new revenue source from rental fees charged for their use. During the first few years of operation, this revenue would be used to pay the debt incurred in installing the facility. Once this debt was erased, the University would clear a surplus of approximately $7,500 annually.

Because of its mutual benefit to both the University and the students, a lighting system for the tennis courts is thus more than justified. The system would initially be installed for courts 1, 2, 3, 7, 8, and 9 only, but could easily be duplicated if the demand warranted expansion. The best design would be one using high-pressure fixtures mounted on 35-foot poles. These poles would be located at the front, center, and back fence lines, one pole at each corner of each court. The total cost of such a system, excluding the cost of the feeder cable to the courts, would be approximately $20,000.

Contents

	Page
Abstract	(i)
Contents	(ii)
Introduction	1
Light Sources	1
Metal Halide	2
Mercury Vapor	3
High-Pressure Sodium	4
Light Source Comparisons	5
Layout Designs	6
Funding	9
Conclusions	9
Recommendations	10
Endnotes	11
Bibliography	12

Appendix A: Current Cost Calculations for 1,000-Watt Fixtures
Appendix B: Comparative Analysis of Light Sources

Lighting the Tennis Courts at Rice University

Introduction

A lighting system for the tennis courts east of the Rice gymnasium is long overdue. During the spring and summer, or about eight months out of the year, these courts are regularly full from 5:00 p.m. until 8:00 p.m. They are relatively empty earlier in the day, due to the extreme heat of the afternoon sun. If the courts were lighted from 8:00 until 11:00, three additional one-hour playing shifts would be provided in the cooler night air.

I first investigated the possible lighting sources available for such a system. Of the nine major light sources available for general lighting purposes, only three were recommended· for outdoor tennis court lighting by the major lighting distributors. These three were: (1) metal halide, (2) mercury vapor, and (3) high-pressure sodium. For this study, only these lamps were considered. After selecting the best lamp for the system, two alternative layout designs were analyzed.

The following study provides for lighting the six courts nearest the gymnasium, courts 1, 2, 3, 7, 8, and 9 only. This design could easily be duplicated for the remaining courts if the demand was sufficient.

Light Sources

The three light sources considered were evaluated on the basis of their lighting characteristics and their relative cost. In each case, 1,000-watt lamps were considered to be the best for the design. The following lighting characteristics were considered:

1. Efficiency of lamps
2. Life expectancy of lamps
3. Colors accented by lamps
4. Colors grayed by lamps
5. Degree of light control for lamps
6. Power requirement in feeder cable to lamps

In addition, the initial installation and annual operating costs of each lamp were considered. The operating cost was based on a three cents per kilowatt-hour electric energy rate with fixed operating requirements for the system: eight months per year, three hours per day, operating at 75 percent of peak due to bad weather (540 hours per year). This cost and the installation cost were based on the latest available cost information as outlined by General Electric Company.[1]

The following paragraphs outline the basic characteristics of each of the light sources considered. Appendix A gives the cost calculations for the lamps. Appendix B contains a comparative analysis of all the characteristics of each light source.

I. Metal Halide
   A. Lighting Characteristics
      1. The efficiency of this lighting system is 91,000 lumens per lamp. On the basis of this level of efficiency, six lamps would be needed to provide the 30-foot-candle capacity needed for one court. A total of 36 lamps would be required for six courts.
      2. The average life of this lamp is 10,000 hours.

3. The colors accented by this lamp are a significant feature since the Layco courts to be lighted have green surfaces. This lamp accents green in addition to yellow and orange, typical tennis ball colors.
4. Only deep red is dulled by this lamp.
5. The lamp beam is generally easier to control than the beam of either the mercury vapor or the sodium lamp.
6. The power required in the feeder line for 36 lamps is 36 kilowatts.

B. Cost
  1. The initial installation cost of a system using this lamp, excluding the cost of erecting poles, would be $12,927. This would include the cost of 36 lamps and luminaires in addition to the labor and wiring cost associated with their installation.
  2. The total annual operating cost of this system would be $702.

II. Mercury Vapor
  A. Lighting Characteristics
    1. The efficiency of this lighting system is 59,000 lumens per lamp. At this level of efficiency, fourteen lamps would be needed for one court. A total of 84 lamps would be required for six courts.
    2. The average life of this lamp is 24,000 hours.
    3. The colors accented by this lamp include orange and yellow, but not green.
    4. Green is grayed by this lamp.
    5. The beam of this lamp is the most difficult one of the three to control.
    6. The power required in the feeder line for 84 lamps is 84 kilowatts.

  B. Cost
    1. The initial installation cost of a system using this lamp, excluding the cost of erecting poles, would be $26,236. This would include the cost of 84 lamps and luminaires in addition to the labor and wiring cost associated with their installation.
    2. The total annual operating cost of this system would be $852.

III. High-Pressure Sodium
  A. Lighting Characteristics
    1. The efficiency of this lighting system is 122,000 lumens per lamp. At this level of efficiency, only four lamps would be needed for one court. A total of 24 lamps would be required for six courts.
    2. The average life of this lamp is 15,000 hours.
    3. The colors accented by this lamp include orange and yellow but not but not green.
    4. Green is grayed by this lamp.

5. This lamp's beam is second only to that of the metal halide lamp in terms of beam directionality.
6. The power required in the feeder line for 24 lamps is 24 kilowatts.

B. Cost
1. The initial installation cost of a system using this lamp, excluding the cost of erecting poles, would be $12,058. This would include the cost of 24 lamps and luminaires in addition to the labor and wiring cost associated with their installation.
2. The total annual operating cost of this system would be only $469.

Light Source Comparisons

Because each light source offers definite advantages, I decided to run a comparative analysis based on the characteristics of each light (see Appendixes A and B). I decided to rate first, second, or third choice in each category by awarding 1,2, or 3 points. In addition, I doubled the effect of cost since this is a greater controlling factor than the general lighting characteristics of the system. In tabular form the ratings are:

Light Source Characteristic	Metal Halide	Mercury Vapor	Sodium
Installation Cost	4 = 2x2	6 = 3x2	2 = 1x2
Operating Cost	4 = 2x2	6 = 3x2	2 = 2x1
Efficiency	2	3	1
Life Expectancy	3	1	2
Colors Accented	1	2	2
Colors Grayed	1	2	2
Light Control	1	3	2
Power Required	2	3	1
Total Points	18	26	14

The lamp with the lowest total points represents the best choice. This is the high-pressure sodium lamp, which is by far the best. In terms of initial installation and annual operating cost, this system is the most economical. In addition, the power requirements would be substantially less than those of any other system. It would therefore cost less to run a line to feed power to the courts since a cable with smaller capacity would be required. No estimate of this cost was made in the report since it would have meant my hiring a consultant.

Layout Designs

Two alternative layout designs were considered after selection of the high-pressure sodium lamp as the best available light source. Each of these designs was evaluated by the following criteria:

1. Construction should cause as little destruction to the existing courts as possible.
2. Lights should be directed in such a way as to cast a minimum amount of light toward the Weiss college west wing.
3. Poles should be placed so there is a minimum of interference to players hitting the ball down the sidelines or the baselines.
4. The cost of pole erection should be minimal.
5. The lighting should be uniform at the nets and on the baselines.

Each of the layout designs uses 35-foot, square, tapered steel poles since these are the cheapest ones available for general lighting purposes.

The illustrations on the following page present the two layout designs considered. Discussion of these two designs is presented in the paragraphs following the illustrations.

Layout Design #1   Layout Design #2

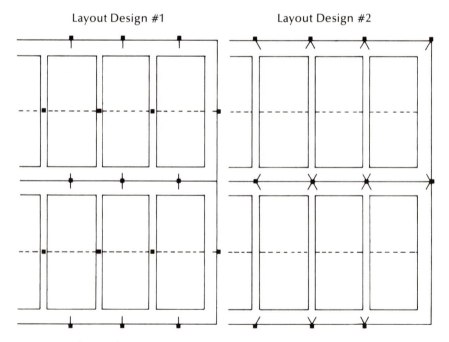

Effects of construction
Layout design #2 would be much better than design #1 from a construction standpoint. Design #1 would require at least six poles at the net, and three others at the center fence. Setting

these poles, particularly those at the net, and then wiring them underground would require a great amount of destruction to the existing court surface. Design #2, on the other hand, would only require three poles at the center fence while the remainder could be erected around the perimeter outside the court area itself.

Effects on Weiss College
With proper shielding and reflecting from the luminaires, either one of these designs could be used with a minimum of light directed toward Weiss College. Therefore, either system would be acceptable under provision #2.

Interference from pole placement
As stated in provision #3, the poles for the system should be placed to interfere as little as possible with players hitting the ball down the sidelines or the baselines. This could present a problem with design #1, since poles are located at the net. Design #2 would present no such problem since all the poles are outside the courts or at the fences.

Costs of pole erection
In terms of cost, at a standard erection rate per pole of $650,[2] design #2 would be far better than design #1. Design #1 with a total of seventeen poles would cost $11,050, while design #2 with only twelve poles would cost $7,800. These cost figures include only the cost of the poles themselves and their erection.

Uniformity of lighting
Finally, design #1 would provide better uniform lighting at the net than would be provided by design #2. Design #2, however, would provide better baseline lighting. Each system would have certain advantages under provision #5.

In summary, design #2 is better or at least as good as design #1 by each criterion considered. Design #2 with high-pressure sodium lamps would be the best one to use for the tennis court lighting system at Rice.

Funding
A fee for using the courts would pay the installation and maintenance costs and generate new revenue for the University. A reasonable fee of $2.50 per court per hour would bring in $8,100 of additional revenue if the lighted courts were used 540 hours per year, as estimated on page two. These funds would easily cover the annual operating costs of $469, leaving $7,631 to be applied to the cost of installation. After the installation cost had been paid, the University could use this yearly surplus for other improvements to athletic facilities for the students.

Conclusions
The high pressure sodium lamp is the best of the three light sources. It is cheaper than either the metal halide or the mercury

vapor lamp in terms of both installation cost and annual operating cost. Its effect on colors is less desirable than that of the metal halide lamp, but the high pressure sodium lamp is the most efficient light source.

Design #2 is better than Design #1. Design #2 not only costs less, but will cause less destruction to the courts during construction. Further, it will interfere less with play at the perimeter of each court.

Recommendations

I recommend that the University install a lighting system for tennis courts 1, 2, 3, 7, 8, and 9 east of the gymnasium. The initial cost of this system, excluding the cost of the feeder cable, would be approximately $20,000. This cost is the approximate sum of the $12,058 cost of 24 high-pressure sodium fixtures plus the $7,800 installation cost for twelve 35-foot, square, tapered steel poles as required for design #2. In addition, the annual operating cost of this system would be $469. These costs would be offset by the $2.50 per court per hour rental fee, which for 540 hours of operating time per court per year, would gross $8,100 annually. The initial investment would be recovered, and the operation would be self-sufficient, in less than three years.

End Notes

1. *High Intensity Discharge Lamps*, Report No. TP-109R, General Electric Company Lamp Business Division, Nela Park, Cleveland, Ohio, March 1975, p. 40.
2. Kenneth C. Kolstad, *Rapid Electrical Estimating and Pricing*. New York: McGraw-Hill Co., Inc., 1974, p. A-27.

Bibliography

High Intensity Discharge Lamps, Report No. TP-109R, General Electric Company Lamp Business Division, Nela Park, Cleveland, Ohio, March 1975.

Kolstad, C. Kenneth. *Rapid Electrical Estimating and Pricing*. New York: McGraw-Hill Co., Inc., 1974.

Planning Facilities for Athletics, Physical Education and Recreation. Harold K. Jack, chairman of committee. Chicago, Illinois: The Athletic Institute; and Washington, D.C.: American Association for Health, Physical Education, and Recreation. 1974.

Williams, Henry G. *Selection Guidelines for Tennis Lighting Systems*. Report No. 260-5255, General Electric Company Lamp Business Division, Nela Park, Cleveland, Ohio, June 1975.

Appendix A
Current Cost Calculations for 1,000-Watt Fixtures

Costs	Type of Fixture		
	Metal Halide	Mercury Vapor	High-Pressure Sodium
Installation Costs:			
Luminaire costs	$ 4,500	$ 8,400	$ 5,520
Wiring costs	5,832	13,860	3,996
Installation labor costs	1,080	2,520	720
Initial lamp costs	1,515	1,456	1,822
Total Installation	$12,927	$26,236	$12,058
Annual Operating Costs:			
Annual lamp costs	$ 76	$ 32	$ 61
Annual maintenance costs	43	42	19
Annual energy costs	583	778	389
Total Annual	$ 702	$ 852	$ 469

Note: These figures are based on current cost figures as given in the following reference: *High Intensity Discharge Lamps*, Report No. TP-109R (General Electric Company Lamp Business Division, Nela Park, Cleveland, Ohio, March 1975), p. 40.

Appendix B
Comparative Analysis of Light Sources

Bases of Comparison	Type of Fixture		
	Metal Halide	Mercury Vapor	· High-Pressure Sodium
Number of fixtures required	36	84	24
Installation costs	$12,927	$26,236	$12,058
Annual operating costs	$ 702	$ 852	$ 469
Efficiency (lumens/lamp)	91,000	59,000	122,000
Life expectancy (hours)	10,000	24,000	15,000
Colors accented	orange, yellow, green	red-orange, yellow	orange-yellow, yellow-orange
Colors grayed	deep red	green	green
Light control	excellent	poor	good
Power requirements (kilowatts)	36	84	24